HTML5 and CSS3

ILLUSTRATED – First Edition

Introductory

HTML5 and CSS3

ILLUSTRATED — First Edition

Introductory

Sasha Vodnik

COURSE TECHNOLOGY
CENGAGE Learning

Australia • Brazil • Japan • Korea • Mexico • Singapore • Spain • United Kingdom • United States

COURSE TECHNOLOGY
CENGAGE Learning™

HTML5 and CSS3—Illustrated Introductory, First Edition

Sasha Vodnik

Vice President, Publisher: Nicole Jones Pinard

Executive Editor: Marjorie Hunt

Associate Acquisitions Editor: Amanda Lyons

Senior Product Manager: Christina Kling Garrett

Associate Product Manager: Kim Klasner

Editorial Assistant: Brandelynn Perry

Director of Marketing: Elisa Roberts

Senior Marketing Manager: Ryan DeGrote

Marketing Coordinator: Kristen Panciocco

Developmental Editor: Marjorie Hopper

Content Project Manager: Matthew Hutchinson

Copy Editor: Troy Lilly

Proofreader: Foxxe Editorial

Indexer: BIM Indexing and Proofreading Services

QA Manuscript Reviewers: John Frietas, Jeff Schwartz, Danielle Shaw, Ashlee Welz Smith, Susan Whalen

Print Buyer: Fola Orekoya

Cover Designer: GEX Publishing Services

Cover Artist: Mark Hunt

Composition: GEX Publishing Services

For product information and technology assistance, contact us at
Cengage Learning Customer & Sales Support, 1-800-354-9706
For permission to use material from this text or product, submit all requests online at **www.cengage.com/permissions**
Further permissions questions can be emailed to
permissionrequest@cengage.com

Trademarks:

Some of the product names and company names used in this book have been used for identification purposes only and may be trademarks or registered trademarks of their respective manufacturers and sellers.

Library of Congress Control Number: 2011920012

ISBN-13: 978-1-111-52789-1
ISBN-10: 1-111-52789-X

Course Technology
20 Channel Center Street
Boston, MA 02210
USA

Cengage Learning is a leading provider of customized learning solutions with office locations around the globe, including Singapore, the United Kingdom, Australia, Mexico, Brazil, and Japan. Locate your local office at:
international.cengage.com/region

Cengage Learning products are represented in Canada by Nelson Education, Ltd.

To learn more about Course Technology, visit **www.cengage.com/coursetechnology**

To learn more about Cengage Learning, visit **www.cengage.com**

Purchase any of our products at your local college store or at our preferred online store
www.cengagebrain.com

Printed in the United States of America
1 2 3 4 5 6 7 8 9 18 17 16 15 14 13 12 11

Brief Contents

Contents

Preface

Welcome to *HTML5 and CSS3—Illustrated Introductory*, First Edition. If this is your first experience with the Illustrated series, you'll see that this book has a unique design: each skill is presented on two facing pages, with steps on the left and screens on the right. The layout makes it easy to learn a skill without having to read a lot of text and flip pages to see an illustration.

This book is an ideal learning tool for a wide range of learners—the "rookies" will find the clean design easy to follow and focused with only essential information presented, and the "hotshots" will appreciate being able to move quickly through the lessons to find the information they need without reading a lot of text. The design also makes this a great reference after the course is over! See the illustration on the right to learn more about the pedagogical and design elements of a typical lesson.

About This Book

This is a brand new book in the Illustrated Series—this is *not* a revision of *HTML Illustrated*, Third Edition by Cox, Reding and Wermers. This book takes a new, fresh approach to teaching HTML5 and CSS3 to develop Web pages and Web sites. Users learn to write and interpret HTML and CSS code using no more than a basic text editor and a browser. Encouraging users to see Web development as team process, sample projects include professionally-designed layouts and Web-ready text, allowing users to focus on building the skills needed to combine these elements into Web pages and Web sites. All code is tested on several widely-used browsers, and all steps can be completed by Windows or Mac users. In addition to basic HTML elements, units cover and incorporate new HTML5 semantic elements. CSS coverage includes downloadable fonts, multicolumn and fluid layouts, and semantically accurate table layouts using only CSS.

Each two-page spread focuses on a single skill.

Introduction briefly explains why the lesson skill is important.

A case scenario motivates the the steps and puts learning in context.

UNIT F

HTML5 and CSS3

Inserting Images

You add an image to an HTML document using the one-sided img element. The element must include two attributes: src, whose value is the path and filename of the image file to display, and alt, which specifies text to display in case the image is unavailable or needs to be read in user agents by software such as screen readers. Table F-2 details all available attributes for the img element. Like span and br, img elements are inline elements by default. You can wrap an img element in its own block element, such as a div element, and align it horizontally using standard block-level alignment techniques. For an image occurring within a paragraph of text, the bottom of an image is aligned with the bottom of the text, which is known as the **baseline**. You add the Lakeland Reeds B&B logo in place of the heading at the top of the page in the Web site. You also replace the bullets separating the sections of the contact information with decorative graphics.

STEPS

1. In your text editor, open HTM F-1.html from the Unit F/Unit folder on the drive and folder where you store your Data Files, insert a blank line before the closing body tag, insert a paragraph element containing your first and last name and the text HTML5 Unit F, save it as index.html, repeat to save HTM F-2.html as rooms.html then use a CSS comment to add the same information to HTM F-3.css and save it as lakeland.css

QUICK TIP
Be sure to type a space before the closing /.

2. In index.html, locate the h1 element, delete the text Lakeland Reeds Bed & Breakfast, leaving the <h1> and </h1> tags, move the </h1> tag to a separate line at the same indent level, then on a blank line between the h1 tags, indent two additional spaces and type <img src="images/lakeland.gif" width="664" height="180" alt="Lakeland Reeds Bed and Breakfast" />
While the width and height attributes are not required, it's highly recommended that you use them to specify the native dimensions of the image. This ensures that if a visual user agent is unable for any reason to display the referenced image, it can maintain a corresponding amount of blank space, preserving the layout of your Web page. Width and height attributes are always in pixels, so it's not necessary to specify units. Figure F-2 shows the code for the img element.

3. In the paragraph element at the bottom of the page containing contact information, replace the first occurrence of the character code • with <img src="images/flourish.gif" width="16" height="16" alt= />, then repeat to replace the second occurrence of the character code with the same HTML code
Figure F-2 shows the completed code for adding images to the main Web page.

4. Save your work, then return to lakeland.css in your text editor

QUICK TIP
Don't make changes to the h1, h2, nav style rule.

5. In the h1 style rule, remove all name–value pairs except font-size, then add the code margin: 0;

6. Save your work, then open index.html in your default browser
Figure F-3 shows index.html with images in a browser.

7. Repeat Steps 2 through 4 to add the logo and decorative graphic to the corresponding elements in rooms.html, then preview your changes

132   Inserting and Working with Images

Tips and troubleshooting advice, right where you need it—next to the step itself.

Large screen shots keep students on track as they complete steps

Brightly colored tabs indicate which section of the book you are in.

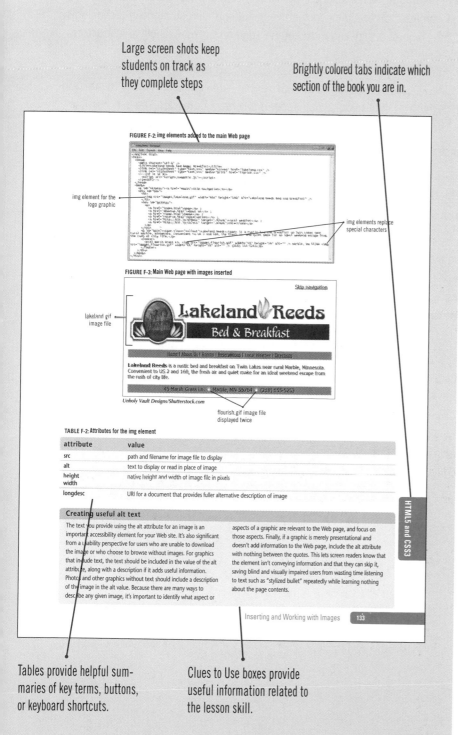

FIGURE F-2: img elements added to the main Web page

img element for the logo graphic

img elements replace special characters

FIGURE F-3: Main Web page with images inserted

Skip navigation

lakeland gif image file

Lakeland Reeds
Bed & Breakfast

Home | About Us | Rooms | Reservations | Local Weather | Directions

Lakeland Reeds is a rustic bed and breakfast on Twin Lakes near rural Marble, Minnesota. Convenient to US 2 and 169, the fresh air and quiet make for an ideal weekend escape from the rush of city life.

45 Marsh Grass Ln. • Marble, MN 55764 • (218) 555-5253

Unholy Vault Designs/Shutterstock.com

flourish.gif image file displayed twice

TABLE F-2: Attributes for the img element

attribute	value
src	path and filename for image file to display
alt	text to display or read in place of image
height width	native height and width of image file in pixels
longdesc	URI for a document that provides fuller alternative description of image

Creating useful alt text

The text you provide using the alt attribute for an image is an important accessibility element for your Web site. It's also significant from a usability perspective for users who are unable to download the image or who choose to browse without images. For graphics that include text, the text should be included in the value of the alt attribute, along with a description if it adds useful information. Photos and other graphics without text should include a description of the image in the alt value. Because there are many ways to describe any given image, it's important to identify what aspect or aspects of a graphic are relevant to the Web page, and focus on those aspects. Finally, if a graphic is merely presentational and doesn't add information to the Web page, include the alt attribute with nothing between the quotes. This lets screen readers know that the element isn't conveying information and that they can skip it, saving blind and visually impaired users from wasting time listening to text such as "stylized bullet" repeatedly while learning nothing about the page contents.

HTML5 and CSS3

Inserting and Working with Images   133

Tables provide helpful summaries of key terms, buttons, or keyboard shortcuts.

Clues to Use boxes provide useful information related to the lesson skill.

Assignments

The lessons use Lakeland Reeds Bed and Breakfast, a fictional company, as the case study. The assignments on the light yellow pages at the end of each unit increase in difficulty. Assignments include:

- **Concepts Review** consist of multiple choice, matching, and screen identification questions.

- **Skills Reviews** are hands-on, step-by-step exercises that review the skills covered in each lesson in the unit.

- **Independent Challenges** are case projects requiring critical thinking and application of the unit skills. The Independent Challenges increase in difficulty, with the first one in each unit being the easiest. Independent Challenges 2 and 3 become increasingly open-ended, requiring more independent problem solving.

- **Real Life Independent Challenges** are practical exercises in which students create documents to help them with their every day lives.

- **Advanced Challenge Exercises** set within the Independent Challenges provide optional steps for more advanced students.

- **Visual Workshops** are practical, self-graded capstone projects that require independent problem solving.

Instructor Resources

The Instructor Resources CD is Course Technology's way of putting the resources and information needed to teach and learn effectively into your hands. With an integrated array of teaching and learning tools that offer you and your students a broad range of technology-based instructional options, we believe this CD represents the highest quality and most cutting edge resources available to instructors today. The resources available with this book are:

- **Instructor's Manual**—Available as an electronic file, the Instructor's Manual includes detailed lecture topics with teaching tips for each unit.

- **Sample Syllabus**—Prepare and customize your course easily using this sample course outline.

- **PowerPoint Presentations**—Each unit has a corresponding PowerPoint presentation that you can use in lecture, distribute to your students, or customize to suit your course.

- **Figure Files**—The figures in the text are provided on the Instructor Resources CD to help you illustrate key topics or concepts. You can create traditional overhead transparencies by printing the figure files. Or you can create electronic slide shows by using the figures in a presentation program such as PowerPoint.

- **Solutions to Exercises**—Solutions to Exercises contains every file students are asked to create or modify in the lessons and end-of-unit material. Also provided in this section, there is a document outlining the solutions for the end-of-unit Concepts Review, Skills Review, and Independent Challenges. An Annotated Solution File and Grading Rubric accompany each file and can be used together for quick and easy grading.

- **Data Files for Students**—To complete most of the units in this book, your students will need Data Files. You can post the Data Files on a file server for students to copy. The Data Files are available on the Instructor Resources CD-ROM, the Review Pack, and can also be downloaded from cengagebrain.com. For more information on how to download the Data Files, see page xvi.

Instruct students to use the Data Files List included on the Review Pack and the Instructor Resources CD. This list gives instructions on copying and organizing files.

- **ExamView**—ExamView is a powerful testing software package that allows you to create and administer printed, computer (LAN-based), and Internet exams. ExamView includes hundreds of questions that correspond to the topics covered in this text, enabling students to generate detailed study guides that include page references for further review. The computer-based and Internet testing components allow students to take exams at their computers, and also saves you time by grading each exam automatically.

Acknowledgements

Reviewers

Thank you to the reviewers who provided opinions and guided decisions during the creation of this book. They are as follows:

Dan Fergus, Brown College

Hazel Freeman, The University of Alabama

David Harden, Santa Rosa Junior College

Sherry Hopkins, Anne Arundel Community College

MaryAnn Kelly, Abby Kelley Foster Charter Public School

Jonathan Meersman, Milwaukee Area Technical College

Colleen Meyer, Cincinnati State Technical and Community College

Special Thanks

We are grateful to Jonathan Meersman, professor at Milwaukee Area Technical College, who provided the vision, inspiration, and initial impetus for creating this book.

Author Acknowledgements

Sasha Vodnik Creating this book has truly been a team effort. Thanks to the many people who helped shape and strengthen what I've written: Marj Hopper, whose feedback and guidance strongly influenced the final content of every page; Christina Kling-Garrett, who kept us focused and on schedule; John Freitas, Ashlee Welz Smith, and Danielle Shaw, whose careful reviews and thoughtful comments on each chapter removed many roadblocks for future users; Brandi Shailer, who set us on all on the path toward creating this book together; Matthew Hutchinson and the folks at GEX, Inc., who carefully transformed my words and pictures into usable, attractive layouts; and John McKelvy, who created all the Web page layouts on which the sites created in this book are based. Additional thanks go to my partner, Jason Bucy, who's helped me stay happy, healthy, and connected to life outside of HTML and CSS while I worked on this book.

Credits

All Web sites created in this book are based on designs by John McKelvy of Oakland, CA.

The images shown in some figures are used by permission from the following sources:

Elena Elisseeva/Shutterstock.com
Ron Rowan Photography/Shutterstock.com
Regien Paassen/Shutterstock.com
Unholy Vault Designs/Shutterstock.com
somchaij/Shutterstock.com
Weldon Schloneger/Shutterstock.com
Jessica Bethke/Shutterstock.com
Jim Gitzlaff/Shutterstock.com
Maxim Tupikov/Shutterstock.com
9507848116/Shutterstock.com
Lario Tus/Shutterstock.com
Jason Bucy
Faithe Wempen/sycamoreknoll.com

Read This Before You Begin

Frequently Asked Questions

What are Data Files?

A Data File is a partially completed file that you use to complete the steps in the units and exercises to create the final document that you submit to your instructor. Each unit opener page lists the Data Files that you need for that unit.

Where are the Data Files?

Your instructor will provide the Data Files to you or direct you to a location on a network drive from which you can download them. For information on how to download the Data Files from cengagebrain.com, see the inside back cover.

What software was used to write and test this book?

This book was written and tested using Notepad on a computer with a typical installation of Microsoft Windows 7 Home, and TextEdit on a computer with a typical installation of Macintosh OS 10.6. All Web pages were tested on the most recent versions of Firefox, Chrome, and Safari for Windows and Mac, as well as Internet Explorer 9, 8, 7, and 6 for Windows. Where Internet Explorer 6 provides quirky results, the text explains the issues and provides suggestions for further research and troubleshooting. File uploading instructions were written and tested using FileZilla on both Windows and Mac.

Do I need to be connected to the Internet to complete the steps and exercises in this book?

Some of the exercises in this book require that your computer be connected to the Internet. If you are not connected to the Internet, see your instructor for information on how to complete the exercises.

What do I do if my screen is different from the figures shown in this book?

This book was written and tested on computers with monitors set at a resolution of 1024 × 768. If your screen shows more or less information than the figures in the book, your monitor is probably set at a higher or lower resolution. If you don't see something on your screen, you might have to scroll down or up to see the object identified in the figures.

COURSECASTS Learning on the Go. Always Available...Always Relevant.

Our fast-paced world is driven by technology. You know because you are an active participant—always on the go, always keeping up with technological trends, and always learning new ways to embrace technology to power your life. Let CourseCasts, hosted by Ken Baldauf of Florida State University, be your guide into weekly updates in this ever-changing space. These timely, relevant podcasts are produced weekly and are available for download at http://coursecasts.course.com or directly from iTunes (search by CourseCasts). CourseCasts are a perfect solution to getting students (and even instructors) to learn on the go!

CENGAGE**brain**.com

Buy. Rent. Access.

Access Student Data Files and other
study tools on **cengagebrain.com**.

For detailed instructions visit
www.cengage.com/ct/studentdownload.

Store your Data Files on a USB drive for maximum efficiency in
organizing and working with the files.

Macintosh users should use a program to expand WinZip or PKZip archives.
Ask your instructor or lab coordinator for assistance.

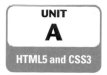

Preparing to Create a Web Site

People and organizations around the world share information using the **World Wide Web**, or Web for short. You can make your own information available on the Web by creating **Web pages**, which are documents formatted to be accessible on the Web, and then publishing them as **Web sites**, which are available to anyone with Web access. Many options are available for creating Web pages, but no matter which method you use, the first step involves a thoughtful planning process. You have just been hired as a Web design intern by Great Northern Web Solutions. For your first project, the art director, Faduma Egal, has assigned you to create a new Web site for Lakeland Reeds Bed & Breakfast, one of Great Northern's clients. Before you start writing Lakeland's Web pages, you'll begin your work by creating a plan for the Web site, setting up a structure for the client's files, and considering the impact of usability, accessibility, and browser compatibility on the pages you'll be creating.

OBJECTIVES

Assemble a project plan

Create a storyboard

Implement Web accessibility standards

Evaluate Web site usability

Manage Web browser compatibility issues

Practice good file management

Configure your FTP client

Upload Web site files

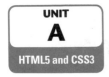

Assembling a Project Plan

Whether you intend to make a single Web page or a large set of interrelated pages available, making information accessible on the Web starts with careful planning. This critical first step involves identifying the goals and objectives, as well as the target audience, of the Web site. Whether you're brainstorming for a personal site or meeting with a client regarding a site you've been hired to create, you sum up your work in this first step with a **project plan**, which is also known as a design document. You hold a planning meeting with Philip Blaine, owner of Lakeland Reeds B&B, to discuss the components he would like included in his new Web site. Figure A-1 shows the project plan you develop based on this meeting.

DETAILS

Important topics to consider in Web site planning include:

- **Identifying Web site goals and objectives**

  You want to ask a client a variety of questions to help understand goals and objectives for the site. For example, "What is the mission of the organization? Why do you want a Web site? What are the short-term goals of the Web site? What are the long-term goals of the Web site? What do you hope to gain by having a Web presence? Who is your target audience? Do your objectives support the needs of your target audience?" The more thorough you are in asking questions of the client, the better prepared you will be to design the Web site.

- **Identifying the target audience**

  It can be helpful to know the target audience for a Web site when choosing a layout and design. Web sites should look different based upon who will be visiting the site and why they are interested in the content. Some potential questions to ask about the target audience might be, "Who are the typical members of your audience? What is the mix of genders? What is the age range? What professions are they in? What is the average education level? Why will people visit this Web site? Will your visitors be using Microsoft Windows, Apple OS X, or another operating system? What size monitors are most common, and at what resolution will the site be viewed? Which Web browsers will they use to view the Web site?" While your client may not have ready answers to all of these questions, getting even a few answers can help prepare you for the design phase.

QUICK TIP

Listing exclusions in the project plan will help reduce the potential for scope creep, which is the expansion of a project beyond the original goals and objectives.

- **Identifying the type of Web site**

  Identifying the type of Web site the owner wants can help to focus the scope of the project. A Web site usually has one of a small number of main functions: a Web presence serving as an online informational brochure; providing important information for special interest groups and nonprofit organizations; showcasing examples of different types of works and designs commonly used by Web design individuals and agencies; providing multiple levels of information with page templates; extracting information from databases; or conducting the sale of products or services and other business transactions through the Internet. It is important to clearly define what the site will include, as well as what the site won't include.

- **Developing a budget**

  Every Web site design project should include a budget that is presented to the client prior to completing any work. The budget should be included in the project plan, which becomes part of the contract.

- **Creating a timeline**

  You should always provide the Web site owner with a timeline that includes the delivery date of the final Web site, along with various implementation milestones along the way. The timeline should always identify who is responsible for which tasks.

Great Northern Web Solutions

Project plan for Lakeland Reeds Bed and Breakfast

Objectives:

- Make general info about the facility and contact info available online
- Enable prospective guests to view the accommodations and grounds
- Allow prospective guests to book a stay online

Target audience:

- 35+
- Live in southern Canada and the upper Midwest U.S.
- Want to "get away from it all"
- Not sure about technical details of users; it's likely many will not be very experienced with the Web

Site type:

- Billboard (while the client wants some e-commerce functionality, they will accomplish this by linking to another site that takes reservations; thus, no advanced functionality is required for this site)

Budget:

- Hien is preparing a few detailed options for the client; this section will be updated when the budget is finalized and the contract is signed

Timeline:

Milestone	Date	Who's responsible
Design mockup submitted for approval	April 1, 2013	Project manager
Draft site published to testing server	April 15, 2013	Project manager
Feedback received from client	April 22, 2013	Phillip Blaine
Client feedback incorporated	May 1, 2013	Project manager
Final feedback from client	May 8, 2013	Phillip Blaine
Final feedback incorporated	May 22, 2013	Project manager
Final signoff from client	June 5, 2013	Phillip Blaine
Site goes live	June 5, 2013	Project manager

Client contact info:

Phillip Blaine

Lakeland Reeds Bed and Breakfast

45 Marsh Grass Ln.

Marble, MN 55764

(218) 555-5253

Deciding how much to charge

Estimating the amount of time a project will take can be difficult, especially for new Web designers. If you work for a Web design agency, the budget will typically be developed by your supervisors. If you are a freelance Web designer, you must place a value on your time that takes many things into consideration, such as the cost of computer equipment and software, supplying your own insurance, advertising, and other expenses. There really is no set hourly or project fee in this industry, as it varies dramatically depending upon the geographic market, competition, and experience level of the Web designer. New Web designers often barter, or trade, their skills for products or services offered by a Web site owner as a means of building a portfolio.

Creating a Storyboard

When you create a Web page or a Web site, it can be helpful to start by getting a clear idea of what you're trying to build. Web designers typically accomplish this by creating a **storyboard**, which is a sketch that outlines the components of each Web page and their places in the layout, as well as the links between the pages in a Web site. On a Web design team, often people responsible for art or design create the storyboard and hand it off to the developers to make into a Web page or Web site. 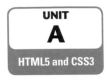 You work with Karl Dixon, one of your colleagues in the art department, to create a storyboard for the Lakeland Reeds Web site based on the project plan you developed.

Storyboarding a Web site involves a few main steps:

- ### Identify components to include
  Before you start sketching, it's important to get a firm handle on all the elements that the Web site you're working on must include. A good place to start is your project plan, which should include a thorough inventory of items that must be part of the Web site; for instance, an existing logo and color scheme that a client already uses in all of their printed materials. You should augment this list with any other essential design elements based on your understanding of the site's target audience and functionality; for example, most multi-page Web sites need a standardized navigation section that provides links to each of the pages.

- ### Sketch possible layouts and then select one
  The next step is to place the elements in a layout that's functional, usable, and, ideally, aesthetically pleasing. This step is often the job of a graphic designer; however, it's a skill that many Web developers without artistic backgrounds have built with study and practice. Whoever does this step, it often involves a series of sketches that either lay out a set of choices or progressively fine-tune a theme. For a simple Web site, a single layout should suffice for all the site's pages; however, if some pages have requirements that are best served by distinct layouts, these layouts need to be finalized in this step as well. Figure A-2 shows the layout for the pages of the Lakeland Reeds Web site.

- ### Map the relationships between Web pages
  Any time you're creating a Web site or a single Web page with links to other Web sites, it's helpful to map out the relationships between pages. This map is a crucial tool when you create the navigation system for the Web site. Figure A-3 lists the pages of the Lakeland Reeds Web site and illustrates the relationships between them, as well as links to external pages.

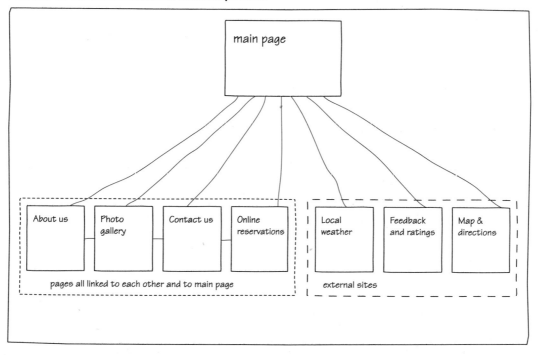

Creating a Web site from a template

An alternative to creating a layout for your Web site is to download a **template**, which is a generic layout that includes a color scheme and element positions, but which uses placeholder images and text. Some templates are available to download and use for free, while others must be purchased from the designer. A Web developer can simply replace the placeholder items with elements specific to the Web site being developed. While a template is not as specifically tailored to the companies or topics of the Web sites where it is used, it can save time in the Web development process and can be an invaluable tool when a site needs to be up right away.

Implementing Web Accessibility Standards

Once you make a Web page publicly available on the Internet, users can access it using a wide variety of **user agents**, which are programs and devices that interpret Web documents. Many Web users view pages with the default settings in popular Web browsers such as Internet Explorer, Firefox, Chrome, and Safari. Some users with disabilities may use custom browser settings, or even specialized software or hardware, to access the Web. While laws in many countries spell out mandatory accessibility standards for government Web sites, building a high level of accessibility into any Web pages you create widens the potential audience for your work, as illustrated in Figure A-4. Thus, as a Web developer, it's important that you understand and implement Web accessibility standards as you create your Web pages in order to make them adaptable to the needs of different users and the capabilities of different user agents. A widely used reference for implementing Web accessibility is the **Web Content Accessibility Guidelines (WCAG)** maintained by the World Wide Web Consortium. To help ensure that the Lakeland Reeds B&B Web site is widely accessible, you review the main tenets of Web accessibility standards.

The WCAG describe techniques for helping your Web content meet the following goals as broadly as possible:

- **Perceivable**

  All of the contents of your Web pages need to be accessible in whatever format a given user is accessing it. This includes ensuring that any information that you convey visually is also available by non-visual means, such as text descriptions for images and videos. Many people with visual impairments access the Web using devices called **screen readers** that read aloud Web page text and descriptions that a user selects. In addition, any audio content should be accompanied by transcripts or written descriptions, which can substitute for many users with auditory impairments.

- **Operable**

  Users interface with computers in different ways. While many users scroll Web pages and click links using a mouse, ensuring that no elements of your Web pages rely on the use of a mouse makes your Web pages more accessible to people with some physical impairments. Web pages also need to allow users to explore and read them at their own paces, and should allow scrolling or self-updating features to be paused, stopped, or hidden. Designs should not include elements known to cause seizures, such as certain frequencies of flashing. Finally, navigation within the site and to external pages should be clearly indicated, easy to understand, and, ideally, redundant.

- **Understandable**

  The language that a Web page is written in should be indicated, and means should be included for users to understand any specialized vocabulary used. Links should not make unexpected drastic changes to the way a Web page is displayed; some warning should be given. When possible, forms that accept user input should include means for identifying common errors and allowing users to correct them.

- **Robust**

  Web pages should be coded according to Web standards, ensuring that they can be accessed by the widest possible variety of programs and devices.

FIGURE A-4: A Web page before and after an accessibility redesign

Text darkened for
Improved text contrast

Navigation bar added to facilitate
moving around site and to make site
organization viewable at a glance

Web accessibility is a team effort

In addition to Web developers' work creating a site, other factors significantly influence Web accessibility. The developers of user agents make decisions that affect how their software and devices interact with Web content, which impacts whether users can access content in specific ways. In addition, some Web content is produced using software that automates the Web development process, and the accessibility choices of the makers of these packages affects the accessibility of the content produced using them. Thus, while Web developers have a crucial role to play in building and maintaining a Web that's available to everyone, it can be useful to see your role as part of a larger team and to recognize when you run against a limitation that you can't realistically fix.

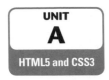
Evaluating Web Site Usability

Even among Web sites on similar topics or in a common area, there's often wide variety in how easy it is for users to accomplish their goals in visiting, whether accessing information or making purchases. It can be tempting to ignore evaluating a Web site's ease of use, known as **usability**, among the many tasks necessary to create and maintain it. However, usability is critically important in determining whether your users are satisfied or frustrated when they leave your Web site, whether the users make return visits, and whether they recommend the site to friends and colleagues. In addition, designing a usable Web site from the beginning is often much easier than improving the usability of an existing Web site. Thinking about who will use your site and what they'll want from it is an important starting point in creating a usable Web resource. As you prepare to work on the Lakeland Reeds Web site, you review Web usability guidelines.

DETAILS

The most usable Web sites share the following attributes, which are highlighted in Figure A-5:

- **Consistent and cohesive**

  All the pages on a Web site should be visually similar enough that users can tell that they're on the same site. Visual design, including a color scheme and logo, plays an important role. In addition, page elements, such as site navigation links, should appear in a consistent place on every page. Your Web site designs should also make use of elements that are standard on most other Web sites, making your Web site instantly familiar to even first-time visitors. Thus, an important part of creating a new Web design is exploring other Web sites sharing similar audiences or topics to get a clear understanding of the standard elements that users may expect to see.

- **Navigable**

  Users often have a specific goal when they visit most Web sites. It's important that your site's opening page makes it clear how users can accomplish the task before them, whether the user wants to find information on a specific topic, buy a product, or make a reservation. In addition, each page should include links that make it clear to users how to move to other areas of the site.

- **Understandable**

  The contents of your Web pages need to make sense to your users. Write text in as simple and straightforward a manner as possible, avoiding technical jargon unless your site targets a specific audience that understands it. Limit your Web page designs to the elements you need; overloading a page with too many options and too much information can overwhelm users and prevent them from getting what they need from your site.

FIGURE A-5: Usability features across a single Web site

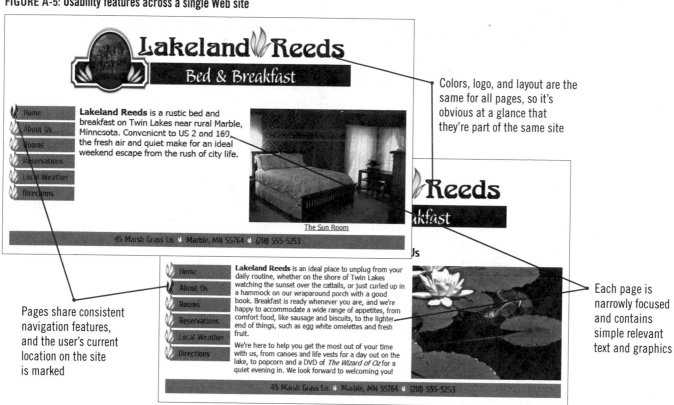

Colors, logo, and layout are the same for all pages, so it's obvious at a glance that they're part of the same site

Pages share consistent navigation features, and the user's current location on the site is marked

Each page is narrowly focused and contains simple relevant text and graphics

Unholy Vault Designs/Shutterstock.com
Faithe Wempen/sycamoreknoll.com
Jason Bucy

Testing usability

Even when you create a Web site with usability in mind, it's easy to overlook some of your users' needs and quirks. Especially for larger Web sites, a crucial part of improving a site's usability is **usability testing**, in which a developer sits down with potential or actual users of the site, asks them to accomplish a task, notes how they go about it and whether they are successful, and asks for their feedback. Often observation of users can point out blind spots that developers have overlooked. Users' feedback may also suggest features that would add a lot of value for your site's visitors.

Managing Web Browser Compatibility Issues

Although everyone who views a given Web page is accessing the same document, different Web browsers translate and display the code differently. In addition to specialized hardware and software such as screen readers, several main Web browsers are in wide use, including Internet Explorer, Firefox, Chrome, and Safari on desktops, notebooks, and tablets, and a number of platform-specific browsers on handheld devices. In addition, each user may be accessing your Web page with an older or newer version of a given browser, and using Windows, OS X, Android, iOS, or another operating system; this multiplies the potential differences in how your page may be presented. While it may be impossible for your Web site to look identical in all versions of all user agents, you can take steps to ensure it looks as close to your original design as possible in many common configurations. 🔲🔲 You prepare for your work on the Lakeland Reeds site by brushing up on development practices for maximizing the consistency of your Web pages across different user agents.

DETAILS

Tips for maximizing browser compatibility:

- **Practice good coding habits**

  While most Web browsers ignore minor coding errors, not all browsers are as forgiving with all errors. Therefore, as you learn Web page code and begin to practice working with it, it is important to stick to good coding habits.

- **Test your Web site with different user agents**

  Because different user agents may render the same code differently, the only way to experience potential discrepancies is to test your Web site in different user agents. While only the largest companies and Web design studios generally own the hardware necessary for exhaustive testing, you should research the user agent configurations that visitors to your site are most likely to be running and make sure you have the hardware and software to test these setups. In addition, software and Web services such as the one shown in Figure A-6 allow you to simulate the user experience in different Web browsers; these can be invaluable in maximizing the visual compatibility of your pages.

- **Validate your HTML and CSS code**

  Sometimes a Web page can display as expected in a user agent in spite of code that doesn't conform to specifications. In this case, it can be useful to put your code through an automated comparison against Web coding standards, a process known as **validation**. Several reputable Web sites offer validation services free of charge. In addition to double-checking code that seems error-free, validation can also help to identify the specific source of an error in your code if the error is difficult to track down.

FIGURE A-6: Gallery of browser previews generated by a Web site

Previews of a single Web page in multiple browsers running on different operating systems

Each preview can be enlarged or opened at full size to see specific details of page appearance

Unholy Vault Designs/Shutterstock.com
Jason Bucy

Practicing Good File Management

Another important step in preparing to create a Web site is to set up a folder and document structure for your Web site on your computer. It's important to keep all the files for your Web site in a common location so you can easily locate them when you want to make changes. In addition, as your Web site becomes larger, the number of individual files will likely mushroom, making organization a must. The main directory on the computer, USB drive, or shared network drive where you will save all of the files for your Web site is known as the **local root folder**. Using this folder only for files that are ready to be published helps you avoid erroneously publishing old or unfinished files. Faduma has supplied you with an automatically generated placeholder Web page for Lakeland Reeds. You create a local root folder for the site and move the provided files into it in preparation for publishing them to the Web.

STEPS

1. **Open your file manager, navigate to the drive and folder where you store your Data Files, open the Unit A folder, then open the Unit folder**

2. **Create a new folder inside the Unit folder**

3. **Rename the new folder wwwroot**

   You'll use the wwwroot folder to store the folders and files for the Lakeland Reeds Web site that are ready to be published to the Web.

4. **Move the index.html file to the wwwroot folder, then move the gnlogo.png file to the wwwroot folder**

   As shown in Figure A-7, the only file left in the Unit folder is htma-1.rtf, which contains your project plan for the Web site. While this file is related to your work on the Web site, you will not publish it to the Web, so it does not go in the wwwroot folder.

5. **Open the wwwroot folder**

   As Figure A-8 shows, the index.html and gnlogo.png files appear in the wwwroot folder.

FIGURE A-7: The wwwroot folder

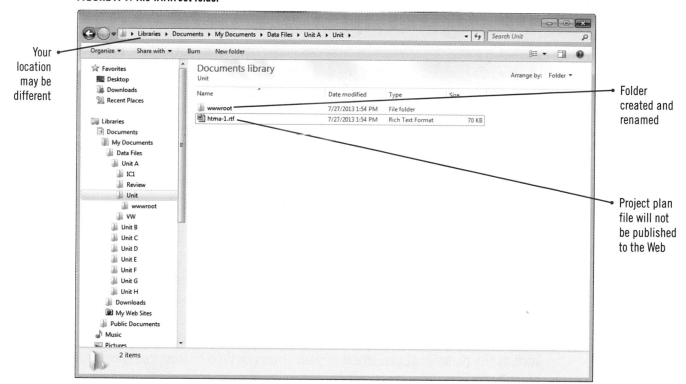

Your location may be different

Folder created and renamed

Project plan file will not be published to the Web

FIGURE A-8: Files to be published

Files ready to be published have been moved to the wwwroot folder

Configuring Your FTP Client

As you develop a Web site, you store your Web documents on your local computer. However, to make your site available to anyone with access to the Web, you need to copy the files to a **Web server**, which is a computer optimized to store and share Web documents and that has an extremely high-speed Internet connection. The most common method of transferring documents to a Web server is **File Transfer Protocol (FTP)**, which is a means of communication specifically created for moving files between two networked computers. While FTP capability is built into most popular operating systems, downloading and installing a dedicated FTP program makes the process much easier. Many such programs, known as **FTP clients**, are downloadable for free online. Before you begin work on the Lakeland Reeds Web site, you configure your FTP client to prepare for uploading your files to the Web.

STEPS

TROUBLE
These steps are for FileZilla, a free FTP client available at www.filezilla-project. org. If you are using a different FTP client, obtain configuration instructions from your instructor or technical support person, or from the documentation that came with the program.

1. **Open your FTP client**

2. **Click File, then click Site Manager**

   FileZilla opens the Site Manager dialog box, which provides options for setting up a new connection to a Web server.

3. **Click the New Site button, type a descriptive name for the Web server you are configuring, such as the name or abbreviation of your school or Web hosting company, then press [Enter]**

4. **Click the Host box, then type the FTP address provided by your instructor, technical support person, or Web host**

5. **Click the Logon Type list arrow, then click Ask for password**

6. **Click the User box, then type the user name provided by your instructor or technical support person**

   Figure A-9 shows the completed Site Manager dialog box.

TROUBLE
If you aren't able to connect to your Web server, ask your instructor or technical support person about other configuration options you might need to select.

7. **Click Connect, type your password, click the Remember password for this session check box to uncheck it, then click OK**

   FileZilla saves the new configuration and tests your connection to the FTP server. Figure A-10 shows a successful connection in FileZilla.

8. **Click the Close button ⊠ to end your FTP connection and exit FileZilla**

FIGURE A-9: Site Manager dialog box

List of Web servers configured for this client

Descriptive name for the Web server

Saves configuration information and tests connection

Address of FTP server

"Normal" stores login information for this connection; "Ask for password" prompts for this information each time you connect

Login name for your Web server

FIGURE A-10: View of connected Web server

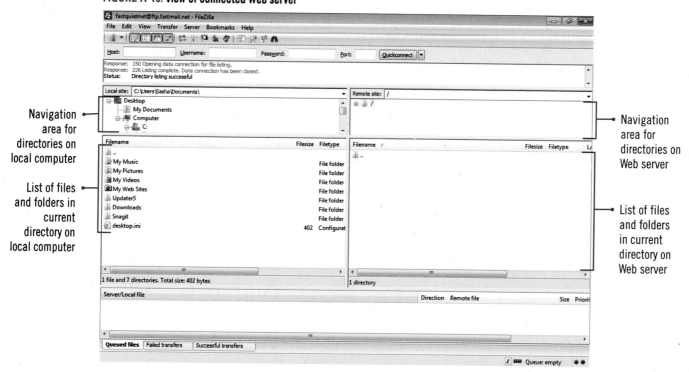

Navigation area for directories on local computer

List of files and folders in current directory on local computer

Navigation area for directories on Web server

List of files and folders in current directory on Web server

Configuring a testing server

As part of the Web development process, it's useful to upload your pages to your Web server for testing purposes before actually making them available to the public. The final upload location for pages on your Web server is not a good location for this purpose, because all pages you upload there are immediately available to the entire World Wide Web, even pages that still contain errors or don't display properly. Instead, Web developers often maintain a separate **testing server** for their projects, which is a location available on a local network or on the Web that is non-publicized and may even require a password for access. When using an FTP client to access a testing server, you use the same local source folder as for final files. The target location, however, may be a different folder on the same Web server, or a different Web host altogether.

Uploading Web Site Files

Once your FTP client is configured to access your Web server, you can upload the files for your Web site and make them available via the Web. 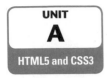 You upload the placeholder Web page for the Lakeland Reeds Web site to the Web host and verify that it was uploaded correctly.

1. **Open your FTP client and connect to your Web server**

2. **Use the Local site directory tree on the left side of the FileZilla window to navigate to the drive and folder where you store your Data Files, open the Unit A folder, open the Unit folder, then open the wwwroot folder**

   The files you moved into the wwwroot folder appear in the Local site file list below the directory tree.

3. **Use the Remote site directory tree on the right side of the FileZilla window to Navigate to the folder designated for your Web pages on the Web server**

   Any Web documents that you copy to this directory are available on the Web.

4. **Right-click a blank area of the Remote site file list, click Create directory, type unit, press [Enter], then double-click the unit folder to open it**

5. **Repeat Step 4 to create a new directory named wwwroot, within the unit directory and then open the new directory**

6. **In the Local site file list, click gnlogo.png, press and hold [Ctrl] (Windows) or [command] (Mac), click index.html, release [Ctrl] or [command], then drag the selected files to the Remote site file list and release the mouse button**

7. **If necessary, enter your password, click the Remember password for this session check box to uncheck it, then click OK for each file**

   The files are copied to your Web server, as shown in Figure A-11.

8. **Click the Close button to end your FTP connection and exit FileZilla**

9. **Open your Web browser, then navigate to the Web publishing address provided by your instructor or technical support person**

   The Lakeland Reeds placeholder page displays, as shown in Figure A-12.

10. **Close your Web browser**

TROUBLE

If you do not see the Web page shown in Figure A-12, be sure you added the /unit/wwwroot directory path to the end of the default path to your Web documents.

FIGURE A-11: Web site files copied to Web server

Files selected
and dragged to
Remote site
file list

Files copied
to Web server

FIGURE A-12: Lakeland Reeds placeholder Web page

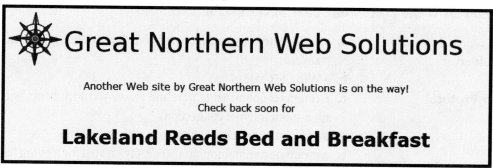

Another Web site by Great Northern Web Solutions is on the way!

Check back soon for

Lakeland Reeds Bed and Breakfast

Practice

Concepts Review

For current SAM information, including versions and content details, visit SAM Central (http://www.cengage.com/samcentral). If you have a SAM user profile, you may have access to hands-on instruction, practice, and assessment of the skills covered in this unit. Since various versions of SAM are supported throughout the life of this text, check with your instructor for the correct instructions and URL/Web site for accessing assignments.

Label each item in the FTP client dialog box shown in Figure A-13.

FIGURE A-13

Match each term with the statement that best describes it.

5. usability
6. local root folder
7. storyboard
8. File Transfer Protocol
9. validation
10. user agent
11. Web server

a. an automated comparison of the code for a Web page against Web coding standards

b. a Web site's ease of use

c. a computer optimized to store and share Web documents, with an extremely high-speed Internet connection

d. a program or device that interprets Web documents

e. a means of communication specifically created for moving files between two networked computers

f. a sketch that outlines the components of each Web page and their places in the layout, as well as the links between the pages in a Web site

g. the main directory on the computer, USB drive, or shared network drive where you save all of the files for a Web site

Select the best answer from the list of choices.

12. The process of identifying the goals and objectives, as well as the target audience, of the Web site is summed up in the _____.
    a. Web server
    b. user agent
    c. project plan
    d. storyboard

13. On a Web design team, often people responsible for art or design create the _____ and hand it off to the developers to make into a Web page or Web site.
    a. storyboard
    b. validator
    c. FTP client
    d. user agent

14. What is one advantage of using a template to create a Web site?
    a. It is guaranteed to create an accessible site.
    b. It can save time in the development process.
    c. You can publish the resulting site without an FTP client.
    d. It doesn't require you to use multiple user agents to check the Web pages you create.

15. What is one advantage of building a high level of accessibility into any Web pages you create?
    a. It widens the potential audience for your work.
    b. It doesn't require you to use multiple user agents to check the Web pages you create.
    c. It eliminates the need to create a storyboard.
    d. You can publish the resulting site without an FTP client.

16. Making a Web site consistent, cohesive, navigable, and understandable helps improve its _____.
    a. project plan
    b. accessibility
    c. storyboard
    d. usability

17. A Web developer can get valuable feedback on a Web site by sitting down with potential or actual users and watching them attempt to accomplish a task, a process known as _____.
    a. storyboarding
    b. validation
    c. usability testing
    d. uploading

Skills Review

1. **Practice good file management.**
   a. Open your file manager.
   b. Navigate to the drive and folder where you store your Data Files, open the Unit A folder, then open the Review folder.
   c. Create an empty folder inside the Review folder and rename it **wwwroot**.
   d. Click and drag the index file to the wwwroot folder, then click and drag the gnlogo file to the wwwroot folder.
   e. View the contents of the wwwroot folder and compare your screen to Figure A-14.

2. **Upload Web site files.**
   a. Open your FTP client and connect to your Web server. If you are using an FTP client other than FileZilla, use the steps provided for your client instead of the steps below to upload the contents of the wwwroot folder to your Web server.
   b. In the Local site directory tree, navigate to the drive and folder where you store your Data Files, open the Unit A folder, open the Review folder, then open the wwwroot folder.

FIGURE A-14

Skills Review (continued)

c. Use the Remote site directory tree on the right side of the FileZilla window to navigate to the folder designated for your Web pages on the Web server.

d. Right-click a blank area of the Remote site file list, create a new folder named **review**, then open the review folder.

e. Repeat Step d to create a new directory named **wwwroot** within the review directory, then open the new directory.

f. In the Local site file list, select the files gnlogo.png and index.html, then drag the files to the Remote site file list.

g. If necessary, enter your password, click the Remember password for this session check box to uncheck it, then click OK for each file.

h. Close your FTP connection and exit your FTP client.

i. Open your Web browser, then navigate to the Web publishing address provided by your instructor or technical support person to view the files you uploaded. Be sure to add the /review/wwwroot directory to the end of your default Web publishing address.

j. Close your Web browser.

Independent Challenge 1

Spotted Wren Garden Center, a local garden shop and plant store, has hired you to create a Web site for their business. Sarah Nguyen, the shop's owner and manager, would like you to create a Web presence as a new avenue of marketing, as well as a means to keep regular customers up to date on seasonal specials and new products. You start your work on the site by setting up a folder structure on your local machine for the Web site, copying the placeholder files that a colleague has created for you to the appropriate folder, creating the necessary folders on your Web server, and uploading and previewing the placeholder files.

a. In your file manager, navigate to the drive and folder where you store your Data Files, open the Unit A folder, then open the IC1 folder.

b. Create a new folder within the IC1 folder named **wwwroot**.

c. Move the index and birdhouse files to the wwwroot directory.

d. Open your FTP client and connect to your Web server.

e. In the Local site directory tree, navigate to the drive and folder where you store your Data Files, open the Unit A folder, open the IC1 folder, then open the wwwroot folder.

f. Use the Remote site directory tree on the right side of the FileZilla window to navigate to the folder designated for your Web pages on the Web server.

g. Create a new folder named **ic1** on the remote server, then open the ic1 folder and create a folder named **wwwroot** within it.

FIGURE A-15

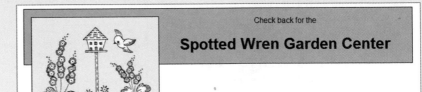

Check back for the

Spotted Wren Garden Center

h. Drag the files index.html and birdhouse.jpg to the Remote site file list to upload them to the Web server, entering your password if necessary.

i. Close your FTP connection, exit your FTP client, then view the page you just uploaded in your Web browser, which should look like the one shown in Figure A-15. Be sure to include **/ic1/wwwroot** in the Web address.

j. Close your Web browser.

Independent Challenge 2

To help build your Web design skills, you have volunteered to create a Web site for the Murfreesboro Recreational Soccer League (MRSL). The league organizes recreational leagues every summer and fall for local, nonprofessional soccer players to get exercise and have fun. You start your work on the site by preparing directory structures on your local computer and your Web server, and researching potential accessibility and usability elements.

a. In your file manager, navigate to the drive and folder where you store your Data files, open the Unit A folder, then open the IC2 folder.

b. Create a new folder within the IC2 folder named **wwwroot**.

c. Open your FTP client and connect to your Web server.

d. Use the Remote site directory tree on the right side of the FileZilla window to navigate to the folder designated for your Web pages on the Web server.

e. Create a new folder named **ic2** on the remote server, then open the ic2 folder and create a folder named **wwwroot** within it. Your remote directory structure should resemble the one shown in Figure A-16.

f. Close your FTP connection, then exit your FTP client.

FIGURE A-16

Advanced Challenge Exercise

- Open your Web browser, then use the search engine of your choice to find and explore at least two recreational sports Web sites.
- Using the "Implementing Web Accessibility" section of this unit as a guide, write a paragraph about each Web site that assesses the site's design in terms of accessibility. Specify at least three details of each Web site and explain why you feel they help or hinder the site's accessibility.
- Using the "Evaluating Web Site Usability" section of this unit as a guide, write a paragraph about each Web site that assesses the site's design in terms of usability. Specify at least three details of each Web site and explain why you feel they help or hinder the site's usability.

Independent Challenge 3

In your new job creating sites for a Web design firm, you've been assigned a new client, Hotel Natoma. The hotel's business manager, Diego Merckx, wants to use the Web to showcase the facility and its amenities. You start your work on the site by preparing directory structures on your local computer and your Web server, and researching potential browser compatibility issues to watch for by exploring similar Web sites.

a. In your file manager, navigate to the drive and folder where you store your Data files, open the Unit A folder, then open the IC3 folder. Create a **wwwroot** folder within the IC3 folder.

b. Open your FTP client, connect to your Web server, and use the Remote site directory tree on the right side of the FileZilla window to Navigate to the folder designated for your Web pages on the Web server.

Independent Challenge 3 (continued)

c. Create a new folder named **ic3** on the remote server, then create a folder named **wwwroot** within the ic3 folder. Your remote directory structure should resemble the one shown in Figure A-17.

d. Close your FTP connection, then exit your FTP client.

Advanced Challenge Exercise

- Open your Web browser, then use the search engine of your choice to find and explore at least two Web sites for small hotels.
- Using a search phrase such as "check browser compatibility," use the search engine of your choice to find a Web site that allows you to check a site's browser compatibility in multiple browsers for free.
- Use the browser compatibility site to use at least three browsers to compare the appearance of one of the hotel sites you explored. Save browser screenshots to the location where you store your Data Files and write a paragraph summarizing any differences in appearance that you notice.

FIGURE A-17

Real Life Independent Challenge

This Independent Challenge requires an Internet connection.

For this Independent Challenge, you will choose a topic or organization of personal interest and create a Web site for or about it. As a first step, you will create a project plan, survey other similar sites, and create a storyboard. Throughout this book, you will design and build the site.

This Real Life Independent Challenge will build from unit to unit, so you must complete the Real Life Independent Challenge in each unit to complete your Web site.

a. Create a project plan for your Web site using the components outlined in the "Assembling a Project Plan" section of this unit and the sample project plan in the htma-1.rtf data file. Include your name at the bottom of the project plan as the contact person. Your course syllabus may be helpful in creating a timeline of components to add to the site, as well as indicating a final publishing date.

b. Open your Web browser, then use the search engine of your choice to find and explore at least two other sites similar to the one you are planning. Write a summary of each site, noting the ways in which the site's focus is similar to and different from the one you are planning, and describing specific aspects of the site that you find less appealing or more appealing. Using the "Implementing Web Accessibility" and "Evaluating Web Site Usability" sections of this unit as a guide, assess the design of each Web site in terms of accessibility and usability.

c. Sketch a storyboard for your Web site, including at least one and no more than five Web pages. If you have a background in graphic design, or have a friend or colleague who's willing to help, sketch an arrangement of elements and include colors, graphics, and any other page elements the site should include.

d. Use your FTP client to connect to your Web server. Create a folder named **rlic**, then create a folder named **wwwroot** within the new folder.

Visual Workshop

Use your file manager and your FTP client to create the folder paths shown in Figure A-18.

FIGURE A-18

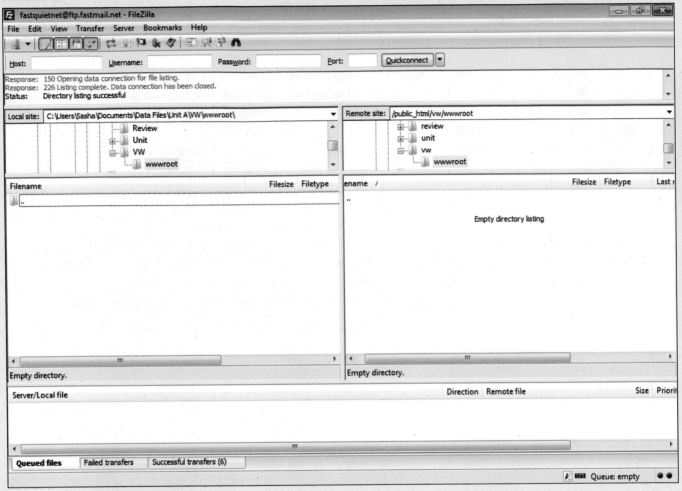

Preparing to Create a Web Site

Getting Started with HTML

After you plan out a Web site, you can begin to create it with nothing more than a basic text editor. Web pages are written in **Hypertext Markup Language (HTML)**, which is a standardized format for specifying the structure of a Web page. You can add HTML code to the text you want to be part of your Web pages in order to indicate the different types of content present. To test your pages and preview their appearance, you can open them in a Web browser or other user agent that interprets your HTML code and represents your Web page contents in a consistent way. Faduma Egal, the art director at Great Northern Web Solutions, has approved the plan you created for the Lakeland Reeds Bed & Breakfast Web site. She wants you to start work on the site by creating a home page containing basic information about the bed and breakfast, including contact information. In this unit, you'll learn more about HTML, and then create and test the main Lakeland Reeds B&B Web page.

OBJECTIVES

Assess the history of HTML

Compare HTML and XHTML

Create an HTML document

Set up the document head and body

Add Web page text

Preview your Web page

Implement one-sided tags

Validate your HTML code

Assessing the History of HTML

HTML was created in 1991 by Tim Berners-Lee. In the succeeding years, the language has undergone several major revisions, along with a couple periods of reinvention when the underlying purpose and direction of the language were reevaluated. Along the way, a few major themes emerged, all of which are important factors in understanding HTML today. ▄▄▄▄▄ You start your work on the Web site by exploring the history of HTML and the factors that have influenced the current version of the language, HTML5.

A few factors have heavily influenced the development of HTML:

- **Process and evolution**

  The first two versions of HTML were defined and published by the **Internet Engineering Task Force (IETF)**. In 1994, the **World Wide Web Consortium (W3C)** was founded to take on the responsibility of maintaining the language's standards, which it continues to do today. Although HTML has gone through several major versions (see Table B-1), in practice the language is constantly under transformation. Through ongoing proposals and debates, the W3C facilitates the process of clarifying and amending the existing specification to incorporate new features while keeping the language consistent. The W3C also maintains a vision for the next steps in the evolution of HTML in an attempt to clarify what developers and software companies want prioritized in future versions of the language.

- **Semantics vs. presentation**

  The publication of HTML 4 in 1997 marked a major turning point in the development of the language. Companies that created Web browser software had begun to anticipate the W3C standards by adding their own extensions to HTML that generally worked only on a particular brand of browser. Between these extensions and a mushrooming of overlapping features codified in previous versions of HTML, it was becoming clear that the language needed to narrow its focus. HTML 4 codified HTML as a **semantic** language, meaning its intended use was to indicate the meanings of elements such as headings and paragraphs in a Web page, but not to tell Web browsers how the elements should appear. The new version of HTML coincided with the rollout of a companion language, **Cascading Style Sheets (CSS)**. CSS is a presentational language, meaning that it's designed for describing the appearance of items.

  Many features of previous HTML versions were presentational rather than semantic and, thus, didn't fit the new model of HTML. However, because so many Web pages had already been written using these features, and existing Web browsers and other user agents supported them, the W3C designated these features as **deprecated**, meaning that, while these features could still be used, their use was no longer recommended, and alternatives to their use were available. This step gave Web designers time to learn new ways of coding and update their Web pages gradually while maintaining support for the current state of the Web.

- **Web application support**

  In the years since the HTML 4.01 specification was finalized, common uses of the Web have changed and grown in significant ways. The core updates that are part of HTML5 include integrated support for new features, such as embedding video, as well as enhancement of longstanding features, such as Web page forms.

TABLE B-1: The evolution of HTML

version	year	major changes
HTML 2.0 & 3.2	1995–97	Codified the current state of HTML
HTML 4 & 4.01	1997–99	Added support for CSS and several newly developed HTML features
HTML5	2008–present	Enriches semantic options, along with new features and enhancements

HTML and Web browser versions

In the early years of the Web, browser creators Microsoft and Netscape added to their browsers proprietary features that weren't supported by their competitors. This provided opportunities for Web developers to add new elements to their Web pages. However, it also meant that any Web page incorporating these features would be displayed differently depending on which browser was used to open it. This situation created difficulties for developers trying to reach the widest possible audience with their Web pages. Eventually, the major browser companies recognized that creating their own features would not be a major key to gaining or maintaining market share, and they have joined with developers to support a largely standards-based Web.

On the flip side, recent updates to Web standards have not always been quickly or fully adopted by makers of browsers and other user agents. As a result, when considering whether to use a particular HTML feature in your Web pages, it's important to research which user agents support it and how widely the supporting user agents are in use. In some cases, implementing new features will need to wait until your target audience has caught up with available Web technologies.

Comparing HTML and XHTML

Efforts to enhance Web standards didn't stop with the publication of the HTML 4.01 specification in 2002. Instead, work began to make HTML interoperable with another markup language known as **Extensible Markup Language (XML)**. The result was a new specification known as **Extensible Hypertext Markup Language (XHTML)**, which for several years was seen as the successor to HTML. Today work continues on both HTML and XHTML, and each has similar, distinct applications. As you prepare to design Web pages, it's important to understand the differences between HTML and XHTML, and when each might be appropriate in your work.

HTML and XHTML both have distinct advantages:

- **XHTML is XML-compliant**

  In addition to HTML, many other markup languages exist for specialized applications. Many of these languages are subsets of XML. Like HTML, XML enables users to describe the structure of a document. However, because XML is a more generic language than HTML, it enables users to describe any kind of document, instead of only Web pages. XHTML grew out of work in the late '90s to make HTML comply with the rules of XML in order to facilitate the interoperation of Web pages with documents coded using other XML-based languages. The first phase of this work resulted in the XHTML 1.1 standard.

  Adapting existing HTML standards to adhere to XML syntax required that Web page authors change a few aspects of the way they write code, which are outlined in Table B-2. You'll see examples of these aspects as you begin to create Web pages.

- **HTML can handle coding errors and quirks**

  As HTML standards changed and grew during the '90s, flexibility became an important part of the language. Even if Web page authors made minor mistakes in writing code, user agents could often interpret the code loosely, rather than hewing unerringly to rules, and successfully display their best interpretations of what the authors intended. XML, however, does not tolerate errors. Thus, if a user agent encounters a coding error while attempting to display a Web page coded in XHTML, the user agent must display an error message rather than read the code more loosely.

  While work initially went forward to create XHTML 2.0 as a successor to XHTML 1.1, some members of the Web standards community dissented. The W3C's focus solely on XHTML as the path forward meant that Web pages containing coding errors would not be displayed correctly or at all. It also meant that any new features under consideration for the next version of XHTML would be unavailable in the billions of existing Web pages written in HTML unless their code was edited to comply with the rules of XHTML. Some community members saw this as an unnecessary barrier and instead began working together to build on the HTML 4.01 standard in order to create a specification that integrated markup features geared toward modern Web usage.

- **Moving forward: coexistence**

  Today, the W3C is improving and expanding both XHTML and HTML, seeing the two as parallel languages with their own reasons to exist. In this book, you'll learn how to create Web pages in both HTML and XHTML, so you can make your own decisions about which language is most appropriate for projects you work on in the future.

TABLE B-2: Differences between HTML and XHTML

aspect	HTML	XHTML
Tag nesting	Tags may be closed out of order	Tags must be closed in the order opened
Tag case	Tags may be written in upper or lower case	Tags must be written in lower case
Tag closure	Closing tags may be omitted for some elements	All opening tags must be matched with closing tags
Attribute-value pairs	Value may occur without attribute name	Attribute-value pair required
Empty elements	Empty elements do not need to be closed	Empty elements must be closed
Script and Style elements	Elements may be placed within HTML document	Elements must be in separate documents and linked to XHTML document
Attribute values	Values may be enclosed within quotes	Values must be enclosed within quotes
ID and Name attributes	Either attribute may be used	ID attribute may be used, but Name attribute prohibited
Character codes for special characters	Codes recommended	Codes required

The W3C and the WHATWG

After XHTML 1.1 was finalized, the W3C moved forward with adding new features to XHTML, and drafted a proposal for XHTML 2.0. However, a number of community members, including several major technology companies, felt that HTML, rather than XHTML, would better serve the future of the Web, and proposed that the W3C change course. When a W3C committee voted against this proposal, these companies formed the **Web Hypertext Application Technology Working Group (WHATWG)** to begin a process of creating a new HTML specification. Over time, the two organizations bridged their differences and agreed to collaborate in creating HTML5, with the W3C coordinating work on XHTML5.

Before finalizing the latest version of HTML, the two organizations are following a process of soliciting input and incorporating feedback from members of the Web community, including makers of user agents and other software and Web developers. As a result, the development process will likely continue for several years before all parties involved finalize a single standard. In the interim, however, different features of the developing specification may become available at different times.

Creating an HTML Document

An HTML document consists solely of text. As a result, you can create a Web page in a text editor such as Notepad, which is included with all current versions of Windows or TextEdit, which is part of Mac OS X. To create a Web page, you enter text that you want to display on the page along with HTML codes known as **tags**, which specify how a user agent should treat each item in the document. While most tags occur in pairs, some tags, known as **one-sided tags**, are used by themselves. ▰▰▰▰▰ You decide to use a text editor to create the home page for the Lakeland Reeds Bed and Breakfast.

STEPS

1. **Start your text editor**
   A new, blank document opens, as shown in Figure B-1.

QUICK TIP
To read more about any HTML tag used in these steps, see Appendix A.

2. **Type <!DOCTYPE html>, then press [Enter]**
   This one-sided tag creates an element known as the **DOCTYPE declaration**, which lets user agents know that the document contents are written in HTML.

3. **Type <html>, press [Enter] twice, then type </html>**
   A tag pair assigns meaning to a Web page **element**, which is a specific component of the page, such as a paragraph or a heading. You place the **opening tag** at the start of the element you are marking and the **closing tag** at the end. HTML tags always start with an opening angle bracket (<) and end with a closing angle bracket (>). A closing tag is the same as its corresponding opening tag except that the opening angle bracket is followed by a slash (/). The text between the angle brackets specifies the HTML element type being applied to the selection. The html tag pair marks the beginning and the end of the Web page.

   Your document should match the one shown in Figure B-2.

4. **If you are using TextEdit on a Mac, click Format, then click Make Plain Text**

5. **Click File, then click Save**
   The Save As dialog box opens.

6. **Navigate to the drive and folder where you store your Data Files, open the Unit B folder, then open the Unit folder**

TROUBLE
If you are using TextEdit on a Mac, uncheck the Hide extension check box if necessary.

7. **In the File name box (Windows) or Save As box (Mac), type index.html**
   The standard name for the main page of a Web site is "index." The .htm or .html extension signifies that a file is written in HTML.

8. **If you are using Notepad in Windows, click the Save as type list arrow, then click All Files (*.*)**

9. **Click Save**
   The index.html file is saved to your storage location.

Other Web page creation software

Many other programs are available that allow you to create Web pages visually by clicking buttons and using drag-and-drop to place items on a page. However, creating your first Web pages by entering HTML directly—sometimes referred to as **hand-coding**—is one of the best ways to get familiar with HTML and the underlying structure of a Web page.

FIGURE B-1: **A blank document in Notepad**

FIGURE B-2: **The basic structure of the Web page**

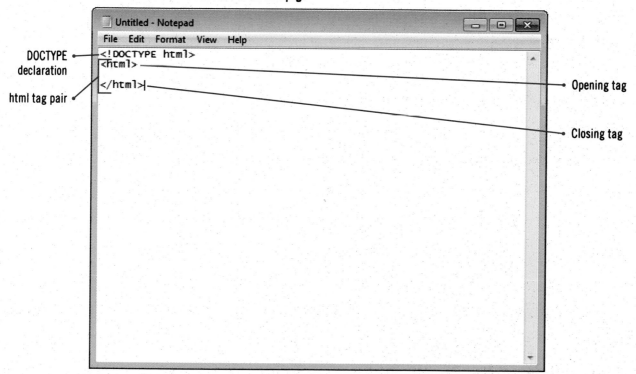

DOCTYPE declaration

html tag pair

Opening tag

Closing tag

Setting Up the Document Head and Body

Within the html tag pair for a Web page, the document contents are divided into two sections. The head section contains elements that are not part of the main Web page, such as the page title that appears in a browser's title bar. The contents of the **body section** are visible in the main window of a Web browser and include elements like paragraphs and headings. Both the head and body tag pairs are located within the html tag pair. This situation is known as **nesting**, and most elements in the code for a Web page are nested within one or more other elements. As you continue creating the structure for the Lakeland Reeds Web page, you add the head and body sections to the page.

STEPS

1. **Click in the blank line between the opening and closing html tags, press [Spacebar] twice, then type <head>**

   Adding two spaces before a nested tag makes it appear indented. As your Web page code becomes longer and more complex, these indentations make it easier to identify the beginning and end of an element at a glance. Figure B-3 shows HTML code with several layers of nested tags that are formatted with indentations.

2. **Press [Enter] twice, press [Spacebar] twice, then type </head>**

3. **Press [Enter], press [Spacebar] twice, then type <body>**

4. **Press [Enter] twice, press [Spacebar] twice, then type </body>**

5. **Click in the blank line between the opening and closing head tags**

6. **Press [Spacebar] four times, type <meta charset="utf-8" />, then press [Enter]**

   The meta element enables you to pass information about a Web page to user agents that open it. The text following the name of the tag in the code you typed is an **attribute**, which you can use to provide additional information about an element. The charset attribute specifies the **character encoding**, which is the system user agents should employ to translate the electronic information representing the page into human-recognizable symbols, such as letters and numbers. Figure B-4 shows the completed Web page structure.

   QUICK TIP
   To save your work without using the menus, you can press **[Ctrl]+[S]** (Windows) or **[command]+ [S]** (Mac).

7. **Save your work**

Describing nested elements

An element nested within another element is called a **child element** of the enclosing element, and the enclosing element is known as the **parent element**. Two elements that are both children of the same element are known as **sibling elements**. In the code

the head element is both a child of the html element and the parent of the meta element. In addition, here the html element is the **grandparent element** of the meta element, which can be referred to as a **grandchild element** of the html element.

```
<html>
  <head>
    <meta charset="utf-8" />
```

FIGURE B-3: **HTML code containing multiple layers of nested elements**

Indentations
indicate
section of
code visually

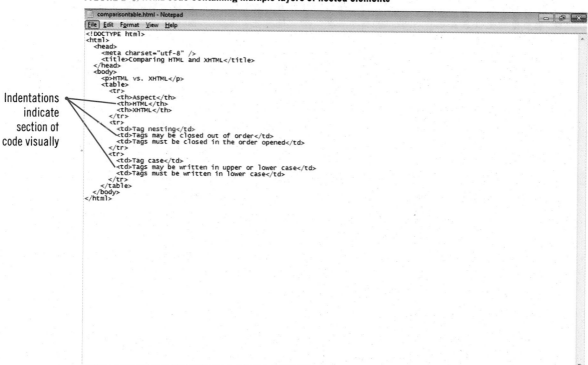

```
comparisontable.html - Notepad
File  Edit  Format  View  Help
<!DOCTYPE html>
<html>
  <head>
    <meta charset="utf-8" />
    <title>Comparing HTML and XHTML</title>
  </head>
  <body>
    <p>HTML vs. XHTML</p>
    <table>
      <tr>
        <th>Aspect</th>
        <th>HTML</th>
        <th>XHTML</th>
      </tr>
      <tr>
        <td>Tag nesting</td>
        <td>Tags may be closed out of order</td>
        <td>Tags must be closed in the order opened</td>
      </tr>
      <tr>
        <td>Tag case</td>
        <td>Tags may be written in upper or lower case</td>
        <td>Tags must be written in lower case</td>
      </tr>
    </table>
  </body>
</html>
```

FIGURE B-4: **Completed Web page structure**

head section

body section

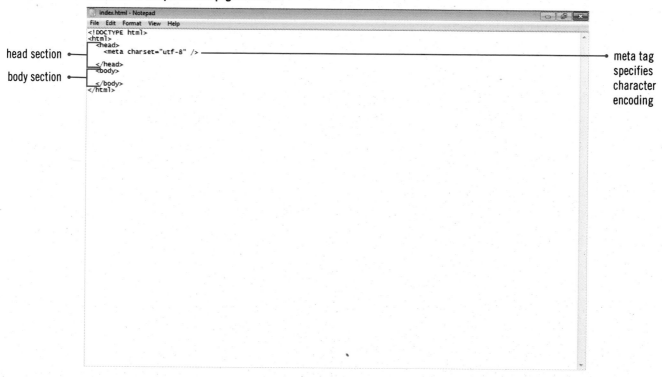

meta tag
specifies
character
encoding

```
index.html - Notepad
File  Edit  Format  View  Help
<!DOCTYPE html>
<html>
  <head>
    <meta charset="utf-8" />
  </head>
  <body>
  </body>
</html>
```

HTML attributes

Many, but not all, HTML elements allow you to set attributes to specify details about a given element's properties. To use an attribute, you provide two pieces of information: an attribute name and the value you are assigning to the attribute. Together, these two pieces are known as an **attribute-value pair**. In the element <meta charset="utf-8" />, *charset* is the attribute name, and *utf-8* is the attribute value. In a tag pair, you specify any attributes in the opening tag, never in the closing one.

Adding Web Page Text

Because an HTML document is simply a plain text document that includes HTML codes, entering text for your Web pages is as simple as typing it. You then add the appropriate HTML tags to specify the element type for each text item on the page. Figure B-5 shows a sketch you created of a simplified initial version of the Lakeland Reeds Web page. You decide to enter the page title that will appear in the title bar of viewers' browsers, along with the basic information about Lakeland Reeds.

QUICK TIP

This line is indented four spaces because it is nested within two elements: html and head.

1. **Click in the blank line above the closing head tag if necessary, press [Spacebar] four times, then type** <title>Lakeland Reeds Bed and Breakfast</title>

   The title element specifies text that appears in the title bar of the Web browser opening the page. This element is part of the document's head section because the text does not appear in the main browser window.

2. **Click in the blank line between the opening and closing body tags, press [Spacebar] four times, then type** <h1>Lakeland Reeds Bed and Breakfast</h1>

   The h1 element represents the highest-level heading on the page.

3. **Press [Enter], press [Spacebar] four times, then type** <p>A country getaway perfect for fishing, boating, biking, or just watching the day go by.</p>

   The p element marks a paragraph of text.

4. **Press [Enter], then type the following text, pressing [Spacebar] four times at the beginning of each line and pressing [Enter] at the end of each line except the last:**

   <p>Philip Blaine, Proprietor

   45 Marsh Grass Ln.

   Marble, MN 55764

   (218) 555-5253</p>

   Your document should look like the one shown in Figure B-6.

5. **Press [Enter], type** <p>, **type your first and last name, type a comma, then type** HTML5 Unit B</p>

6. **Save your work**

Adding comments to your HTML code

In addition to marking text that appears on your Web pages, you can create text elements in your Web page code that user agents ignore. These elements, known as **comments**, are not rendered by user agents and are viewable only by people who examine the HTML code of your Web pages. Comments can be especially helpful when you are creating or adding on to a large, complex Web document or Web site, or when other Web developers will be working with your code—now or in the future. Common uses for comments include explaining what a particular section of HTML does or pointing out the beginning and end of parts of a Web page containing numerous HTML elements. The comment tag pair begins with <!-- and ends with -->.

FIGURE B-5: Sketch of the Web page

Heading in browser title bar or tab

Main page heading

Business description

Contact information

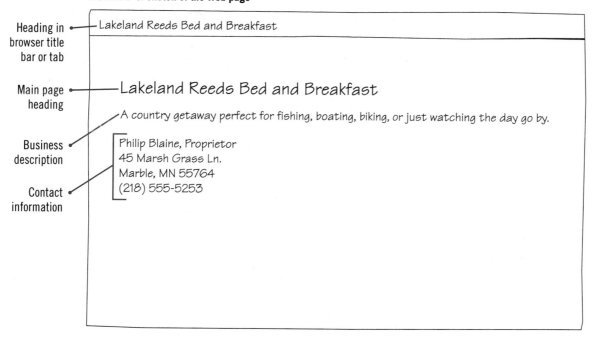

FIGURE B-6: Title, h1, and p elements entered

title element

h1 element

p element for business description

p element for contact information

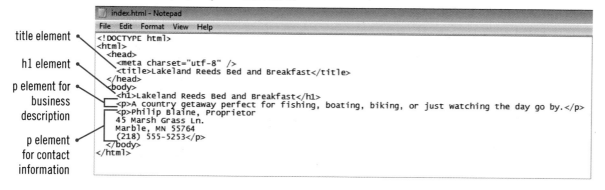

HTML5 and CSS3

Previewing Your Web Page

An important step in the process of creating a Web page is to **preview** it, which involves opening it in one or more user agents and examining the result. When a Web page isn't interpreted as expected by a user agent, you can research the problem and make corrections to the code before publishing the page. In addition, because different user agents can interpret the same page with slight differences, it's good practice to test your pages with multiple user agents. ▆▆▆▆ You decide to preview your Lakeland Reeds Web page in a browser.

STEPS

TROUBLE

If your Web page does not match Figure B-6, return to Notepad, compare your code to Figure B-7, edit as necessary, and save the file, then repeat Step 2 to preview your edited Web page.

1. **Using your file manager, navigate to the drive and folder where you store your Data Files, open the Unit B/Unit folder, then double-click index.html**

   The Web page opens in your system's default Web browser, as shown in Figure B-7. The address information runs together on a single line, rather than appearing on multiple lines as in the code.

2. **If multiple browsers are installed on your system, return to your file manager, right-click (Windows) or control-click (Mac) index.html, point to Open with, then click another browser name in the list**

   The Web page opens in a non-primary browser.

3. **If your Web page is open in two browsers, note any differences between them in the way the page is displayed**

   Often differences in the way each browser displays, or **renders**, a Web page are subtle, such as slight variations in the space between lines. Figure B-8 shows a Web page that is displayed differently in multiple browsers.

Why browsers display Web pages differently

The display of Web pages in HTML5 starts with the standards created by the W3C and the WHATWG. The standards list and describe all the available elements, along with parameters for how user agents should handle them. User agents are built around software known as **rendering engines** that translate Web page elements into visual, auditory, or tactile representations based on these standards. Because the standards require some interpretation, no two engines render the same HTML code in exactly the same way. In addition, the creators of rendering engines do not always implement all of the current standards in their software. Because the audience for your Web pages will almost always be using a number of different user agents, it's important to test your code in a variety of popular browsers and on multiple operating systems (such as Windows 7, Windows XP, and Mac OS X).

FIGURE B-7: Previewing the Web page

Contents of
title element
displayed in tab

Browser displays
h1 element as
a heading

Browser displays
p elements as
standard text

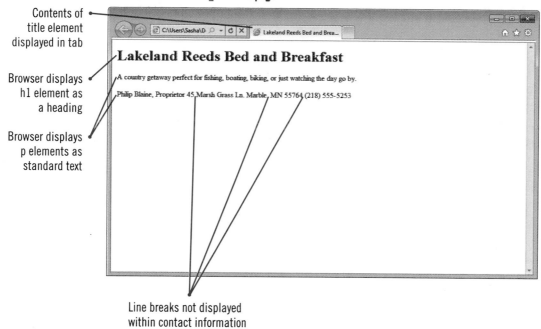

Line breaks not displayed
within contact information

FIGURE B-8: Rendering differences between browsers

Browsers align and format
title text differently

Slight differences in font
size in different browsers

Copyright © 2010 Cengage Learning

Implementing One-Sided Tags

While you add most elements to a Web page using tag pairs, some elements require only a single tag. Instead of affecting text or other elements on the page, these one-sided elements generally represent a specific occurrence of an item or a behavior. You enter a one-sided element by typing a single tag. ▰▰▰ Although pressing [Enter] to insert line breaks in your HTML code is useful for making your code easier to understand, user agents ignore line breaks inserted this way when processing HTML code. To make the Lakeland Reeds address and phone number appear on multiple lines, you decide to add HTML line break codes that browsers will incorporate into the page layout.

STEPS

1. **In your text editor, click at the beginning of the line that reads 45 Marsh Grass Ln., then use ➞ and ← if necessary to position the insertion point immediately to the left of the 4**

QUICK TIP

Be sure to type a space between the r and the /.

2. **Press [Backspace] (Windows) or [delete] (Mac) five times to remove the indentation and move the street address to the end of the previous line, then type
**

   The br element inserts a line break. As a result, the text "45 Marsh Grass Ln." will be displayed on a new line when a user opens the document in a browser. Table B-3 summarizes the Web page elements you have implemented in your Web page.

3. **Click at the beginning of the line that reads Marble, MN 55764, then use ➞ and ← if necessary to position the insertion point immediately to the left of the first M**

4. **Press [Backspace] (Windows) or [delete] (Mac) five times, then type
**

5. **Click at the beginning of the line that reads (218) 555-5253</p>, then use ➞ and ← if necessary to position the insertion point immediately to the left of the (**

6. **Press [Backspace] (Windows) or [delete] (Mac) five times, then type
**

   Your document should look like the one shown in Figure B-9.

7. **Press [Ctrl][S] (Windows) or [command][s] (Mac)**

   Your changes are saved.

8. **Return to your primary Web browser, then click your browser's Refresh or Reload button**

   The browser loads the updated version of the Web page. The address and phone number now appear on multiple lines, as shown in Figure B-10.

9. **If you previously opened index.html in a second browser, refresh or reload the page to see the changes in that browser as well**

FIGURE B-9: HTML document containing line breaks

```
index.html - Notepad
File  Edit  Format  View  Help
<!DOCTYPE html>
<html>
   <head>
      <meta charset="utf-8" />
      <title>Lakeland Reeds Bed and Breakfast</title>
   </head>
   <body>
      <h1>Lakeland Reeds Bed and Breakfast</h1>
      <p>A country getaway perfect for fishing, boating, biking, or just watching the day go by.</p>
      <p>Philip Blaine, Proprietor<br />45 Marsh Grass Ln.<br />Marble, MN 55764<br />(218) 555-5253</p>
   </body>
</html>
```

Line break elements inserted to
break up contact information onto
multiple lines in browsers

FIGURE B-10: Web page displaying line breaks

Lakeland Reeds Bed and Breakfast

A country getaway perfect for fishing, boating, biking, or just watching the day go by.

Philip Blaine, Proprietor
45 Marsh Grass Ln.
Marble, MN 55764
(218) 555-5253

Line break elements divide
up contact information onto
multiple lines

TABLE B-3: Basic Web page elements

element	function	code sample

html	marks the beginning and the end of the Web page	`<html>`
		 web page contents
		 `</html>`

head	contains elements that are not part of the main Web page	`<head>`
		 head contents, such as title and meta elements
		 `</head>`

body	includes contents that are visible in the main window of a Web browser	`<body>`
		 body contents, such as p and h1 elements
		 `</body>`

meta	enables you to pass information about a Web page to user agents that open it	`<meta charset="utf-8" />`
title	specifies text that appears in the title bar of the Web browser opening the page	`<title>Lakeland Reeds</title>`
p	marks a paragraph of text	`<p>Escape to the lake!</p>`
h1	represents the highest-level heading on the page	`<h1>Lakeland Reeds</h1>`
br	inserts a line break	`45 Marsh Grass Ln. Marble, MN 55764`

Validating Your HTML Code

You've seen that previewing your Web pages can be useful for spotting problems with your code and making sure that your Web pages display as expected for your users. Another tool is validation, which is an automated process of comparing code you've written against the HTML5 coding standards. When previewing a page reveals an error in your code that's difficult to track down, validation can sometimes be useful in identifying the specific source of the problem. In addition, sometimes a user agent can interpret a Web page as expected in spite of code that doesn't conform to specifications. In this case, validating your code and correcting errors can help to ensure that your code will continue to work with future versions of both user agents and HTML standards, which may not continue to deal seamlessly with erroneous coding. ▓▓▓▓ Faduma has given you the Web address of an online code validator and asks you to give her a validation report of the page you've created.

STEPS

1. **Open your Web browser, click in the** Address Bar, **type** http://validator.w3.org/, **then press [Enter]**
   The Web page opens for the validation service provided by the W3C, as shown in Figure B-11.

2. **Click the** Validate by File Upload tab
   Because your page is not yet published on the Internet, you'll upload your file directly to the w3.org Web site for validation.

3. **Click** Browse **or** Choose File, **navigate to the drive and folder where you store your Data Files, open the** Unit B/Unit folder, **then double-click** index.html

TROUBLE

If your document does not successfully validate as HTML5, return to your text editor, compare your document to Figure B-9 and make any necessary changes, then save your work and revalidate your file.

4. **Click** Check
   The browser uploads your document to the w3.org Web site and the result page opens, as shown in Figure B-12.

5. **Scroll down to read the validation results, including any Notes or Warnings**

6. **If you have space on a Web server for publishing your documents, create a local root folder within the Unit folder, move** index.html **to the local root folder, upload the file to your Web publishing location, then open** index.html **in your browser from the published location to verify that the upload was successful**

7. **Close any open browsers, then close your text editor.**

FIGURE B-11: W3C Validator Web page

Click for
options to
upload your
html file

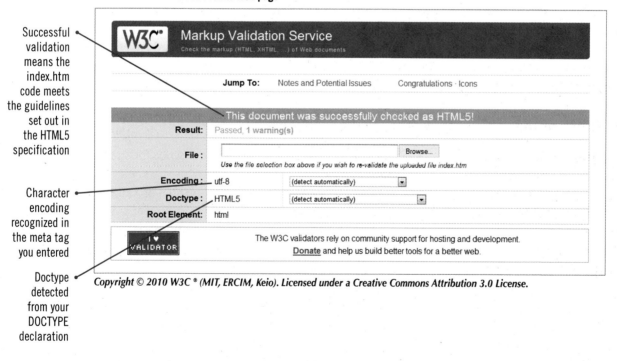

FIGURE B-12: Validation results Web page

Successful
validation
means the
index.htm
code meets
the guidelines
set out in
the HTML5
specification

Character
encoding
recognized in
the meta tag
you entered

Doctype
detected
from your
DOCTYPE
declaration

Practice

For current SAM information, including versions and content details, visit SAM Central (http://www.cengage.com/samcentral). If you have a SAM user profile, you may have access to hands-on instruction, practice, and assessment of the skills covered in this unit. Since various versions of SAM are supported throughout the life of this text, check with your instructor for the correct instructions and URL/Web site for accessing assignments.

Concepts Review

Refer to Figure B-13 to answer the following questions.

FIGURE B-13

```
    index.html - Notepad
a
    File  Edit  Format  View  Help
b   <!DOCTYPE html>
    <html>
       <head>
c        <meta charset="utf-8" />
         <title>Lakeland Reeds Bed and Breakfast</title>
d      </head>
       <body>
e        <h1>Lakeland Reeds Bed and Breakfast</h1>
         <p>A country getaway perfect for fishing, boating, biking, or just watching the day go by.</p>
f        <p>Philip Blaine, Proprietor<br />45 Marsh Grass Ln.<br />Marble, MN 55764<br />(218) 555-5253</p>
       </body>
g   </html>
```

1. Which tag marks the beginning of a paragraph?
2. Which tag marks the beginning of the highest-level heading?
3. Which tag marks the beginning of text that appears in the title bar of a Web browser?
4. Which tag creates a line break?
5. Which tag marks the beginning of page contents that are visible in the main window of a Web browser?
6. Which tag marks the beginning of a Web page?
7. Which tag marks the beginning of code that does not appear in the main browser window?

Match each HTML term with the statement that best describes it.

8. Hypertext Markup Language
9. World Wide Web Consortium
10. Extensible Markup Language
11. Extensible Hypertext Markup Language
12. Web Hypertext Application Technology Working Group

a. a generic language that enables users to describe the structure of any kind of document
b. a version of HTML that complies with the rules of XML
c. a standardized format for specifying the structure of a Web page
d. group responsible along with the W3C for the development of HTML5
e. organization founded to take on the responsibility of maintaining the standards of HTML

Select the best answer from the list of choices.

13. Which type of language is HTML?

  a. presentational

  b. deprecated

  c. semantic

  d. one-sided

14. Which is the companion language to HTML used to describe the appearance of elements?

  a. WHATWG

  b. CSS

  c. XHTML

  d. XML

15. Which element lets user agents know that the document contents are written in HTML?

  a. title

  b. html

  c. body

  d. DOCTYPE declaration

16. Which type of tag do you place at the end of an element you are marking?

  a. deprecated

  b. closing

  c. one-sided

  d. opening

17. What is the term for opening a Web page in one or more Web browsers and examining the result?

  a. tagging

  b. hand-coding

  c. validation

  d. previewing

Skills Review

1. Create an HTML document.

  a. Open a new document in your text editor.

  b. Type **<!DOCTYPE html>**, then press [Enter].

  c. Type **<html>**, press [Enter] twice, then type **</html>**.

  d. If you are using TextEdit on a Mac, click Format, then click Make Plain Text.

  e. Click File, then click Save.

  f. Navigate to the drive and folder where you store your Data Files, open the Unit B folder, then open the Review folder.

  g. In the File name box (Windows) or Save As box (Mac), type **index.html**.

  h. If you are using Notepad in Windows, click the Save as type list arrow, then click All Files (*.*).

  i. Click Save.

2. Set up the document head and body.

  a. Click in the blank line between the opening and closing html tags, press [Spacebar] twice, then type **<head>**.

  b. Press [Enter] twice, press [Spacebar] twice, then type **</head>**.

  c. Press [Enter], press [Spacebar] twice, then type **<body>**.

  d. Press [Enter] twice, press [Spacebar] twice, then type **</body>**.

  e. Click in the blank line between the opening and closing head tags, press [Spacebar] four times, type **<meta charset="utf-8" />**, then press [Enter].

  f. Save your work.

3. Add Web page text and one-sided tags.

  a. Click in the blank line above the closing head tag if necessary, press [Spacebar] four times, then type **<title>Big J's Deep Dish Pizza</title>**.

  b. Click in the blank line between the opening and closing body tags, press [Spacebar] four times, then type **<h1>Big J's Deep Dish Pizza</h1>**.

  c. Press [Enter], press [Spacebar] four times, then type **<p>Authentic Chicago-style deep dish pizza—eat in, carry out, or call for delivery.</p>**.

  d. Press [Enter], insert four spaces, then type the following text:
    **<p>150 St. Joseph St.
Toronto, ON M5S 2C3
(416) 555-3337</p>**

  e. Press [Enter], type **<p>**, type your first and last name, type a comma, then type **HTML5 Unit B, Skills Review</p>**.

  f. Save your work.

Skills Review (continued)

4. Preview your Web page.

    a. Using your file manager, navigate to the drive and folder where you store your Data Files, open the Review folder, double-click index.html, then compare your screen to Figure B-14.

    b. If multiple browsers are installed on your system, return to your file manager, right-click (Windows) or control-click index.html, point to Open with, then click another browser name in the list.

    c. If your Web page is open in multiple browsers, note any differences between them in the way the page is displayed.

5. Validate your HTML code.

    a. Open your Web browser, click in the Address Bar, type **http://validator.w3.org/**, then press [Enter].

    b. Click the Validate by File Upload tab.

    c. Click Browse or Choose File, navigate to the drive and folder where you store your Data Files, open the Unit B/Review folder, then double-click index.html.

    d. Click Check.

    e. Scroll down to read the validation results, including any Notes or Warnings.

    f. If requested by your instructor, save or print the validation results.

    g. If you have space on a Web server for publishing your documents, create a local root folder within the Review folder, move index.html to the local root folder, upload index.html to your Web publishing location, then open index.html in your browser from the published location to verify that the upload was successful.

    h. Close any open browsers, then close your text editor.

FIGURE B-14

Big J's Deep Dish Pizza

Authentic Chicago-style deep dish pizza--eat in, carry out, or call for delivery.

150 St. Joseph St.
Toronto, ON M5S 2C3
(416) 555-3337

Independent Challenge 1

Spotted Wren Garden Center, a local garden shop and plant store, has hired you to create a Web site for their business. Sarah Nguyen, the shop's owner and manager, would like you to create a Web presence as a new avenue of marketing, as well as a means to keep regular customers up to date on seasonal specials and new products.

    a. Open a new document in your text editor, type **<!DOCTYPE html>**, then press [Enter].

    b. Type **<html>**, press [Enter], press [Spacebar] twice, type <head>, then press [Enter].

    c. Press [Spacebar] four times, type **<meta charset="utf-8" />**, then press [Enter] twice.

    d. Press [Spacebar] twice, type **</head>**, then press [Enter].

    e. Press [Spacebar] twice, type **<body>**, then press [Enter] twice.

    f. Press [Spacebar] twice, type **</body>**, press [Enter], then type **</html>**.

    g. Click File, click Save, navigate to the drive and folder where you store your Data Files, open the Unit B folder, then open the IC1 folder.

    h. Click the File name box (Windows) or Save As box (Mac), then type **index.html**.

    i. Click the Save as type list arrow and click All Files (*.*) (Windows), or click the File Format list arrow and click HTML (Mac), then click Save.

    j. Click in the blank line above the closing head tag, press [Spacebar] four times, then type **<title>Spotted Wren Garden Center</title>**.

    k. Click in the blank line between the opening and closing body tags, press [Spacebar] four times, then type **<h1>Spotted Wren Garden Center</h1>**.

Getting Started with HTML

Independent Challenge 1 (continued)

l. Press [Enter], press [Spacebar] four times, then type **<p>For your year-round garden and yard needs, with a focus on the unusual and hard to find.</p>**.

m. Press [Enter], insert four spaces, then type the following text:

**<p>548 N. 58th St.
Omaha, NE 68132
(402) 555-9736</p>**

n. Press [Enter], type **<p>**, type your first and last name, type a comma, then type **HTML5 Unit B, Independent Challenge 1</p>**.

o. Save your work.

p. Use your file manager to navigate to the drive and folder where you store your Data Files, then open the Unit B/IC1 folder. Double-click index.html to view the Web page in your default browser and compare your screen to Figure B-15.

q. If multiple browsers are installed on your system, return to your file manager, right-click (Windows) or control-click (Mac) index.html, point to Open with, then click another browser name in the list, noting any differences between the browsers in the way the page is displayed.

FIGURE B-15

> # Spotted Wren Garden Center
>
> For your year-round garden and yard needs, with a focus on the unusual and hard to find.
>
> 548 N. 58th St.
> Omaha, NE 68132
> (402) 555-9736

r. In your Web browser, open http://validator.w3.org/, then click the Validate by File Upload tab.

s. Click Browse or Choose File, navigate to the drive and folder where you store your Data Files, open the IC1 folder, then double-click index.html.

t. Click Check, then scroll down to read the validation results, including any Notes or Warnings.

u. If requested by your instructor, save or print the validation results.

v. If you have space on a Web server for publishing your documents, create a local root folder within the IC1 folder, move index.html to the local root folder, upload index.html to your Web publishing location, then open index.html in your browser from the published location to verify that the upload was successful.

w. Close any open browsers, then close your text editor.

Independent Challenge 2

To help build your Web design skills, you have volunteered to create a Web site for the Murfreesboro Recreational Soccer League (MRSL). The league organizes recreational leagues every summer and fall for local, nonprofessional soccer players to get exercise and have fun. You decide to start by creating a Web page with a basic description of the league along with contact information.

a. Open a new document in your text editor, type **<!DOCTYPE html>**, then press [Enter].

b. Enter the opening and closing html, head, and body tags. Be sure to indent the head and body tags two spaces.

c. On an empty line between the opening and closing head tags, press [Spacebar] four times, then type **<meta charset="utf-8" />**.

d. Click File, click Save, navigate to the drive and folder where you store your Data Files, open the Unit B folder, then open the IC2 folder. Click the File name box (Windows) or Save As box (Mac), then type **index.html**. Click the Save as type list arrow and click All Files (*.*) (Windows), or click the File Format list arrow and click HTML (Mac), then click Save.

e. Add a blank line in the head section, press [Spacebar] four times, then type **<title>Murfreesboro Regional Soccer League</title>**.

f. Add a blank line in the body section, press [Spacebar] four times, then type **<h1>Murfreesboro Regional Soccer League</h1>**.

Independent Challenge 2 (continued)

Advanced Challenge Exercise

- Beneath the h1 element, add a blank line, press [Spacebar] four times, then type **<h2> Part of the North American Recreational Soccer Association</h2>** to create a second-level heading.

g. Add a blank line in the body section, press [Spacebar] four times, then type **<p>Get exercise, have fun, and build your soccer skills playing with us. Teams for beginners as well as experienced players.</p>**.

h. Below the paragraph you just entered, enter four spaces, then add the following text:
**<p>c/o Davies Sporting Goods
418 N. Sartoris St.
Murfreesboro, TN 37130
(615) 555-2255</p>**

i. Press [Enter], type **<p>**, type your first and last name, type a comma, then type **HTML5 Unit B, Independent Challenge 2</p>**.

j. Save your work.

k. Using your file manager, navigate to the drive and folder where you store your Data Files, open the Unit B/IC2 folder, then double-click index.html to view the Web page in your default browser and compare your screen to Figure B-16.

FIGURE B-16

> ### Murfreesboro Regional Soccer League
>
> **Part of the North American Recreational Soccer Association**
>
> Get exercise, have fun, and build your soccer skills playing with us. Teams for beginners as well as experienced players.
>
> c/o Davies Sporting Goods
> 418 N. Sartoris St.
> Murfreesboro, TN 37130
> (615) 555-2255

l. If multiple browsers are installed on your system, return to your file manager, right-click (Windows) or control-click (Mac) index.html, point to Open with, then click another browser name in the list and note any differences between the browsers in the way the page is displayed.

m. In your Web browser, open http://validator.w3.org/, then click the Validate by File Upload tab.

n. Click Browse or Choose File, navigate to the drive and folder where you store your Data Files, open the Unit B/IC2 folder, then double-click index.html.

o. Click Check, then scroll down to read the validation results, including any Notes or Warnings.

p. If requested by your instructor, save or print the validation results.

q. If you have space on a Web server for publishing your documents, create a local root folder within the IC2 folder, move index.html to the local root folder, upload index.html to your Web publishing location, then open index.html in your browser from the published location to verify that the upload was successful.

r. Close any open browsers, then close your text editor.

Independent Challenge 3

In your new job creating sites for a Web design firm, you've been assigned a new client, Hotel Natoma. The hotel's business manager, Diego Merckx, wants to use the Web to showcase the facility and its amenities.

a. Open a new document in your text editor and enter a DOCTYPE declaration.

b. Enter the opening and closing html, head, and body tags. Be sure to indent the head and body tags.

c. In the head section, add a meta tag to specify the document's character encoding.

d. Save your file as **index.html** to the Unit B/IC3 folder on the drive and folder where you store your Data Files. Be sure to Click the Save as type list arrow and click All Files (*.*) (Windows), or click the File Format list arrow and click HTML (Mac), before you click Save.

e. In the head section, add a title element that displays the text **Hotel Natoma**.

f. In the body section, add a heading 1 element that displays the text **Hotel Natoma**.

Independent Challenge 3 (continued)

g. Add a paragraph element to the body section that displays the text **A low-impact, Earth-friendly home base in the center of everything San Francisco has to offer**.

h. Below the paragraph you just entered, add a paragraph element with line breaks to display the following contact information:

568 Natoma St.
San Francisco, CA 94103
(415) 555-8378

i. Press [Enter], type **<p>**, type your first and last name, type a comma, then type **HTML5 Unit B, Independent Challenge 3</p>**.

> ## Hotel Natoma
>
> A low-impact, Earth-friendly home base in the center of everything San Francisco has to offer.
>
> 568 Natoma St.
> San Francisco, CA 94103
> (415) 555-8378

j. Save your work, then preview your page in your default Web browser. If multiple browsers are installed on your system, open your page in a secondary browser and note any differences between the two browsers in the way the page is displayed. Compare your screen to Figure B-17.

k. If you have space on a Web server for publishing your documents, create a local root folder within the IC3 folder, move index.html to the local root folder, upload index.html to your Web publishing location, then open index.html in your browser from the published location to verify that the upload was successful.

l. In your Web browser, open http://validator.w3.org/.

Advanced Challenge Exercise

■ If you published your Web page, enter the Web address to open your Web page in the Address box, then click Check.

m. If you did not publish your Web page in Step j, click the Validate by File Upload tab.

n. Navigate to the location of the file you created, click Check, then scroll down to read the validation results.

o. If requested by your instructor, save or print the validation results.

p. Close any open browsers, then close your text editor.

Real Life Independent Challenge

This assignment builds on the personal Web site you started planning in Unit A. In this project, you will create the basic structure of your main Web page and add text to the page.

a. In your text editor, create the structuring tags for your Web site, including a DOCTYPE statement, a character encoding statement, and html, head, and body sections. Save the file as **index.html** to the Unit B/RLIC folder on the drive and folder where you store your Data Files.

b. Add a title element and a heading element. If you choose, the heading text may be different than the title text.

c. Create paragraph elements containing any text shown on your Web site sketch. Include a paragraph element containing your first and last name, and the text **HTML5 Unit B, Real Life Independent Challenge**.

d. Save your work, preview the page, and make any changes to the code that may be necessary.

e. Validate your code using the validator at w3.org.

Visual Workshop

Use a text editor to create the Web page shown in Figure B-18. Include a paragraph element after the content shown that contains your first and last name and the text **HTML5 Unit B, Visual Workshop**. When you are finished, save your work as **index.html** to the Unit B/VW folder on the drive and folder where you store your Data Files. Preview the Web page in your default Web browser, validate your code using the online validator at w3.org, then close your browser and your text editor.

FIGURE B-18

Revisions Bookstore and Cafe

Custom brewed coffee and hand-selected books. Special orders are our specialty.

412 N. 25th St.
Richmond, VA 23223
(804) 555-2565

Getting Started with CSS

Files You Will Need:

To view a list of files needed for this unit, see the Data Files Grid in the back of the book.

Early versions of HTML included both semantic and presentational elements; for example, you could use the i element to format text as italic or the center element to center another element horizontally on the page. Presentational tags such as these made Web page code dense and complex, made changing the appearance of a Web page a significant undertaking because of the many individual tags to be edited, and had to be repeated on every page of a Web site to create a common layout and appearance. Early Web developers recognized that another solution was needed, and through the W3C, helped create Cascading Style Sheets (CSS) as a separate, complementary language for presentation. CSS code can be included in an HTML document, but CSS follows its own syntax rules. As you continue your work on the Lakeland Reeds Bed & Breakfast Web site, your supervisor, Faduma Egal, has asked you to add some layout features to the site. In this unit, you'll learn about CSS and integrate CSS formatting into your Web documents.

OBJECTIVES

Assess style rules

Create an embedded style sheet

Implement an id selector

Implement the div element

Implement a class selector

Create an external style sheet

Link to an external style sheet

Validate your CSS code

Assessing Style Rules

Rather than adding formatting elements to a Web page as in previous versions of HTML, CSS adds style information to elements defined in the HTML code for a Web page. You add CSS to an HTML document by inserting **style rules**, which are lines or blocks of CSS code that specify the presentation of Web page elements. Version 2.1 of the CSS standard has been in wide use for years, but recent additions and enhancements to the language have given rise to CSS3. As you prepare to integrate CSS into the Lakeland Reeds Web site, you review style rule structure and syntax.

CSS code builds on a few basic concepts:

- **Style rule syntax**

  A style rule is composed of two main parts. The rule starts with one or more **selectors**, which identify the HTML element or elements to which the style rule applies. One or more **name-value pairs** follow the selector(s); each pair specifies a CSS **property** to apply to the selector(s) and the value to assign to the property. Each name-value pair ends with a semicolon, and all of the name-value pairs declared for a selector are enclosed in a single set of curly braces. For instance, the style rule

  ```
  h1 {
      text-align: center;
      width: 40em;
      }
  ```

  centers the text of any h1 heading in a Web document and sets its width to 40 ems.

- **Kinds of selectors**

  CSS allows several selector types. The most general selectors are the names of HTML elements, such as h1 or p, which are known as **type selectors**. These selectors apply associated name/value pairs to every instance of the specified element in the associated Web document. For instance, the style rule in the previous paragraph centers the text and sets the width of any h1 heading in the HTML document, even if there is more than one. Likewise, a style rule using a p selector would apply the properties it specifies to all of a document's p elements.

QUICK TIP

Appendix B lists the most commonly used properties from CSS versions 1 and 2, along with some of the most widely supported CSS3 properties.

- **Types of name-value pairs**

  CSS supports properties for many aspects of Web page presentation, including fonts, text, tables, lists, background, borders, and positioning. Multiple properties are defined for each area, enabling control over specific details of presentation. Table C-1 lists the properties you will use in this unit. Allowable values are specific to each property and vary widely, including keywords such as "centered," numerical values expressed in percentages or units of measurement, and relative measurements such as "smaller." If you're unsure of the allowable values for a property, you can look them up in online CSS references such as the one at www.w3c.org.

TABLE C-1: CSS properties and values

group	affects	properties	allowable values	notes
Text alignment	the horizontal alignment of text.	text-align	**left**, **right**, **center**, **justify**, **inherit** (same value as enclosing element)	
Dimensions	the dimensions of an element, excluding border, padding, and margins.	width, height, max-width, max-height, min-width, min-height	*value* in em, pixels, or another supported unit, *percent* of the enclosing element, **inherit** (same value as enclosing element), **auto** (default)	
Border	the properties of the border around an element.	border-width, border-top-width, border-right-width, border-bottom -width, border-left-width	**thin**, **medium**, **thick**, *value* in em, pixels, or another supported unit	Specify width for all borders with border-width property, or use individual properties for specific sides.
		border-style, border-top-style, border-right-style, border-bottom-style, border-left-style	**dotted**, **dashed**, **solid**, **double**, **groove**, **ridge**, **inset**, **outset**	Specify style for all borders with border-style property, or use individual properties for specific sides.
		border-color, border-top-color, border-right-color, border-bottom-color, border-left-color	color as a *name* from cross-browser compatibility list, *rgb code* in the format rgb (*rrr,ggg,bbb*), or *hexadecimal code* in the format #*rrggbb*, **transparent**, **inherit** (value of enclosing element)	Specify color for all borders with border-color property, or use individual properties for specific sides.
		border	*width style color*	Shorthand property combining width, style, and color into a single declaration.
Padding	the space between element contents and border.	padding, padding-top, padding-right, padding-bottom, padding-left	*value* in em, pixels, or another supported unit, *percent* of the enclosing element.	Specify padding for all borders with padding property, or use individual properties for specific sides.
Margins	the space outside of the element border.	margin, margin-top, margin-right, margin-bottom, margin-left	*value* in em, pixels, or another supported unit, *percent* of the enclosing element, **auto** (default)	Specify margins for all borders with margins property, or use individual properties for specific sides.

Spacing your CSS code

Web page rendering engines recognize name-value pairs after a selector as starting after an opening curly brace { and ending with the closing curly brace }. As long as a semicolon follows each value, any number of spaces, tabs, and new lines can occur within a set of name-value pairs. As a result, the appearance of CSS code can vary widely. Some developers prefer to keep all name-value pairs on the same line as the selector, as shown at the top of Figure C-1, to keep their code compact and make it obvious which pairs are associated with which selector. Others prefer to give each name-value pair its own line, often indented beneath its selector, as shown at the bottom of Figure C-1, to make the code easier to read and parse. While the code shown in this book uses the latter format, don't be surprised to see the former—as well as other variations—in other examples of CSS that you may encounter. While you may be required to follow a given code format by an employer or client, such formatting is most often a matter of personal taste.

FIGURE C-1: Two alternative ways of entering CSS code

```
<style type="text/css">
  h1 {text-align: center;}
  #contact {text-align:right; padding-right:15px;}
  #box {border-width:3px; border-style:solid; border-color:black; width:800px; margin-left:auto; margin-right:auto;}
  .maintext {text-align:left; width:60%; margin-left:auto; margin-right:auto;}
</style>
```

```
<style type="text/css">
  h1 {
    text-align: center;
  }
  #contact {
    text-align: right;
    padding-right: 15px;
  }
  #box {
    border-width: 3px;
    border-style: solid;
    border-color: black;
    width: 800px;
    margin-left: auto;
    margin-right: auto;
  }
  .maintext {
    text-align: center;
    width: 60%;
    margin-left: auto;
    margin-right: auto;
  }
</style>
```

Creating an Embedded Style Sheet

While there are a few different ways to apply CSS styles to Web page elements, creating an embedded style sheet is the most straightforward solution for affecting the presentation of a single Web page. An **embedded style sheet** is a section of CSS code entered in the head element of an HTML document. You insert CSS code in a style element with an attribute specifying that the contents are written in CSS. You have created basic Web documents for each of the pages in the Lakeland Reeds B&B Web site. In addition, the art department at Great Northern Web Solutions has provided you a sketch of a visual layout for the site. You start your work with CSS by creating a style rule to center the main heading text.

STEPS

1. **Start your text editor, click** File, **click** Open **(or choose the appropriate options in your program for selecting a file), then navigate to the** Unit C/Unit folder **on the drive and folder where you store your Data Files**

2. **Select the file** HTM C-1.html, **then click** Open **(or choose the appropriate program-specific option to open the file)**

3. **Insert a blank line before the closing body tag, insert a paragraph element containing your first and last name and the text** HTML5 Unit C, **then save the file as** index.html

4. **Open** index.html **in your browser**

   In addition to your personal info, the Web page contains a level 1 heading, a level 2 heading, and two additional paragraphs.

5. **Return to your text editor, click at the end of the line containing the title element, then press** [Enter]

6. **Press** [Spacebar] **four times, type** <style type="text/css">, **press** [Enter] **twice, press** [Spacebar] **four times, then type** </style>

   You will enter your CSS code between the opening and closing style tags. The attribute "type" and value "text/css" in the opening tag specify that the code within the style element follows the rules of CSS.

7. **Click in the blank line between the opening and closing style tags, press** [Spacebar] **six times, type** h1 {, **press** [Enter], **press** [Spacebar] **eight times, type** text-align: center;, **press** [Enter], **press** [Spacebar] **eight times, then type** }

   The text-align property determines the horizontal alignment of text. This style rule center-aligns all text within h1 elements. Compare your document to Figure C-2.

8. **Save your document, return to your default browser, then click the** Refresh **or** Reload **button to view changes to your Web document**

   As Figure C-3 shows, the first line of text, which is an h1 element, is centered horizontally in the browser window.

FIGURE C-2: Type style rule

Embedded
stylesheet

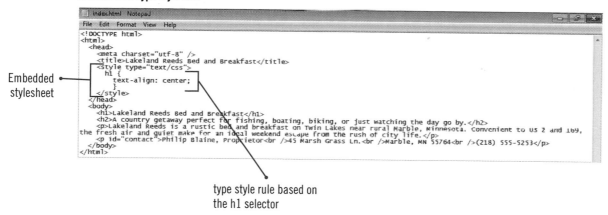

type style rule based on
the h1 selector

FIGURE C-3: Type style rule implemented Web page text styled by style rule

h1 heading
text centered
horizontally
on the
Web page

Lakeland Reeds Bed and Breakfast

A country getaway perfect for fishing, boating, biking, or just watching the day go by.

Lakeland Reeds is a rustic bed and breakfast on Twin Lakes near rural Marble, Minnesota. Convenient to US 2 and 169, the fresh air and quiet make for an ideal weekend escape from the rush of city life.

Philip Blaine, Proprietor
45 Marsh Grass Ln.
Marble, MN 55764
(218) 555-5253

Implementing an id Selector

Sometimes instead of affecting the presentation of all the elements of a certain type, you want to make changes that affect only a single element. For instance, maybe a certain p element requires a different alignment or size from all the other p elements in a document. HTML allows you to add the id attribute to the opening tag for an element to give the element a name. You can then create a special type of selector known as an **id selector** to create CSS code that applies to that element alone. An id selector is simply a pound sign (#) followed by the id value for the element. Any name-value pairs following this selector apply only to the element with the specified id attribute value. The main Lakeland Reeds Web page contains several paragraph elements. The visual style for the page has one of them, the contact information, right-aligned. You use an id attribute and id selector to change the appearance of the contact information.

1. **In your text editor, scroll down if necessary to the paragraph that begins <p>Philip Blaine, Proprietor**

2. **In the opening <p> tag, click to position the insertion point between the p and the >, then press [Spacebar]**

3. **Type id="contact"**
   The paragraph containing the contact information is assigned the unique id value "contact".

4. **If necessary, scroll up to view the embedded style sheet, click after the closing brace for the h1 style rule, press [Enter], then press [Spacebar] six times**

5. **Type #contact { then press [Enter]**

6. **Press [Spacebar] eight times, type text-align: right;, then press [Enter]**
   The default value of text-align is "left", which aligns the left edges of each line of text in an element. Specifying a value of "right" lines up the right edges of the text instead and aligns the right edge of the element with the right edge of the enclosing element.

7. **Press [Spacebar] eight times, then type }**
   Compare your completed code to Figure C-4.

8. **Save your document, return to your default browser, then click the Refresh or Reload button to view changes to your Web document**
   As Figure C-5 shows, the contact information at the bottom of the page is right-aligned.

FIGURE C-4: Style rule using id selector

Style rule
based on id
selector

```
index.html - Notepad
File  Edit  Format  View  Help
<!DOCTYPE html>
<html>
  <head>
    <meta charset="utf-8" />
    <title>Lakeland Reeds Bed and Breakfast</title>
    <style type="text/css">
      h1 {
        text-align: center;
      }
      #contact {
        text-align: right;
      }
    </style>
  </head>
  <body>
    <h1>Lakeland Reeds Bed and Breakfast</h1>
    <h2>A country getaway perfect for fishing, boating, biking, or just watching the day go by.</h2>
    <p>Lakeland Reeds is a rustic bed and breakfast on Twin Lakes near rural Marble, Minnesota. Convenient to US 2 and 169,
the fresh air and quiet make for an ideal weekend escape from the rush of city life.</p>
    <p id="contact">Philip Blaine, Proprietor<br />45 Marsh Grass Ln.<br />Marble, MN 55764<br />(218) 555-5253</p>
  </body>
</html>
```

Attribute value matches id
selector for new style rule

FIGURE C-5: Results of style rule based on id selector

Lakeland Reeds Bed and Breakfast

A country getaway perfect for fishing, boating, biking, or just watching the day go by.

Lakeland Reeds is a rustic bed and breakfast on Twin Lakes near rural Marble, Minnesota. Convenient to US 2 and 169, the fresh air and quiet make for an ideal weekend escape from the rush of city life.

Philip Blaine, Proprietor
45 Marsh Grass Ln.
Marble, MN 55764
(218) 555-5253

Contact information is
right-aligned

Implementing a style rule with multiple selectors

Sometimes you want to assign the same presentation properties to multiple types of elements. While you could create a style rule and duplicate it for each type selector, an easier way is to add multiple type selectors to a single rule. To do this, simply type the selectors with a comma after each one except the last. Adding a space after each comma is optional, but it helps make the code easier to read. After the final selector, type an opening curly brace and enter name-value pairs as you would for any other style rule. For example, you could create a style rule to center-align both the h1 element and the element with the id "stores" using the following code:

```
h1, #stores {
text-align: center;
}
```

There's no limit to the number of element types that you can include in a single rule. In fact, many Web developers start their style sheets with a rule for 10–20 element types to apply a collection of global settings.

Implementing the div Element

Sometimes you want to affect the presentation of a section of a Web document that's not itself a single element. One strategy to accomplish this is to enclose the relevant code in another element and then specify styles for the enclosing element. Even though you can apply whatever changes you want to the contents of an element, many HTML elements describe their contents semantically; for example, the contents of an h1 element are assumed to be the highest level heading, while creating a p element implies that it contains a paragraph of text. However, HTML includes a generic element free of semantic meaning for cases where the section isn't a single element: the div element. Thus, you can assign CSS styles to a section of a Web document by enclosing the relevant block of HTML code in a div element, using the tag pair <div></div>. ▓▓▓▓ The visual design for the Lakeland Reeds Web page encloses the page content in a black box with a fixed width. You enclose the page contents in a div element and add the CSS code to change the visual layout of its contents.

STEPS

1. **In your text editor, click after the opening <body> tag, then press [Enter]**

2. **Press [Spacebar] four times, then type <div id="box">**

3. **At the bottom of the document, click after the closing </p> tag for the element containing the contact information, press [Enter], press [Spacebar] four times, then type </div>**
   The div element contains all the elements between the opening and closing tags.

4. **At the top of the body section, click before the opening <h1> tag, then press [Spacebar] two times**
   Because you are adding another element to your code, you need to increase the indentation of tags that occur within the new tag pair.

5. **Repeat Step 4 to add two spaces before the opening <h2> tag and before both of the opening <p> tags, as shown in Figure C-6, and also before the opening <p> tag for your name**

6. **If necessary, scroll up to view the embedded style sheet, click after the closing brace for the #contact style rule, press [Enter], press [Spacebar] six times, type #box { , then press [Enter]**

QUICK TIP
Be sure to indent each line of code with eight spaces to keep your embedded style sheet easily readable.

7. **Press [Spacebar] eight times, type border-width: 0.25em;, press [Enter], then add the remaining name-value pairs shown in Figure C-6**
   The specification "em" is a relative unit of measure that represents the current font size. If a user customizes font sizes for a browser, elements specified in em resize as well, preserving your Web page layout. The padding property creates blank space between the div element and elements nested inside it.

8. **If necessary, press [Enter] to create a blank line, press [Spacebar] eight times, then type }**
   Compare your completed code to Figure C-6.

9. **Save your document, return to your default browser, then click the Refresh or Reload button to view the changes to your Web document**
   The page contents are now surrounded by a black border that is horizontally centered on the screen, as shown in Figure C-7.

FIGURE C-6: div element added

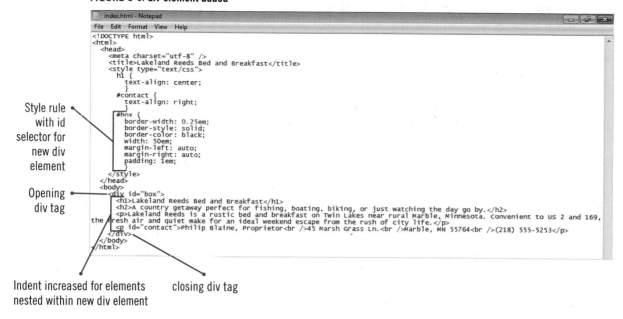

Style rule with id selector for new div element

Opening div tag

Indent increased for elements nested within new div element

closing div tag

FIGURE C-7: Results of new div element and style rule

Lakeland Reeds Bed and Breakfast

A country getaway perfect for fishing, boating, biking, or just watching the day go by.

Lakeland Reeds is a rustic bed and breakfast on Twin Lakes near rural Marble, Minnesota. Convenient to US 2 and 169, the fresh air and quiet make for an ideal weekend escape from the rush of city life.

Philip Blaine, Proprietor
45 Marsh Grass Ln.
Marble, MN 55764
(218) 555-5253

Contents of div element surrounded by 0.25-em-thick, solid black box

Box centered in browser window

Using HTML5 semantic elements

The div element is a useful tool for applying styles to elements or groups of elements that don't fit semantically into common HTML tags. However, the added semantic value of more specific tags can enhance the interpretation of your Web pages by user agents and increase the value of the information indexed by search engines. To bridge this gap, HTML5 defines a set of elements that serve the same function as the div element, but that include semantic value. These elements include *section*, *article*, *header*, and *footer*. Some extra coding is required to make these elements work in older versions of Internet Explorer, so you should make sure you understand how to implement them, and be sure to test any pages that use them in affected browsers. However, whenever practical, implementing these semantic elements in your Web pages adds an extra level of information and can help you create a richer experience for your users.

Implementing a class Selector

Sometimes you want to apply a style rule to multiple elements in a Web document without adding an additional layer of HTML code. While the id attribute limits a given value to a single instance in a Web page, you can create a selector that applies to any number of elements on a page using the HTML class attribute, which does not have this limit. A **class selector** creates a style rule based on values assigned to elements using the HTML class attribute. This allows you to apply a style rule to an unlimited number of separate elements. A class selector consists of a period followed by a class attribute value. 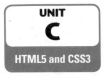 Your final step in implementing the visual design for the Lakeland Reeds Web page is to change the width and alignment of the two paragraphs that appear before the contact information. You add a class attribute to the two elements containing these paragraphs and then add a style rule to modify their presentation.

STEPS

1. **In your text editor, scroll down if necessary to the opening tag for the h2 element, click to position the insertion point between the 2 and the >, press [Spacebar], then type** class="maintext"

2. **In the opening <p> tag for the paragraph that begins "Lakeland Reeds is a rustic bed and breakfast", click to position the insertion point between the p and the >, press [Spacebar], then type** class="maintext"

   The h2 element and the first p element are both assigned the class value *maintext*.

3. **If necessary, scroll up to view the embedded style sheet, click after the closing brace for the #box style rule, press [Enter], then press [Spacebar] six times**

4. **Type** .maintext { **then press [Enter]**

5. **Press [Spacebar] eight times, type** text-align: center;, **then press [Enter]**

   QUICK TIP
   Be sure to indent each line of code with eight spaces to keep your embedded style sheet easily readable.

6. **Add the remaining name-value pairs shown in Figure C-8**

   Using a percentage value with the width property resizes an element relative to the size of the element enclosing it—in this case, the div element that creates the border. Setting the margin-left and margin-right properties to auto centers a non-text element within the element enclosing it.

7. **If necessary, press [Enter] to create a blank line after the last name-value pair, press [Spacebar] eight times, then type** }

   Compare your completed code to Figure C-8.

8. **Save your document, return to your default browser, then click the Refresh or Reload button to view changes to your Web document**

   As Figure C-9 shows, the h2 element and the p element that follows it are narrower than the surrounding border and centered within the border.

FIGURE C-8: Style rule Implemented using class selector

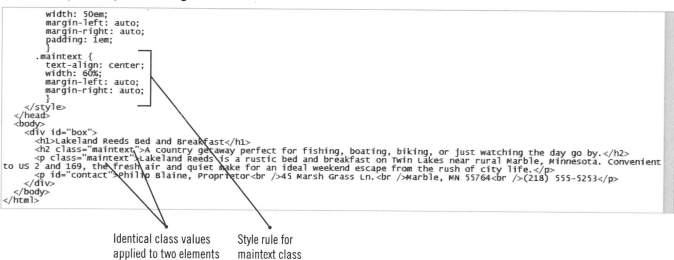

```
        width: 50em;
        margin-left: auto;
        margin-right: auto;
        padding: 1em;
        }
     .maintext {
        text-align: center;
        width: 60%;
        margin-left: auto;
        margin-right: auto;
        }
     </style>
  </head>
  <body>
     <div id="box">
        <h1>Lakeland Reeds Bed and Breakfast</h1>
        <h2 class="maintext">A country getaway perfect for fishing, boating, biking, or just watching the day go by.</h2>
        <p class="maintext">Lakeland Reeds is a rustic bed and breakfast on Twin Lakes near rural Marble, Minnesota. Convenient
to US 2 and 169, the fresh air and quiet make for an ideal weekend escape from the rush of city life.</p>
        <p id="contact">Philip Blaine, Proprietor<br />45 Marsh Grass Ln.<br />Marble, MN 55764<br />(218) 555-5253</p>
     </div>
  </body>
</html>
```

Identical class values
applied to two elements

Style rule for
maintext class

FIGURE C-9: Results of style rule based on class selector

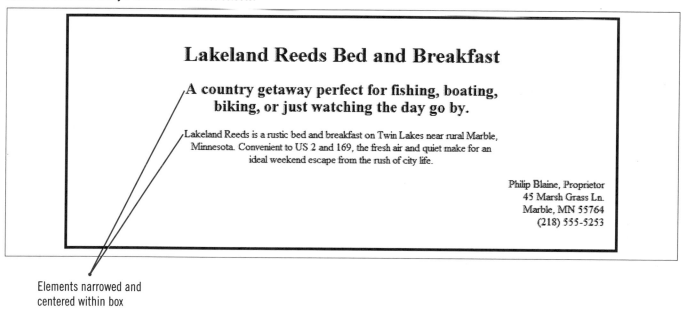

Elements narrowed and
centered within box

Inserting multiple attributes

There is no limit to the number of attributes you can include in a single HTML element. Thus, you can apply multiple style rules to a single element using any combination of a single id attribute and one or more class attributes. For example, you might assign a class to every paragraph in a given section of a Web page, along with an id for the first paragraph in the section to add extra elements to its style. The code for the opening tag might look as follows:

```
<p class="point1" id="opener1">
```

If multiple rules applied to the same element specify values for the same attribute, the value from the last rule in the style sheet is applied. This means it's important to take care with the order of rules in your style sheets. If your pages do not appear as you expect, verify that the order of rules is correct.

Creating an External Style Sheet

An embedded style sheet works well for a stand-alone Web page. However, as your Web presence grows into multiple pages, it becomes impractical to implement a given style change on every page; it also becomes challenging to keep embedded style sheets consistent between multiple pages. Instead, it's helpful to transition a growing Web site to an **external style sheet**, which is a separate file containing style information that multiple Web pages can link to. ▄▄▄▄ As you prepare to create more pages for the Lakeland Reeds Web site, you move the style information for the current page to an external style sheet in order to make the appearance of the site easier to modify as the site grows.

STEPS

1. **In your text editor, scroll up if necessary to view the embedded style sheet, select all the code between the opening and closing style tags, click Edit, then click Cut**

   The contents of the embedded style sheet are removed from the Web document and placed on the clipboard.

2. **Save index.html, click File, click New, then in the new document that opens, type /* Lakeland Reeds Bed and Breakfast */ and press [Enter]**

   In CSS code, any text between /* and */ is treated as a comment and ignored by user agents. Comments are useful for describing the contents of your documents for other Web developers who may need to make changes to them in the future.

3. **Click Edit, click Paste, press [Enter], then add a comment including your first and last name along with the text HTML5 Unit C**

   The embedded style sheet code is pasted into the new document, as shown in Figure C-10.

4. **If you are using TextEdit on a Mac, click Format, then, if necessary, click Make Plain Text**

QUICK TIP

If you are using TextEdit on a Mac, if a dialog box opens asking which file extension to use, click Use .css.

5. **Click File, click Save, navigate to the Unit C/Unit directory on the drive and folder where you store your Data Files, type lakeland.css, click the Encoding list arrow if necessary and click UTF-8, then click Save**

   Your external style sheet is saved with the filename "lakeland.css".

6. **Close lakeland.css, then if necessary, reopen index.html in your text editor**

7. **Select the lines containing the opening and closing <style> tags along with any blank lines between them, then press Delete**

8. **If necessary, click after the closing </title> tag, then press [Enter] to insert a blank line**

QUICK TIP

Because the contents of an external style sheet are written entirely in CSS, the file uses the extension .css instead of .html.

9. **Press [Spacebar] four times, then type <link rel="stylesheet" type="text/css" href="lakeland.css" />**

   Figure C-11 shows the Web page code with the external style sheet reference inserted. The link element makes the contents of an external file available in the HTML document. The values for the rel and type attributes specify that user agents should read the external document as a style sheet written in CSS. The href attribute specifies the filename of the external style sheet.

10. **Save your document, return to your default browser, then click the Refresh or Reload button**

   Your Web page appears just as it did when you were using an embedded style sheet. Even though you removed the style rules previously defined in the HTML document, you added a reference to the external document containing the rules. As a result, your browser still has access to the same style information and renders the Web page according to the same guidelines.

FIGURE C-10: External style sheet

CSS comment

Style rules moved from embedded style sheet

```
/* Lakeland Reeds Bed and Breakfast */
h1 {
    text-align: center;
}
#contact {
    text-align: right;
}
#box {
    border-width: 0.25em;
    border-style: solid;
    border-color: black;
    width: 50em;
    margin-left: auto;
    margin-right: auto;
    padding: 1em;
}
.maintext {
    text-align: center;
    width: 60%;
    margin-left: auto;
    margin-right: auto;
}
```

FIGURE C-11: Web page linked to external style sheet

link element loads contents of external css document

```
<!DOCTYPE html>
<html>
  <head>
    <meta charset="utf-8" />
    <title>Lakeland Reeds Bed and Breakfast</title>
    <link rel="stylesheet" type="text/css" href="lakeland.css" />
  </head>
  <body>
    <div id="box">
      <h1>Lakeland Reeds Bed and Breakfast</h1>
      <h2 class="maintext">A country getaway perfect for fishing, boating, biking, or just watching the day go by.</h2>
      <p class="maintext">Lakeland Reeds is a rustic bed and breakfast on Twin Lakes near rural Marble, Minnesota. Convenient
to US 2 and 169, the fresh air and quiet make for an ideal weekend escape from the rush of city life.</p>
      <p id="contact">Philip Blaine, Proprietor<br />45 Marsh Grass Ln.<br />Marble, MN 55764<br />(218) 555-5253</p>
    </div>
  </body>
</html>
```

Filename of external style sheet

Implementing Inline styles

In addition to embedded and external style sheets, you can also incorporate CSS properties into an HTML document using inline styles. An **inline style** is a style rule inserted into the opening tag of an element using the style attribute. Figure C-12 shows an example of an inline style. Inline styles do not offer many of the benefits provided by other methods of applying styles. For instance, changing a style applied inline requires locating the style within HTML code, rather than simply looking at an embedded or external style sheet. Because of this and other drawbacks, many Web developers avoid using inline styles.

FIGURE C-12: An inline style

```
<h1 style="text-align: center;">Lakeland Reeds Bed and Breakfast</h1>
```

Linking to an External Style Sheet

Once you create an external style sheet for a Web site, you can apply the style rules it contains to every page on the site simply by adding to each HTML document a link element referencing the style sheet file. If you later decide to make changes to the layout of your Web site, any change you make to the external style sheet is reflected immediately on all the pages that link to it. ▰▰▰ You have created a second page for the Lakeland Reeds Web site and added to it the same class and id attributes that you used on the main Web page. You add a link in the new Web document to the external style sheet file you created in order to implement on the new page the same style rules you already created.

STEPS

QUICK TIP
If you are using TextEdit on a Mac, in the Open dialog box, click the **Ignore Rich Text Commands check box** to select it for any HTML file you open.

1. **In your text editor, open the file** HTM C-2.html **from the** Unit C/Unit folder **on the drive and folder where you store your Data Files, then save it as** aboutus.html

   As Figure C-13 shows, the file contains an element with an id value of "contact", a div element with an id value of "box", and multiple elements with the class value of "maintext".

2. **Insert a blank line before the closing body tag, then insert a paragraph element containing your first and last name and the text** HTML5 Unit C

3. **Open** aboutus.html **in your browser**

   All the page elements are left-aligned, and the page resembles the main Lakeland Reeds page at the beginning of the unit.

4. **Return to your text editor, click at the end of the line containing the title element, then press [Enter]**

5. **Press [Spacebar] four times, then type** <link rel="stylesheet" type="text/css" href="lakeland.css" />

   This is the same link code you inserted into index.html. Figure C-13 shows the completed code for the Web document.

6. **Save your document, return to your default browser, then click the** Refresh or Reload button **to view the changes to the About Us page**

   The browser now renders the Web page with a layout similar to the main page of the Web site.

7. **Reopen** lakeland.css **in your text editor, then in the .maintext style rule, change the value for** text-align **from** center **to** left

8. **Save your document, close your text editor, return to your default browser, then click the** Refresh or Reload button **to view the changes to the About Us page**

   As Figure C-14 shows, the h2 heading and the paragraphs below it are now left-aligned rather than center-aligned.

9. **Reopen** index.html **in your default browser**

   As shown in Figure C-14, the changes in the main page match the changes in the About Us page because the presentation of both documents is based on the external style sheet in lakeland.css.

FIGURE C-13: About Us page with link to external style sheet

```
aboutus.html - Notepad
File  Edit  Format  View  Help
<!DOCTYPE html>
<html>
   <head>
      <meta charset="utf-8" />
      <title>Lakeland Reeds Bed and Breakfast - About Us</title>
      <link rel="stylesheet" type="text/css" href="lakeland.css" />
   </head>
   <body>
      <div id="box">
         <h1>Lakeland Reeds Bed and Breakfast</h1>
         <h2 class="maintext">About Us</h2>
         <p class="maintext">Lakeland Reeds is an ideal place to unplug from your daily routine, whether on the shore of Twin
Lakes watching the sundown over the cattails or just curled up in a hammock on our screened wraparound porch with a good
book.  Breakfast is ready whenever you are, and we're happy to accommodate a wide range of appetites, from comfort food like
sausage and biscuits to the lighter end of things, such as egg white omelettes and fresh fruit.</p>
         <p class="maintext">We're here to help you get the most out of your time with us, from canoes and life vests for a day
out on the lake, to DVDs and popcorn for a quiet evening in. We look forward to welcoming you!</p>
         <p id="contact">Philip Blaine, Proprietor<br />45 Marsh Grass Ln.<br />Marble, MN 55764<br />(218) 555-5253</p>
      </div>
   </body>
</html>
```

Every document linking to an external
style sheet uses the same code for the
link element

FIGURE C-14: Multiple pages styled with a single style sheet

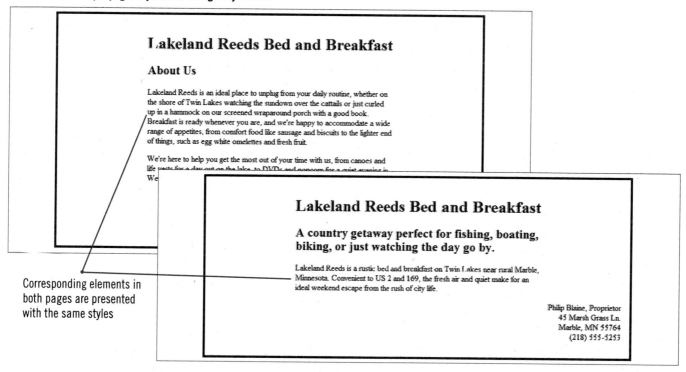

Corresponding elements in
both pages are presented
with the same styles

Combining embedded and external style sheets

Sometimes a Web page on a Web site you're developing might require styling that the site's other pages don't need. You can include style rules that apply only to one page in an external style sheet. However, as your Web site grows larger, you want to minimize the size of an external style sheet to avoid increasing the download time for your Web site and thereby delaying users who want to view your pages. In fact, it's fairly common to combine both embedded and external styles in the same Web site.

Because styles can be applied based on external or embedded style sheets, inline styles, or a browser's default settings, an element may be subject to multiple contradictory values for a given property. To resolve such conflicts, CSS includes rules of precedence for

determining which style rule to follow in a conflict: inline styles have the highest priority, followed by embedded styles, external styles, and finally browser settings. This process of determining precedence is known as **cascading** and results in all available styles coalescing into a single virtual style sheet for the user agent's reference in rendering content.

For some user agents, the order of embedded and external style sheets in your code changes the default order of precedence. To ensure that your Web pages follow standard cascading order when using both kinds of style sheets, be sure to always place the link element to an external style sheet before the style element for an embedded style sheet.

Validating Your CSS Code

Even when your CSS code works in your browser testing, it's important to validate it against CSS rules. Validation helps ensure the compatibility of your code with user agents other than those you test on, and goes a long way toward ensuring that your code remains usable through the continual enhancement and expansion of the CSS specification. There are several reputable online validators available that allow you to either copy and paste code from an embedded style sheet or upload a .css file for checking. ▓▓▓ You upload your external style sheet to a CSS validator on the W3C Web site to verify that it complies with the rules of CSS.

STEPS

QUICK TIP

You can find alternative validators by searching on the phrase **CSS validator** in a search engine.

1. **Open your Web browser, click in the Address Bar, type** http://jigsaw.w3.org/css-validator/, **then press [Enter]**

   The Web page opens for the CSS validation service provided by the W3C, as shown in Figure C-15.

2. **Click the By file upload tab**

   Because your Web site is not yet published on the Internet, you'll upload your file directly to the w3.org Web site for validation.

3. **Click Browse or Choose File, navigate to the drive and folder where you store your Data Files, open the Unit C/Unit folder, then double-click lakeland.css**

4. **Click More Options, if necessary click the Profile list arrow and click CSS Level 3, then click Check**

   The browser uploads your style sheet to the w3.org Web site and the result page opens, as shown in Figure C-16.

5. **Scroll down to read the validation results, including any notes or warnings**

6. **If you have space on a Web server for publishing your documents, create a local root folder within the Unit folder, move index.html, aboutus.html, and lakeland.css to the local root folder, then upload the files to your Web publishing location**

7. **Open index.htm in your browser from the published location to verify that the upload was successful, then open aboutus.html from the published location**

8. **Close any open browsers, then close your text editor**

FIGURE C-15: W3C CSS Validation Service Web page

Click to
display
options for
uploading
your file

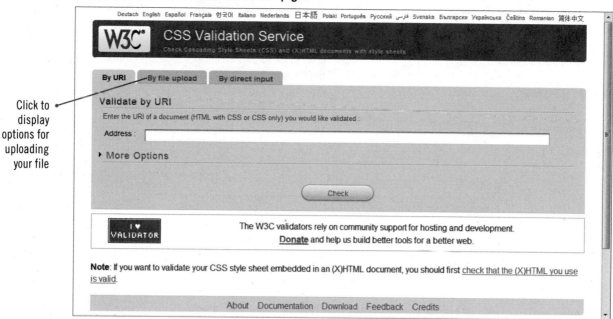

FIGURE C-16: W3C CSS Validator results for lakeland.css

Practice

Concepts Review

For current SAM information, including versions and content details, visit SAM Central (http://www.cengage.com/samcentral). If you have a SAM user profile, you may have access to hands-on instruction, practice, and assessment of the skills covered in this unit. Since various versions of SAM are supported throughout the life of this text, check with your instructor for the correct instructions and URL/Web site for accessing assignments.

Refer to Figure C-17.

FIGURE C-17

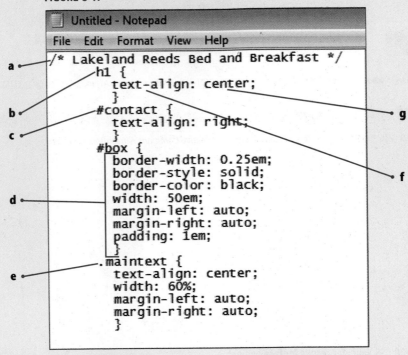

```
Untitled - Notepad
File  Edit  Format  View  Help
/* Lakeland Reeds Bed and Breakfast */
    h1 {
        text-align: center;
    }
    #contact {
        text-align: right;
    }
    #box {
        border-width: 0.25em;
        border-style: solid;
        border-color: black;
        width: 50em;
        margin-left: auto;
        margin-right: auto;
        padding: 1em;
    }
    .maintext {
        text-align: center;
        width: 60%;
        margin-left: auto;
        margin-right: auto;
    }
```

1. Which item is the value assigned to a CSS property?
2. Which item is ignored by a user agent?
3. Which item specifies a set of presentation rules?
4. Which item is a CSS property?
5. Which selector is based on the value of an HTML id attribute?
6. Which selector is based on the value of an HTML class attribute?
7. Which selector is based on the name of an HTML element?

Match each term with the statement that best describes it.

8. style rule
9. name-value pair
10. embedded style sheet
11. external style sheet
12. type selector
13. id selector
14. class selector

a. a selector that applies the specified name-value pairs only to the element with the specified id

b. a line or block of CSS code that specifies the presentation of Web page elements

c. a selector that creates a style rule based on values assigned to elements using the HTML class attribute

d. the most general type of selector, which is the name of an HTML element

e. a separate file containing style information that multiple Web pages can link to

f. a section of CSS code that specifies a CSS property to apply to the selector(s) and the value to assign to the property

g. a section of CSS code entered in the head element of an HTML document

Select the best answer from the list of choices.

15. Which part of a style rule identifies the HTML element or elements to which the style rule applies?

a. selector

b. property

c. value

d. the code between the opening and closing braces

16. A style rule ends with which of the following?

a. */

b. </style>

c. ;

d. }

17. A CSS comment ends with which of the following?

a. */

b. :

c. ;

d. </style>

18. A name-value pair ends with which of the following?

a. :

b. </style>

c. ;

d. }

19. An embedded style sheet ends with which of the following?

a. */

b. </style>

c. ;

d. :

20. Which is the most straightforward solution for affecting the presentation of single Web page?

a. inline styles

b. embedded style sheet

c. external style sheet

d. div element

21. Which of the following enables you to modify the presentation of multiple Web pages with a single change?

a. inline styles

b. embedded style sheet

c. external style sheet

d. div element

22. Which of the following is a class selector?

a. text-align: right

b. #lilac

c. .ideas

d. p

Skills Review

1. Create an embedded style sheet.

  a. Open the file HTM C-3.html in your text editor from the Unit C/Review folder on the drive and folder where you store your Data Files, then save it to the same folder as **index.html**.

  b. Preview index.html in your browser.

  c. Return to your text editor, then add a new line below the line containing the title element.

  d. Insert four spaces, type an opening style tag that specifies a data type of **text/css**, add two new lines, insert four spaces, then type a closing style tag.

  e. Click in the blank line between the opening and closing style tags, insert six spaces, insert a type selector for the h1 element followed by an opening curly brace, add a new line, insert eight spaces, add a name-value pair that left-aligns text, add a new line, insert eight spaces, then insert a closing curly brace.

  f. Save your document.

2. Implement an id selector.

  a. In your text editor, scroll down if necessary to the paragraph that begins with <p>150 St. Joseph St.

  b. In the opening <p> tag, click to position the insertion point between the p and the >, then insert a space.

  c. Insert an id attribute with a value of **contact**.

  d. If necessary, scroll up to view the embedded style sheet, insert a new line below the closing brace for the h1 style rule, then insert six spaces.

  e. Insert an id selector for the value "contact", then type an opening curly brace.

  f. Add a new line, insert eight spaces, then insert a name-value pair that right-aligns text.

  g. Add a new line, insert eight spaces, then insert a closing curly brace.

  h. Save your document, then return to your default browser and refresh the Web page to view your changes.

Skills Review (continued)

3. **Implement the div element.**

   a. In your text editor, add a blank line below the opening <body> tag.

   b. Insert four spaces, then insert a div tag with the id value of **box**.

   c. Add a blank line below the closing </p> tag for the element containing the contact information, insert four spaces, then insert a closing div tag.

   d. Add two spaces before the opening tag for the h1 element, then repeat for the h2 element and all three p elements.

   e. Add a new line beneath the contact style rule, insert six spaces, add an id selector for the value "box", then type an opening curly brace.

   f. Insert a name-value pair that sets each of the following on its own line, indented eight spaces:

     • border width to **0.5em**.

     • border style to **solid**.

     • border color to **red**.

     • element width to **30em**.

     • left margin to **auto**.

     • right margin to **auto**.

     • padding to **1em**.

   g. Add a new line, insert eight spaces, then insert a closing curly brace.

   h. Save your document, then return to your default browser and refresh the Web page to view your changes.

4. **Implement a class selector.**

   a. In the opening h2 tag, click to position the insertion point between the 2 and the >, then insert a space

   b. Insert a class attribute with a value of **maintext**.

   c. Repeat Steps a and b for the opening p tags for the paragraphs that begin "Eat in" and "Voted".

   d. Add a new line below the closing brace for the box style rule.

   e. Insert six spaces, add a class selector for the value "maintext", then type an opening curly brace.

   f. Add a new line, insert eight spaces, then insert a name-value pair that left-aligns text.

   g. Add a new line, insert eight spaces, then type a closing curly brace.

   h. Save your document, then return to your default browser and refresh the Web page to view your changes. Compare your Web page to Figure C-18.

5. **Create an external style sheet.**

   a. In the embedded style sheet, cut all the code between the opening and closing style tags.

   b. Save index.html, open a new file, then create a CSS comment containing the text **Big J's Deep Dish Pizza**.

   c. Add a new line, then paste the contents of the embedded style sheet.

   d. Add a comment containing your first and last name and the text **HTML5 Unit C, Skills Review**.

   e. If you are using TextEdit on a Mac, click Format, then click Make Plain Text.

   f. Save your work as **bigj.css** to the Unit C/Review directory on the drive and folder where you store your Data Files.

   g. Close the file, then reopen index.html in your text editor from the same directory.

   h. Delete the lines containing the opening and closing <style> tags along with any blank lines between them.

   i. Add a blank line below the line containing the title element, insert four spaces, then insert a link element that points to bigj.css.

FIGURE C-18

Big J's Deep Dish Pizza

Authentic Chicago-style pies

Eat in, carry out, or call for delivery.

Voted "Best Pizza Joint" by the Toronto Times!

150 St. Joseph St.
Toronto, ON M5S 2C3
(416) 555-3337

Skills Review (continued)

j. Insert a blank line before the closing body tag, then insert a paragraph element containing your first and last name and the text **HTML5 Unit C, Skills Review**.

k. Save your document, then return to your default browser and refresh the Web page to view your changes.

6. **Link to an external style sheet.**

a. In your text editor, open the file HTM C-4.html from the Unit C/Review folder on the drive and folder where you store your Data Files, then save it as **history.html**.

b. Preview history.html in your browser.

c. In your text editor, add a blank line beneath the line containing the title element, insert four spaces, then insert a link element that points to the bigj.css style sheet.

d. Insert a blank line before the closing body tag, then insert a paragraph element containing your first and last name and the text **HTML5 Unit C, Skills Review**.

e. Save the document, then reload history.html in your default browser.

f. Reopen bigj.css in your text editor, then in the maintext style rule, change the value for text alignment from center to left.

g. Save your document, close your text editor, then refresh history.html in your default browser. Compare your Web page to Figure C-19.

h. Refresh index.html in your default browser.

7. **Validate your CSS code.**

a. Open **http://jigsaw.w3.org/css-validator/** in your Web browser.

b. Click the By file upload tab.

c. Click Browse or Choose File, then select bigj.css from the Unit C/Review folder in the drive and folder where you store your Data Files.

d. Use the More Options link to set the Profile to CSS Level 3, then click Check.

e. Scroll down to read the validation results, including any notes or warnings.

f. If you have space on a Web server for publishing your documents, create a local root folder within the Review folder, move index.html, history.html, and bigj.css to the local root folder, then upload the files to your Web publishing location.

g. Open index.html in your browser from the published location to verify that the upload was successful, then open history.html from the published location.

h. Close any open browsers, then close your text editor.

FIGURE C-19

Big J's Deep Dish Pizza

History

In 1972, Torontoite Jan Mercutio returned home from a trip to Chicago with a craving for authentic deep-dish pie. Unsatisfied by the local offerings, she practiced up in her kitchen and began inviting friends over to sample the results of her tests. They clearly enjoyed what she whipped up, as her otherwise well-mannered friends were soon asking to come to dinner in numbers that threatened to overwhelm her. Wanting to accommodate the hunger she'd fed, though, Jan put her head to figuring out how to make her pizza more widely available. In 1974, she opened the first Big J's Deep Dish Pizza restaurant on St. Joseph St., and local residents and visitors alike have continued to join the ranks of her fans ever since.

Jan has added two locations and expanded Big J's menu to include salads and calzones, while continuing to serve pizza worth travelling for in a comfortable, friendly setting. Big J's Pizza has been awarded the "Best Pizza" distinction by the Toronto Times reader survey a total of 5 times. We invite you to come by one of our locations and find out what all the excitement is about.

150 St. Joseph St.
Toronto, ON M5S 2C3
(416) 555-3337

Independent Challenge 1

Sarah Nguyen, the owner and manager of the Spotted Wren Garden Center, is happy with your work so far on the company's Web site. She'd like you to add some presentation elements to the Web page you created, so you incorporate some CSS style rules.

a. Open the file HTM C-5.html in your text editor from the Unit C/IC1 folder on the drive and folder where you store your Data Files, then save it to the same folder as **index.html**.

b. In the head section, add opening and closing style tags, then insert a blank line between them.

c. Create a style rule that uses a class selector to center the text of the h1 and h2 headings and the paragraph containing the contact information.

d. Create a style rule that uses an id selector to left-align the text of the first paragraph element.

Independent Challenge 1 (continued)

e. Create a style rule that uses an id selector to right-align the text of the second paragraph element.

f. Insert a div element that contains the headings and the first two paragraph elements. Create a style rule that uses an id selector to style the div element with a width of **30em**, padding of **1em**, a **0.25em solid green** border, and left and right margins set to **auto**.

g. Insert a blank line before the closing body tag, then insert a paragraph element containing your first and last name and the text **HTML5 Unit C, Independent Challenge 1**.

h. Save your work, then preview your Web page in a browser. Compare your screen to Figure C-20. If necessary, make corrections to your code.

i. Validate your CSS code using the validator at **http://jigsaw.w3.org/css-validator/**.

j. If you have space on a Web server for publishing your documents, create a local root folder within the IC1 folder, move index.html to the local root folder, upload the file to your Web publishing location, then open the file in your browser from the published location.

k. Close your browser and your text editor.

FIGURE C-20

Spotted Wren Garden Center

For your year-round garden and yard needs

Looking for something unusual or hard to find?

Ask us!

548 N. 58th St. :: Omaha, NE 68132 :: (402) 555-9736

Independent Challenge 2

As you continue developing the Web site for the Murfreesboro Regional Soccer League, you decide to add presentation features to the Web pages. You've created two Web pages for the site, so you create an external style sheet.

a. Open the file HTM C-6.html in your text editor from the Unit C/IC2 folder on the drive and folder where you store your Data Files, then save it to the same folder as **index.html**. Open HTM C-7.html, then save it as **started.html**. Insert a blank line before the closing body tag in each document, then insert a paragraph element containing your first and last name and the text **HTML5 Unit C, Independent Challenge 2**. Save your work and preview both files in a Web browser.

b. Open a new document, enter a CSS comment containing the name of the organization, then save the document with the name **mrsl.css**.

c. Create a style rule that uses a type selector to center the text of h1 elements. Create a duplicate rule to style h2 elements.

d. Create a style rule for the main page content that uses a class selector to left-align text.

e. Create a style rule for the contact information that uses an id selector to right-align text.

f. Create a style rule to create a box that uses an id selector to set a width of **40em**, padding of **1em**, a **0.5em solid black** border, and left and right margins to **auto**.

Advanced Challenge Exercise

■ Combine the style rules for h1 and h2 elements into a single style rule.

■ Combine the style rules for the border width, style, and color into a single rule. Use the property **border**, inserting the values for width, style, and color with spaces between them and a semicolon only after the color value. Be sure to delete the border-width, border-style, and border-color properties.

g. In index.html, add an id attribute to the element containing the contact information that references the style rule you created in Step e, then add class attributes that reference the style rule you created in Step d to all elements in the body section except the headings and contact information.

h. In index.html, insert a div element that contains all the contents of the body section except the contact information. Give the element an id value that matches the selector for the style rule you created in Step f.

i. At the bottom of your external style sheet document, insert a comment containing your first and last name and the text **HTML5 Unit C, Independent Challenge 2**.

Independent Challenge 2 (continued)

j. Save your work, add link elements that reference your external style sheet to index.html and started.html, then save these files.

k. Preview index.html and started.html in a Web browser. Compare your documents to Figure C-21 and Figure C-22. If necessary, make corrections to your code.

FIGURE C-21

Murfreesboro Regional Soccer League

Part of the North American Recreational Soccer Association

Get exercise, have fun, and build your soccer skills playing with us.

Teams for beginners as well as experienced players.

MRSL
c/o Davies Sporting Goods
418 N. Sartoris St.
Murfreesboro, TN 37130
(615) 555-2255

FIGURE C-22

Murfreesboro Regional Soccer League

Part of the North American Recreational Soccer Association

The MRSL is open to players of all levels who want to play soccer in a relaxed, friendly environment. Even if you've never played soccer before, the MRSL is a great place to start.

To get a feel for our league, we recommend you call us at the number below or stop by Davies Sporting Goods to talk to one or our coordinators and get the details on our next all-team practice or workshop day. Then come kick around the ball with us and meet other players in the league.

If you're interested in joining up, you'll need to complete some paperwork and pay $65 for a seasonal membership ($40 for seniors and students).

We look forward to seeing you on the field!

MRSL
c/o Davies Sporting Goods
418 N. Sartoris St.
Murfreesboro, TN 37130
(615) 555-2255

l. Validate your CSS code using the validator at http://jigsaw.w3.org/css-validator/.

m. If you have space on a Web server for publishing your documents, create a local root folder within the IC2 folder, move index.html, started.html, and mrsl.css to the local root folder, upload the files to your Web publishing location, then open the Web pages in your browser from the published location.

n. Close your browser and your text editor.

Independent Challenge 3

As you continue your work on the Web site for Hotel Natoma, you incorporate a color scheme and basic text alignment using CSS.

a. Open the file HTM C-8.html in your text editor from the Unit C/IC3 folder on the drive and folder where you store your Data Files, then save it to the same folder as **index.html**. Open HTM C-9.html, then save it as **nearby.html**. Insert a blank line before the closing body tag in each document, then insert a paragraph element containing your first and last name and the text **HTML5 Unit C, Independent Challenge 3**. Save your work and preview both files in a Web browser.

b. Open a new document, enter a CSS comment containing the name of the organization, then save the document with the name **natoma.css**.

c. Create style rules to apply the following presentation details, adding HTML attributes to both Web documents when necessary:

- center the text of h1 elements
- right-align the contact information
- left-align the remaining text

Advanced Challenge Exercise

■ Add CSS code to the external style sheet to create a **0.25em solid** border. Use the name **darkgreen** for the border color. Set the left and right margins to **auto**, set the padding to **1em**, and set the width to **30em**. Add HTML code as needed to both index.html and nearby.html to apply this style so it surrounds all of the page contents.

■ Combine the style rules for the border width, style, and color into a single rule. Use the property **border**, inserting the values for width, style, and color with spaces between them and a semicolon only after the color value. Be sure to delete the border-width, border-style, and border-color properties.

Independent Challenge 3 (continued)

■ Add CSS code to the external style sheet to create a **0.25em solid** border Use the name **darkblue** for the border color, and use a single rule to style the border. Set the left and right margins to **auto**, set the padding to **1em**, and set the width to **27em**. Add HTML code as needed to both index.html and nearby.html to apply this style so it that surrounds only the heading, as shown in Figure C-23 and Figure C-24. (*Hint*: This border is nested within the border surrounding the page contents, so the HTML element you use to create it should also be nested within the element used to create the border for the page.)

FIGURE C-23

Hotel Natoma

A low-impact, Earth-friendly home base in the center of everything San Francisco has to offer.

568 Natoma St.
San Francisco, CA 94103
(415) 555-8378

FIGURE C-24

Hotel Natoma

What's Nearby

Asian Art Museum
City Hall
Civic Center Plaza
United Nations Plaza
Cable Car turnaround
Union Square

568 Natoma St.
San Francisco, CA 94103
(415) 555-8378

d. Save your work, add link elements that reference your external style sheet to index.html and nearby.html, then save these files.

e. Preview index.html and nearby.html in a Web browser. Compare your documents to Figure C-23 and Figure C-24. If necessary, make corrections to your code.

f. Validate your CSS code using the validator at **http://jigsaw.w3.org/css-validator/**.

g. If you have space on a Web server for publishing your documents, create a local root folder within the IC3 folder, move index.html, nearby.html, and natoma.css to the local root folder, upload the files to your Web publishing location, then open the Web pages in your browser from the published location.

h. Close your browser and your text editor.

Real Life Independent Challenge

This assignment builds on the personal Web site you have worked on in previous units. You will create one or more additional Web pages and specify presentational aspects for your Web site.

a. Copy any files you created in Unit B from the Unit B/RLIC folder to Unit C/RLIC.

b. Referring to the storyboard you created in Unit A, create any Web pages you didn't create in Unit B. Include a paragraph element at the bottom of each document containing your first and last names and the text **HTML5 Unit C, Real Life Independent Challenge**.

c. Using either the layout you sketched in Unit A, or drawing ideas from one or more Web pages similar to yours and whose design you like, plan style enhancements to add to your site. Include at least one text alignment property and at least one div element. Implement at least one of each of the following:

- type selector
- id selector
- class selector

d. Add the style rules, HTML attributes, and HTML elements necessary to implement the style enhancements from Step c. If your site contains only one page, use an embedded style sheet; otherwise, create an external style sheet and link to it from each Web page.

e. Preview each of your Web pages. Make any necessary edits to the HTML or CSS.

f. Validate your CSS code using the validator at **http://jigsaw.w3.org/css-validator/**.

g. If you have space on a Web server for publishing your documents, create a local root folder within the RLIC folder, move all of your Web documents and external style sheets to the local root folder, upload the files to your Web publishing location, then open the Web pages in your browser from the published location.

Visual Workshop

In your text editor, open the file HTM C-10.html from the /Unit C/VW directory on the drive and folder where you store your Data Files. Save the file as **index.html**, then preview it in a browser. Use your text editor to add the necessary presentational code to make your Web page match the one shown in Figure C-25. Use the color **royalblue** for the top border and **lightblue** for the bottom one. After the content shown, include a paragraph element that contains your first and last name and the text **HTML5 Unit C, Visual Workshop**. Validate your CSS using the online validator at **http://jigsaw.w3.org/css-validator/**. If you have space on a Web server, create a local root folder within the VW folder, move index.html to the local root folder, upload the file to your Web publishing location, then open the Web page in your browser from the published location. Close your browser and text editor.

FIGURE C-25

Revisions Bookstore and Cafe

Custom brewed coffee and hand-selected books.

Special orders are our specialty.

412 N. 25th St.
Richmond, VA 23223
(804) 555-2565

Formatting Text with CSS

**Files You
Will Need:**

To view a list of files
needed for this
unit, see the Data
Files Grid in the
back of the book.

CSS and HTML support many properties and elements that let you customize the appearance of text in your Web pages. You can use styles to change the font, size, and color of text, and you can style text with bold, italic, and other variations. As you continue your work on the Lakeland Reeds Bed and Breakfast Web site, you begin to implement the text formatting specified in the site design.

OBJECTIVES   Assess Web fonts

Declare a font family

Declare font sizes

Implement bold and italics

Change font colors

Change background colors

Use special characters

Provide alternative style sheets

Assessing Web Fonts

When you create a document in a word processing program, you can format text with any font installed on your computer. You can likewise format Web page text with different fonts, but you are limited by the fonts available on your *users'* machines. This limitation makes it a challenge to ensure that your Web pages appear consistently on different computers. ▰▰▰ Karl Dixon, one of your colleagues in the art department at Great Northern Web Solutions, has created a mock-up of the main Lakeland Reeds B&B Web page with text formatting. As you prepare to incorporate the fonts and other text characteristics into the Web page, you review strategies for working with fonts in Web pages.

DETAILS

A few strategies have evolved for implementing fonts consistently on the Web:

QUICK TIP

"arial, helvetica, sans-serif" is a widely used sans-serif font stack. However, as more fonts become widely installed, tahoma and verdana have become popular additions.

- **Specifying multiple font families**

  You specify the font family for the text of an element using the CSS font-family property. The value consists of names of one or more **font families**, which are collections of single typefaces and their variants. For example, the Arial font family contains characters in the standard Arial typeface, including italic and bold versions of those characters. While you can specify a single font family as the property value, doing so is usually not a good idea. Every operating system has some font families installed by default, but different operating systems often have different fonts installed, meaning that not every browser or user agent will have a given font available for rendering. To bridge this discrepancy, CSS enables you to use a font stack as the value of the font-family property. A **font stack** is a list of font families in order of preference, separated by commas. For example, the CSS name-value pair

  `font-family: tahoma, arial;`

  specifies that a user agent should display the text of associated elements in Tahoma font, but if that's not available, the user agent should use Arial instead. Figure D-1 shows text using the above style rule in a browser with Tahoma and a browser without that font.

QUICK TIP

Even though some font names are commonly capitalized, entering them in all lower case in style rules helps keep your code consistent and easier to read.

- **Specifying a generic font family**

  CSS also defines five **generic font families**, which are groupings of font families according to shared characteristics. Two generic font families are based on whether a font incorporates **serifs**, which are small finishing strokes at the ends of lines making up each character. A font that uses these strokes is known as a **serif font**, while a font without these strokes is called a **sans-serif font**. Table D-1 shows examples of all five generic font families.

  You can add the name of a generic font family to the end of a font stack to provide guidance to user agents when your other font family choices are not available. For example,

  `font-family: tahoma, arial, sans-serif;`

  instructs user agents without access to either Tahoma or Arial to instead use the default sans-serif font on the user's system. You surround any font family name or generic font family name containing more than one word with quotes (for instance, "times new roman").

QUICK TIP

Some fonts for creating printed materials are not licensed for use as downloadable fonts. Always verify that you have permission to use a particular font on your Web site before doing so.

- **Implementing downloadable fonts**

  Recent user agents can also download and apply fonts that are not installed on a user's computer. To implement such fonts, you upload one or more files containing elements of a font family you want to use to your Web publishing location or reference a licensed downloadable font available on a public server. You also add an @**font-face rule** to your style sheet, which is a variation of a style rule that indicates the font name and the location of the necessary files. You can then refer to the font by name in font-family value lists. Because not all user agents implement the @font-face rule, you should continue to name alternative font families for user agents that don't support downloadable fonts.

Lakeland Reeds Bed and Breakfast

About Us

Lakeland Reeds is an ideal place to unplug from your daily routine, whether on the shore of Twin Lakes watching the sunset over the cattails, or just curled up in a hammock on our wraparound porch with a good book. Breakfast is ready whenever you are, and we're happy to accommodate a wide range of appetites, from comfort food, like sausage and biscuits, to the lighter end of things, such as egg white omelettes and fresh fruit.

We're here to help you get the most out of your time w[...] for a day out on the lake, to popcorn and a DVD of *The* [...] in. We look forward to welcoming you!

Text displayed in Arial

Text displayed in Tahoma

Lakeland Reeds Bed and Breakfast

About Us

Lakeland Reeds is an ideal place to unplug from your daily routine, whether on the shore of Twin Lakes watching the sunset over the cattails, or just curled up in a hammock on our wraparound porch with a good book. Breakfast is ready whenever you are, and we're happy to accommodate a wide range of appetites, from comfort food, like sausage and biscuits, to the lighter end of things, such as egg white omelettes and fresh fruit.

We're here to help you get the most out of your time with us, from canoes and life vests for a day out on the lake, to popcorn and a DVD of *The Wizard of Oz* for a quiet evening in. We look forward to welcoming you!

Philip Blaine, Proprietor
45 Marsh Grass Ln.
Marble, MN 55764
(218) 555-5253

TABLE D-1: **Generic font families**

generic font family	examples	characteristics	best for
Serif	Times New Roman Georgia	Finishing strokes at the end of each line making up a character	Headings on computer screens and other backlit displays
Sans-serif	Arial Tahoma	Lack of serifs ("sans" is French for "without")	Paragraphs of text on computer screens and other backlit displays
Monospace	Courier New Lucida Console	Each character uses the same amount of horizontal space	Code samples
Cursive	Monotype Corsiva Comic Sans	Flowing strokes that simulate handwritten text	Decorative purposes only, not main Web page text, as font families in these groups can be difficult to read
Fantasy	Papyrus **Impact**	Exaggerated style	

Choosing a downloadable font format

While the most common user agents support @font-face rules, several formats exist for downloadable fonts. While the Web Open Font Format (WOFF) is in line to become a standard, supporting older browsers and other user agents requires that you make each font available in multiple formats and that you specify the location of each file in your code. Table D-2 describes the most common downloadable font formats.

TABLE D-2: **Common downloadable font formats**

abbreviation	name	works with
TTF	TrueType Font	Most browsers except Internet Explorer and iPhone
EOT	Embedded OpenType	Internet Explorer
SVG	Scalable Vector Graphics	iPhone and iPad
WOFF	Web Open Font Format	Recent versions of all major browsers

Declaring a Font Family

To specify fonts in your CSS code, you use the font-family property. The property value is a font stack that includes one or more font family names and ends with a generic font family name. ![icon] To customize the Web site and enhance the readability of text, you create style rules to change the fonts for heading and body text for the Lakeland Reeds B&B Web site.

STEPS

1. **Start your text editor then open the file HTM D-1.html from the Unit D/Unit folder on the drive and folder where you store your Data Files**

2. **Insert a blank line before the closing body tag, insert a paragraph element containing your first and last name and the text HTML5 Unit D, then save the file as aboutus.html**

3. **Open HTM D-2.css in your text editor, add a new comment containing your first and last name and the text HTML5 Unit D beneath the existing comment, then save the file as lakeland.css**

4. **Open aboutus.html in your browser**

   Figure D-2 shows the current appearance of the About Us Web page.

QUICK TIP

Tahoma was developed for enhanced readability on computer screens, and is installed on almost every Windows and Mac system.

5. **Return to lakeland.css in your text editor, insert a blank line above the closing curly brace for the #box style rule, press [Spacebar] twice, then type font-family: tahoma, arial, helvetica, sans-serif;**

   This style rule specifies the font for all text within the element with the id "box". User agents without access to the first choice, tahoma, should look next for arial, then, if necessary, for helvetica. If none of these are available, the text should be displayed in the user agent's default sans-serif font.

6. **Open stylesheet.css in your text editor, select all the code below the opening comment, click Edit, click Copy, then close stylesheet.css**

   Downloadable fonts often include a CSS @font-face rule containing descriptors optimized to work with a wide range of user agents. Table D-3 outlines the most commonly used descriptors in an @font-face rule.

7. **In lakeland.css, insert a blank line below the opening comment, click Edit, then click Paste**

   The code you copied is pasted into the style sheet, as shown in Figure D-3. An @font-face rule provides user agents the font name, file names, and file locations for a downloadable font.

QUICK TIP

"times new roman" is enclosed in quotes because the font name is more than one word.

8. **Insert a blank line above the closing curly brace for the h1, h2 style rule, press [Spacebar] twice, then type font-family: CuprumFFURegular, georgia, "times new roman", times, serif;**

   This name-value pair specifies CuprumFFURegular, the downloadable font you referenced with the @font-face rule, as the first choice for h1 and h2 elements. Figure D-3 shows the completed code.

TROUBLE

If the Tahoma font is not installed on your computer, the body text of your Web page may differ from Figure D-4.

9. **Save your work, then refresh aboutus.html in your browser**

   As Figure D-4 shows, the default heading and body text are replaced with the fonts you specified.

Linking to externally hosted fonts

Instead of using fonts located on your Web server in your Web pages, many companies that create and license fonts enable you to link to fonts on their Web servers. To do so, you add an additional link element to your HTML file using a Web address provided by the host as the value for the href attribute. The address links to a font-specific style sheet on a Web server run by the font provider, making it unnecessary for you to add an @font-face rule to your own style sheet document.

FIGURE D-2: **The About Us Web page**

Lakeland Reeds Bed and Breakfast

About Us

Lakeland Reeds is an ideal place to unplug from your daily routine, whether on the shore of Twin Lakes watching the sunset over the cattails, or just curled up in a hammock on our wraparound porch with a good book. Breakfast is ready whenever you are, and we're happy to accommodate a wide range of appetites, from comfort food, like sausage and biscuits, to the lighter end of things, such as egg white omelettes and fresh fruit.

We're here to help you get the most out of your time with us, from canoes and life vests for a day out on the lake, to popcorn and a DVD of The Wizard of Oz for a quiet evening in. We look forward to welcoming you!

Philip Blaine, Proprietor
45 Marsh Grass Ln.
Marble, MN 55764
(218) 555-5253

FIGURE D-3: **@font-face rule and font-family properties added**

@font-face rule references downloadable font

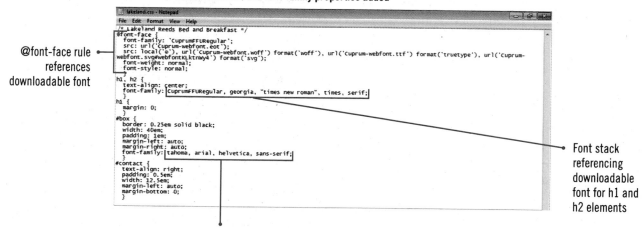

Font stack referencing downloadable font for h1 and h2 elements

Font stack for element with id "box"

FIGURE D-4: **New fonts implemented**

Headings styled with CuprumFFURegular font

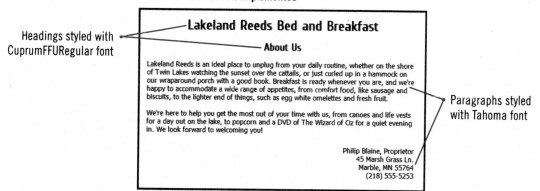

Lakeland Reeds Bed and Breakfast

About Us

Lakeland Reeds is an ideal place to unplug from your daily routine, whether on the shore of Twin Lakes watching the sunset over the cattails, or just curled up in a hammock on our wraparound porch with a good book. Breakfast is ready whenever you are, and we're happy to accommodate a wide range of appetites, from comfort food, like sausage and biscuits, to the lighter end of things, such as egg white omelettes and fresh fruit.

We're here to help you get the most out of your time with us, from canoes and life vests for a day out on the lake, to popcorn and a DVD of The Wizard of Oz for a quiet evening in. We look forward to welcoming you!

Paragraphs styled with Tahoma font

Philip Blaine, Proprietor
45 Marsh Grass Ln.
Marble, MN 55764
(218) 555-5253

TABLE D-3: **common @font-face descriptors**

descriptor	value	purpose
font-family	*family-name*	Creates the name you use to reference the font in all of your CSS code.
src	local(*name*), url(*url*), format(*format*), where *name* is the name of an installed font family, *url* is the remote location of the font, and *format* is the format	Provides parameters for user agents to locate the font family and understand its formatting. Different formats require different combinations of local, url, and format, and Internet Explorer 6 compatibility requires specific formatting.
font-weight	normal, bold, 100, 200, 300, 400, 500, 600, 700, 800, or 900	Specify the font-weight, font-style, and font-stretch values for which the font family should be used. Using these descriptors, you can import several variants of the same font family, use the same font-family name for all of them, and enable user agents to apply bold, italic, condensed, or expanded versions where appropriate.
font-style	normal, italic, or oblique	
font-stretch	normal, ultra-condensed, extra-condensed, condensed, semi-condensed, semi-expanded, expanded, extra-expanded, ultra-expanded	

Declaring Font Sizes

You can specify the font size of an element using the CSS font-size property. This property changes the font size of any Web page element that includes text. You can specify font-size values in many different units, but the most widely supported are percent and em. ▰▰▰ The Lakeland Reeds B&B Web site incorporates both h1 and h2 elements. While you can plan on an h1 heading appearing larger than an h2 heading, different browsers may assign different font sizes to a given heading level. For this reason, it's useful to specify font sizes for headings in your style sheets in order to standardize the visual display of headings in different browsers. You specify the font sizes for the h1 and h2 elements in your style sheet.

STEPS

1. **In lakeland.css, insert a blank line above the closing curly brace for the h1 style rule, press [Spacebar] twice, then type** font-size: 2em;

   You specify the font size in em to ensure that it can scale up or down in different user agents and remain proportional to the rest of the Web page.

2. **Insert a blank line after the closing curly brace for the h1 style rule, type** h2 {, **then press [Enter]**

3. **Press [Spacebar] twice, type** font-size: 1.5em;, **then press [Enter]**

4. **Press [Spacebar] twice, then type** }

   Your style sheet should match the one shown in Figure D-5.

5. **Save your work, then refresh aboutus.html in your browser**

   Compare your Web page to Figure D-6. Because the font sizes you specified match the defaults for many Web browsers, you may notice no difference in the appearance of your Web page.

Working with headings

In addition to the h1 element, which specifies a top-level heading, HTML supports additional heading elements for lower-level headings from h2 through h6. Browsers commonly display headings in bold with the default serif font using a spectrum of font sizes, with h1 as the largest heading and h6 as the smallest, as shown in Table D-4. You could achieve the visual formatting of a heading using the div element; however, using elements that specify the functions of their content—in this case, headers—creates additional possibilities for how different user agents interpret and render the elements. In addition, incorporating such semantic elements offers more opportunities for page layout features using more advanced Web development techniques. For example, you could include code that automatically generates an outline at the top of a Web page based on the heading elements in the page.

TABLE D-4: Relative font sizes for heading elements

element	sample formatting
h1	# Heading text
h2	## Heading text
h3	### Heading text
h4	#### Heading text
h5	##### Heading text
h6	###### Heading text

FIGURE D-5: Font size properties incorporated into style sheet

Font sizes
styled for
headings

```
/* Lakeland Reeds Bed and Breakfast */
@font-face {
  font-family: 'CuprumFFURegular';
  src: url('Cuprum-webfont.eot');
  src: local('☺'), url('Cuprum-webfont.woff') format('woff'), url('Cuprum-webfont.ttf') format('truetype'), url('Cuprum-
webfont.svg#webfontKLktnwy4') format('svg');
  font-weight: normal;
  font-style: normal;
  }
h1, h2 {
  text-align: center;
  font-family: CuprumFFURegular, georgia, "times new roman", times, serif;
  }
h1 {
  margin: 0;
  font-size: 2em;
  }
h2 {
  font-size: 1.5em;
  }
#box {
  border: 0.25em solid black;
  width: 40em;
  padding: 1em;
  margin-left: auto;
  margin-right: auto;
  font-family: tahoma, arial, helvetica, sans-serif;
  }
#contact {
  text-align: right;
  padding: 0.5em;
  width: 12.5em;
  margin-left: auto;
  margin-bottom: 0;
  }
```

FIGURE D-6: Web page displaying updated font sizes

Headings
reflect font
sizes set in
style sheet

Lakeland Reeds Bed and Breakfast

About Us

Lakeland Reeds is an ideal place to unplug from your daily routine, whether on the shore of Twin Lakes watching the sunset over the cattails, or just curled up in a hammock on our wraparound porch with a good book. Breakfast is ready whenever you are, and we're happy to accommodate a wide range of appetites, from comfort food, like sausage and biscuits, to the lighter end of things, such as egg white omelettes and fresh fruit.

We're here to help you get the most out of your time with us, from canoes and life vests for a day out on the lake, to popcorn and a DVD of The Wizard of Oz for a quiet evening in. We look forward to welcoming you!

Philip Blaine, Proprietor
45 Marsh Grass Ln.
Marble, MN 55764
(218) 555-5253

Implementing Bold and Italics

CSS enables you to modify Web page text in a number of ways. Two of the most common are making text bold and italic. You can make text bold using the font-weight property, while the font-style property allows you to add italics. Bold and italic styles are often applied to words or phrases, rather than to entire paragraphs or pages. Thus, you often need a way to indicate the section of a paragraph to format. You can use the span element for this purpose. The **span element** is a generic element, like div; however, it allows you to isolate a specific section of a larger element. You use the font-weight property to apply bold to the name of the B&B at the start of the first paragraph. You also use the font-style property to italicize the title of the DVD in the second paragraph.

STEPS

1. **Return to aboutus.html in your text editor, place the insertion point just to the left of the L in the name Lakeland Reeds at the start of the first p element, then type <span id="callout">**

2. **Place the insertion point just to the right of the s at the end of the word Reeds, then type </span>**

   Figure D-7 shows the code for the span element. The span element transforms the text it contains into an object on the Web page to which you can apply styles. Including an id attribute allows you to create a style rule that affects only the contents of this span element.

3. **Return to lakeland.css in your text editor, insert a blank line at the end of the document, type #callout {, press [Enter], press [Spacebar] twice, type font-weight: bold;, press [Enter], press [Spacebar] twice, then type }**

   Figure D-8 shows the #callout style rule in the style sheet.

4. **Return to aboutus.html in your text editor, place the insertion point just to the left of the T at the start of the name The Wizard of Oz near the end of the second p element, then type <span id="title">**

5. **Place the insertion point just to the right of the z at the end of the word Oz, then type </span>**

   Your completed Web page code should match Figure D-7.

6. **Save your work, return to lakeland.css in your text editor, insert a blank line at the end of the document, type #title {, press [Enter], press [Spacebar] twice, type font-style: italic;, press [Enter], press [Spacebar] twice, then type }**

   Your completed style sheet should match Figure D-8.

7. **Save your work, then refresh aboutus.html in your browser**

   As shown in Figure D-9, the name Lakeland Reeds in the first paragraph appears in bold, and the movie title The Wizard of Oz is displayed in italics.

Comparing block-level and inline elements

The W3C separates HTML elements into two types: block-level and inline. **Block-level elements** are the larger chunks that structure a Web page, such as headings and paragraphs. **Inline elements** are more fine-grained elements that appear within block-level elements; a word or phrase within a paragraph is one example of an inline element. In general, a block-level element starts on a new line, while an inline element continues on the same line as the previous element. The div and span elements share a common purpose, as generic elements that enable you to style sections of Web page text without adding any default formatting. The only difference between the two is that div is a block-level element, while span is an inline element.

FIGURE D-7: HTML document incorporating span elements

```
aboutus.html - Notepad
File  Edit  Format  View  Help
<!DOCTYPE html>
<html>
  <head>
    <meta charset="utf-8" />
    <title>Lakeland Reeds Bed and Breakfast - About Us</title>
    <link rel="stylesheet" type="text/css" href="lakeland.css" />
  </head>
  <body>
    <div id="box">
      <h1>Lakeland Reeds Bed and Breakfast</h1>
      <h2>About Us</h2>
      <p><span id="callout">Lakeland Reeds</span> is an ideal place to unplug from your daily routine, whether on the shore
of Twin Lakes watching the sunset over the cattails, or just curled up in a hammock on our wraparound porch with a good book.
 Breakfast is ready whenever you are, and we're happy to accommodate a wide range of appetites, from comfort food, like
sausage and biscuits, to the lighter end of things, such as egg white omelettes and fresh fruit.</p>
        <p>we're here to help you get the most out of your time with us, from canoes and life vests for a day out on the lake,
to popcorn and a DVD of <span id="title">The Wizard of Oz</span> for a quiet evening in. We look forward to welcoming you!
</p>
        <p id="contact">Philip Blaine, Proprietor<br />45 Marsh Grass Ln.<br />Marble, MN 55764<br />(218) 555-5253</p>
    </div>
  </body>
</html>
```

Span elements added to enable you to
style sections of larger elements

FIGURE D-8: Style sheet with properties for bold and italic text

```
lakeland.css - Notepad
File  Edit  Format  View  Help
/* Lakeland Reeds Bed and Breakfast */
@font-face {
  font-family: 'CuprumFFURegular';
  src: url('Cuprum-webfont.eot');
  src: local('☺'), url('Cuprum-webfont.woff') format('woff'), url('Cuprum-webfont.ttf') format('truetype'), url('Cuprum-
webfont.svg#webfontKLktnwy4') format('svg');
  font-weight: normal;
  font-style: normal;
  }
h1, h2 {
  text-align: center;
  font-family: CuprumFFURegular, georgia, "times new roman", times, serif;
  }
h1 {
  margin: 0;
  font-size: 2em;
  }
h2 {
  font-size: 1.5em;
  }
#box {
  border: 0.25em solid black;
  width: 40em;
  padding: 1em;
  margin-left: auto;
  margin-right: auto;
  font-family: tahoma, arial, helvetica, sans-serif;
  }
#contact {
  text-align: right;
  padding: 0.5em;
  width: 12.5em;
  margin-left: auto;
  margin-bottom: 0;
  }
#callout {
  font-weight: bold;
  }
#title {
  font-style: italic;
  }
```

Use the font-weight property to style text as bold

Use the font-style property to style text in italic

FIGURE D-9: Web page displaying bold and italic text

Lakeland Reeds Bed and Breakfast

About Us

Lakeland Reeds is an ideal place to unplug from your daily routine, whether on the shore of Twin Lakes watching the sunset over the cattails, or just curled up in a hammock on our wraparound porch with a good book. Breakfast is ready whenever you are, and we're happy to accommodate a wide range of appetites, from comfort food, like sausage and biscuits, to the lighter end of things, such as egg white omelettes and fresh fruit.

We're here to help you get the most out of your time with us, from canoes and life vests for a day out on the lake, to popcorn and a DVD of *The Wizard of Oz* for a quiet evening in. We look forward to welcoming you!

Philip Blaine, Proprietor
45 Marsh Grass Ln.
Marble, MN 55764
(218) 555-5253

Text styled with the font-weight property appears in bold

Text styled with the font-style property appears in italics

Formatting Text with CSS

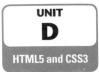
Changing Font Colors

CSS allows you to specify the color of text and many other Web page elements by using the color property. You can specify a color in four different ways: as a name, in hexadecimal format, in rgb format, and in hsl format. Table D-5 provides an overview of these systems. Earlier versions of CSS supported 16-color names, and CSS3 enlarged that list to include a larger standardized list of 147 colors that all major browsers support. However, these names severely limit the range of colors available. The hexadecimal and rgb systems allow you to provide values for the amounts of red, green, and blue that create the color you want to use, resulting in over 16 million possibilities. Using the **hexadecimal system**, the value starts with a pound sign (#), followed by six digits, which may include the numbers 0–9 and the letters a–f. The first two digits specify the red value, the middle two digits indicate the green value, and the final pair of digits represents the blue value. With the **rgb system**, you provide a set of comma-separated values known as an **rgb triplet**. Each value ranges from 0–255 or 0–100%, which represent the amounts of red, green, and blue in the color. CSS3 added support for the **hsl system**, which enables you to create colors by specifying values or percentages for hue, saturation, and light. You format the name of the owner at the bottom of the Web page in dark green using an rgb triplet.

STEPS

1. **Return to** aboutus.html **in your text editor, place the insertion point just to the left of the P at the start of the name** Philip Blaine **near the bottom of the document, then type** <span id="name">

2. **Place the insertion point just to the right of the r at the end of the word** Proprietor, **then type** </span>

   Figure D-10 shows the code for the span element.

QUICK TIP

Many free Web-based utilities provide rgb values for a color you select. Try searching on the phrase **rgb selector** in a search engine to find some of these utilities.

3. **Save your work, then return to** lakeland.css **in your text editor**

4. **Insert a blank line at the end of the document, then enter the following style rule:**

   ```
   #name {
       color: rgb(0,82,0);
   }
   ```

   Figure D-11 shows the #name style rule in the style sheet.

5. **Save your work, then refresh** aboutus.html **in your browser**

   As shown in Figure D-12, the line "Philip Blaine, Proprietor" in the contact information at the bottom of the page appears in dark green.

TABLE D-5: CSS color systems

color system	format	advantages	disadvantages
name	*name* where *name* is CSS3 list of 147 colors	Names are easier to remember and harder to enter incorrectly.	Limited color selection
hexadecimal	#*rrggbb* or #*rgb* where *rr* (or *r*) is the red value, *gg* (or *g*) is the green value, and *bb* (or *b*) is the blue value in hexadecimal absolute value (00–FF or 0–F)	Can specify over 16 million colors	Format is not intuitive; values are not easy to remember and harder to proofread
rgb	rgb(*rrr*,*ggg*,*bbb*) where *rrr* is the red value, *ggg* is the green value, and *bbb* is the blue value in absolute value (0–255) or percent (0%–100%)	Can specify over 16 million colors; format more intuitive than hexadecimal; can create using graphic design software	Values are not easy to remember and harder to proofread
hsl	hsl(*hhh*,*sss*,*lll*) where hhh is the hue value in degrees (0–360), sss is the saturation value in percent (0%–100%), and lll is the light value in percent (0%–100%)	More intuitive than rgb-based systems; not based on the use of CRT monitors	Not widely supported by older browsers

FIGURE D-10: Span element added with id "name"

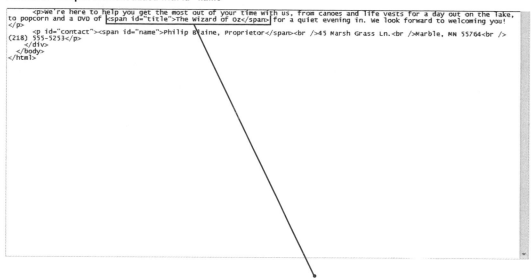

```
        <p>We're here to help you get the most out of your time with us, from canoes and life vests for a day out on the lake,
to popcorn and a DVD of <span id="title">The Wizard of Oz</span> for a quiet evening in. We look forward to welcoming you!
</p>
        <p id="contact"><span id="name">Philip Blaine, Proprietor</span><br />45 Marsh Grass Ln.<br />Marble, MN 55764<br />
(218) 555-5253</p>
    </div>
  </body>
</html>
```

Code for span element to enable you to style the
first line of the contact information

FIGURE D-11: CSS code to style font color

Style rule
for span
element
encompassing
first line of
contact
information

```
#contact {
  text-align: right;
  padding: 0.5em;
  width: 12.5em;
  margin-left: auto;
  margin-bottom: 0;
}
#callout {
  font-weight: bold;
}
#title {
  font-style: italic;
}
#name {
  color: rgb(0,82,0);
}
```

Font color styled using
rgb color value

FIGURE D-12: Font color changed

Lakeland Reeds Bed and Breakfast

About Us

Lakeland Reeds is an ideal place to unplug from your daily routine, whether on the
shore of Twin Lakes watching the sunset over the cattails, or just curled up in a hammock
on our wraparound porch with a good book. Breakfast is ready whenever you are, and
we're happy to accommodate a wide range of appetites, from comfort food, like sausage
and biscuits, to the lighter end of things, such as egg white omelettes and fresh fruit.

We're here to help you get the most out of your time with us, from canoes and life vests
for a day out on the lake, to popcorn and a DVD of *The Wizard of Oz* for a quiet evening
in. We look forward to welcoming you!

Philip Blaine, Proprietor
45 Marsh Grass Ln.
Marble, MN 55764
(218) 555-5253

Font color within
span element
changed using
color property

Using colors judiciously

Although rgb values make over 16 million colors available for use on
your Web pages, it's best not to try to use all of them at once. In
fact, some of the best visual designs use only two or three colors,
with one or two of them reserved for small-scale applications with
specific purposes.

Changing Background Colors

In addition to text, you can set color properties for other aspects of many Web page elements. The ability to modify background colors is particularly important when working with Web page text. For Web page usability, it's important that text contrasts with its background. The default white background for a Web page works fine with the default text color of black, as well as with other dark text colors. However, light-colored text is difficult or impossible to read without changes to the background color. You can change the background color for an entire Web page or for a specific element, allowing you to use different text colors for different elements. 🖌️ You add a background color to the contact information at the bottom of the Web page. You also style the h1 element with text and background colors.

1. **Return to lakeland.css in your text editor, insert a blank line above the closing curly brace for the h1 style rule, press [Spacebar] twice, type color: white;, press [Enter], press [Spacebar] twice, then type background: rgb(0,82,0);**

   You can use multiple ways of specifying colors in the same style sheet. The color name "white" is part of the CSS3 list of 147 color names. The code you entered sets the text of h1 elements to white and creates a dark green background for contrast.

2. **Insert a blank line above the closing curly brace for the #contact style rule, press [Spacebar] twice, then type background: rgb(218,165,32);**

   This name-value pair creates a goldenrod background behind the contact information at the bottom of the Web page.

QUICK TIP

You can set the background property for the body element to change the background color for the entire Web page.

3. **Insert a blank line above the closing curly brace for the #box style rule, press [Spacebar] twice, then type background: rgb(255,255,185);**

   The background property for the element with the id "box" sets the background color for the Web page text to a light yellow. Figure D-13 shows the new name-value pairs in the style sheet.

4. **Save your work, then refresh aboutus.html in your browser**

   The title "Lakeland Reeds Bed and Breakfast" appears in white with a dark green background, and the contact information is displayed with a goldenrod background.

5. **Return to lakeland.css in your text editor, insert a blank line above the closing curly brace for the h1 style rule, press [Spacebar] twice, then type padding: 0.25em;**

   Increasing the padding adds space between the edges of the text and the outer border of the heading element.

6. **Insert a blank line above the closing curly brace for the #name style rule, press [Spacebar] twice, then type font-weight: bold;**

   Figure D-13 shows the style sheet containing the new code.

7. **Save your work, then refresh aboutus.html in your browser**

   Figure D-14 shows your Web page with background colors and line height applied.

FIGURE D-13: Properties inserted to change font color and background colors

```
lakeland.css - Notepad
File  Edit  Format  View  Help
/* Lakeland Reeds Bed and Breakfast */
@font-face {
    font-family: 'CuprumFFURegular';
    src: url('Cuprum-webfont.eot');
    src: local('☺'), url('Cuprum-webfont.woff') format('woff'), url('Cuprum-webfont.ttf') format('truetype'), url('Cuprum-
webfont.svg#webfontKLktrnwy4') format('svg');
    font-weight: normal;
    font-style: normal;
}
h1, h2 {
    text-align: center;
    font-family: CuprumFFURegular, georgia, "times new roman", times, serif;
}
h1 {
    margin: 0;
    font-size: 2em;
    color: white;
    background: rgb(0,82,0);
    padding: 0.25em;
}
h2 {
    font-size: 1.5em;
}
#box {
    border: 0.25em solid black;
    width: 40em;
    padding: 1em;
    margin-left: auto;
    margin-right: auto;
    font-family: tahoma, arial, helvetica, sans-serif;
    background: rgb(255,255,185);
}
#contact {
    text-align: right;
    padding: 0.5em;
    width: 12.5em;
    margin-left: auto;
    margin-bottom: 0;
    background: rgb(218,165,32);
}
#callout {
    font-weight: bold;
}
#title {
    font-style: italic;
}
#name {
    color: rgb(0,82,0);
    font-weight: bold;
}
```

color and background properties implemented together to maintain contrast

background properties for individual screen elements

FIGURE D-14: About Us page with styled background colors

Light font color contrasts with dark background for legibility

Lakeland Reeds Bed and Breakfast

About Us

Lakeland Reeds is an ideal place to unplug from your daily routine, whether on the shore of Twin Lakes watching the sunset over the cattails, or just curled up in a hammock on our wraparound porch with a good book. Breakfast is ready whenever you are, and we're happy to accommodate a wide range of appetites, from comfort food, like sausage and biscuits, to the lighter end of things, such as egg white omelettes and fresh fruit.

We're here to help you get the most out of your time with us, from canoes and life vests for a day out on the lake, to popcorn and a DVD of *The Wizard of Oz* for a quiet evening in. We look forward to welcoming you!

Philip Blaine, Proprietor
45 Marsh Grass Ln.
Marble, MN 55764
(218) 555-5253

Background colors changed using background property

Understanding hexadecimal values

The two rgb color systems—using a triplet of rgb values or using hexadecimal values—allow you to specify the same 16.7 million colors. Each value in an rgb triplet can range from 0 to 255, giving you 256 possible values (1–255, plus the value 0). Hexadecimal values provide the same range in only two digits. The standard decimal numbering system allows 10 possibilities for each digit: the numbers 0–9. Hexadecimal (from roots meaning "six" and "ten") offers 16 possibilities for each digit: the numbers 0–9 plus the letters A–F.

Many common colors are represented in hexadecimal notation with repeating pairs of digits (such as #00DDFF). CSS supports shortening these values to three digits, with the assumption that any three-digit hexadecimal value represents the color created by doubling each digit. Thus, a user agent would interpret the hexadecimal value #0DF as #00DDFF.

Using Special Characters

You add most text to your Web pages simply by typing it. However, there is a handful of common characters that run the risk of being misinterpreted by user agents as computer instructions rather than as plain text. To employ these characters in your Web pages, you represent them with **character references**, which are specially formatted codes that represent characters in the HTML document character set. Character references always begin with an ampersand (&) and end with a semicolon (;). The rest of the code consists of either a pound sign (#) followed by numbers or an English language abbreviation for the associated character name. Every character has a number code, but only a few commonly used characters also have an abbreviation-based alternative. Character references exist for any character you can type; however, the only characters for which it's important to use the codes are those listed in Table D-6. ▰▰▰▰▰ You replace the "and" in the name of the business with an ampersand symbol in both the main page heading and the title element to match the appearance of the organization name on signs and other branded materials.

STEPS

1. **Return to** aboutus.html **in your text editor, then locate the title element**

2. **Delete the word** and **in the name** Lakeland Reeds Bed and Breakfast**, type &, then, if necessary, insert a space before and after the character reference**

3. **Locate the h1 element**

4. **Delete the word** and **in the name** Lakeland Reeds Bed and Breakfast**, type &, then, if necessary, insert a space before and after the character reference**

   Figure D-15 shows the special characters inserted in the code for the Web page.

5. **Save your work, then refresh** aboutus.html **in your browser**

   As shown in Figure D-16, the word "and" in the browser title bar and in the main Web page heading is replace with the ampersand (&) symbol.

6. **Use a validator to check your documents for conformance with the HTML5 and CSS3 specifications, then make any edits necessary to resolve issues and revalidate until both documents pass**

Inserting characters not on the keyboard

In addition to inserting characters that shouldn't be typed directly into HTML code, you can use character references to add symbols to your Web pages that aren't visibly available on a keyboard. Such symbols may include bullet characters, accented letters, and international currency symbols. You can use a search engine to locate one of the many available online references and look up the character reference for any character you might want to use.

FIGURE D-15: Codes for special characters inserted in Web page

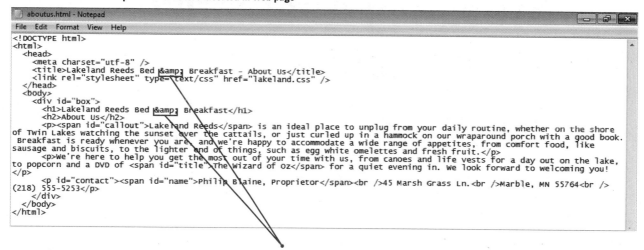

Character codes representing ampersands

FIGURE D-16: About Us page incorporating special characters

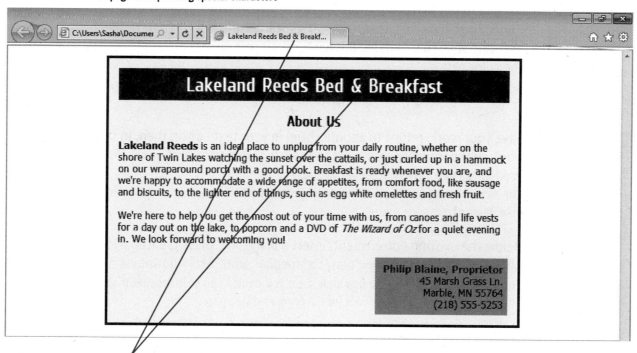

& character codes translated
by browser into ampersands

TABLE D-6: Important character references

character	character name	decimal numeric character reference	named character reference
&	ampersand	&#38;	&amp;
'	apostrophe	&#39;	' (does not work in Internet Explorer)
>	greater-than sign	&#62;	&gt;
<	less-than sign	&#60;	&lt;
"	quotation mark	&#34;	&quot;

Providing Alternative Style Sheets

Web pages can be accessed on computer screens, as printouts, and via a number of other types of user agents. Because these destinations can vary widely in factors like size, resolution, and contrast, styling created for one output is not always ideal on others. To accommodate these differences, HTML allows you to link to multiple style sheets in the same Web document, using the media attribute of the link element to specify which type of device should use each style sheet. Table D-7 describes the available values for the media attribute. ██████ You want to make sure the Lakeland Reeds Web pages are legible when printed, so you create and link a second style sheet for printed output.

STEPS

1. **Return to lakeland.css in your text editor, then save a copy of the document as llprint.css**

2. **In the h1 style rule, delete the color and background properties and their values**

   This change reverts the format for the main heading to black text on a white background.

3. **In the #box style rule, remove the background and border name-value pairs, in the #contact style rule, remove the background pair, then, in the #name style rule, remove the color pair**

   Removing these pairs removes the border and the font and background colors from the page contents in printed output. Figure D-17 shows the completed style sheet.

4. **Save your work, return to aboutus.html in your text editor, then, in the link element, position the insertion point just to the left of the word href, press [Spacebar], type media="screen", then press [Spacebar]**

   The "screen" value for the media attribute specifies that the lakeland.css style sheet is optimized for viewing on a standard computer screen.

5. **Below the existing link element, insert a blank line, press [Spacebar] four times, then type <link rel="stylesheet" type="text/css" media="print" href="llprint.css" />**

   The new element links to the new style sheet you created and specifies that it should be used for printed output. Figure D-18 shows the code for the completed Web page.

6. **Save your work, then refresh aboutus.html in your browser**

   The browser continues to apply the lakeland.css style sheet, so the appearance doesn't change.

7. **If available in your browser, view a print preview of the current page**

   As shown in Figure D-19, the text appears in black with a white background and no border.

8. **Close the print preview, validate llprint.css, then, if you have space on a Web server for publishing your documents, create a local root folder within the Unit folder. Move all the files in the Unit folder to the local root folder, upload the files to your Web publishing location, then open aboutus.htm in your browser from the published location to verify that the upload was successful**

9. **Close your browser, then close your text editor**

FIGURE D-17: Style sheet for printed versions of the Web site

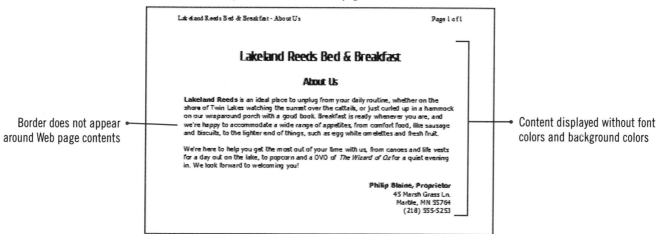

```
liprint.css - Notepad
File  Edit  Format  View  Help
/* Lakeland Reeds Bed and Breakfast */
@font-face {
    font-family: 'CuprumFFURegular';
    src: url('Cuprum-webfont.eot');
    src: local('☺'), url('Cuprum-webfont.woff') format('woff'), url('Cuprum-webfont.ttf') format('truetype'), url('Cuprum-
webfont.svg#webfontKLktrwy4') format('svg');
    font-weight: normal;
    font-style: normal;
    }
h1, h2 {
    text-align: center;
    font-family: CuprumFFURegular, georgia, "times new roman", times, serif;
    }
h1 {
    margin: 0;
    font-size: 2em;
    padding: 0.25em;
    }
h2 {
    font-size: 1.5em;
    }
#box {
    width: 40em;
    padding: 1em;
    margin-left: auto;
    margin-right: auto;
    font-family: tahoma, arial, helvetica, sans-serif;
    }
#contact {
    text-align: right;
    padding: 0.5em;
    width: 12.5em;
    margin-left: auto;
    margin-bottom: 0;
    }
#callout {
    font-weight: bold;
    }
#title {
    font-style: italic;
    }
#name {
    font-weight: bold;
    }
```

FIGURE D-18: Link elements for multiple style sheets

link element added for new style sheet with media value of "print"

media attribute added to original link element with value set to "screen"

```
aboutus.html - Notepad
File  Edit  Format  View  Help
<!DOCTYPE html>
  <html>
    <head>
      <meta charset="utf-8" />
      <title>Lakeland Reeds Bed &amp; Breakfast - About Us</title>
      <link rel="stylesheet" type="text/css" media="screen" href="lakeland.css" />
      <link rel="stylesheet" type="text/css" media="print" href="llprint.css" />   </head>
    <body>
      <div id="box">
        <h1>Lakeland Reeds Bed &amp; Breakfast</h1>
```

FIGURE D-19: Print preview of About Us Web page

Lakeland Reeds Bed & Breakfast - About Us   Page 1 of 1

Lakeland Reeds Bed & Breakfast

About Us

Border does not appear around Web page contents

Lakeland Reeds is an ideal place to unplug from your daily routine, whether on the shore of Twin Lakes watching the sunset over the cattails, or just curled up in a hammock on our wraparound porch with a good book. Breakfast is ready whenever you are, and we're happy to accommodate a wide range of appetites, from comfort food, like sausage and biscuits, to the lighter end of things, such as egg white omelettes and fresh fruit.

Content displayed without font colors and background colors

We're here to help you get the most out of your time with us, from canoes and life vests for a day out on the lake, to popcorn and a DVD of *The Wizard of Oz* for a quiet evening in. We look forward to welcoming you!

Philip Blaine, Proprietor
45 Marsh Grass Ln.
Marble, MN 55764
(218) 555-5253

TABLE D-7: Values for link element media attribute

media type	intended use
all	All devices
aural	Screen reader
braille	Tactile feedback device
handheld	Device with a small screen
print	Printed output and print preview on a screen
projection	Projection device
screen	Computer screen
tty	Teletype or similar terminal
tv	Low-resolution display with limited colors, like a non-high-definition television

Practice

Concepts Review

For current SAM information, including versions and content details, visit SAM Central (http://www.cengage.com/samcentral). If you have a SAM user profile, you may have access to hands-on instruction, practice, and assessment of the skills covered in this unit. Since various versions of SAM are supported throughout the life of this text, check with your instructor for the correct instructions and URL/Web site for accessing assignments.

Refer to Figure D-20.

FIGURE D-20

1. Which item makes text bold?
2. Which item changes the color of an element's text?
3. Which item lets user agents know where to find a downloadable font?
4. Which item changes the color of an element's background?
5. Which item makes text italic?
6. Which item changes the size of an element's text?
7. Which item specifies a font family to apply to an element's text?

Match each term with the statement that best describes it.

8. **block-level element**
9. **character reference**
10. **rgb system**
11. **inline element**
12. **generic font family**
13. **hexadecimal system**
14. **font stack**

a. a system for specifying color on a Web page in which you provide red, green, and blue values represented with numbers 0–9 and letters a–f

b. a fine-grained element, such as a word or phrase within a paragraph

c. a system for specifying color on a Web page in which you provide red, green, and blue values represented as one-, two-, or three-digit numbers

d. a grouping of font families according to shared characteristics

e. a specially formatted string of characters that represents a character in the HTML document character set

f. a list of font families in order of preference, separated by commas

g. one of the larger chunks that structures a Web page, such as a heading or a paragraph

Select the best answer from the list of choices.

15. You specify the font family for the text of an element using the CSS _____ property.
    - a. font-weight
    - b. font-family
    - c. font-style
    - d. font-color

16. You format Web page text as bold using the CSS _____ property.
    - a. font-weight
    - b. font-family
    - c. font-style
    - d. font-size

17. You specify the size of Web page text using the CSS _____ property.
    - a. font-weight
    - b. font-color
    - c. font-family
    - d. font-size

18. You format Web page text as italic using the CSS _____ property.
    - a. font-style
    - b. font-color
    - c. font-family
    - d. font-size

19. The _____ element is a generic element that allows you to isolate a specific section of a larger element.
    - a. div
    - b. span
    - c. p
    - d. h1

20. Sans-serif is an example of a(n) _____.
    - a. font stack
    - b. inline element
    - c. font family
    - d. generic font family

21. When is it important to use a character reference to add a character to a Web page?
    - a. for any character you enter in a Web document
    - b. in place of any numerical digit
    - c. in place of a few special characters that run the risk of being misinterpreted by user agents as computer instructions
    - d. to insert any non-English-language character

22. Which attribute of the link element lets you specify the intended use of an external style sheet?
    - a. media
    - b. type
    - c. rel
    - d. href

Skills Review

1. **Declare a font family.**
    - a. Start your text editor then open the file HTM D-3.html from the Unit D/Review folder on the drive and folder where you store your Data Files.
    - b. Insert a blank line before the closing body tag, insert a paragraph element containing your first and last name and the text **HTML5 Unit D, Skills Review**, then save the file as **history.html**.
    - c. Open HTM D-4.css in your text editor, add a new comment containing your first and last name and the text **HTML5 Unit D, Skills Review** beneath the existing comment, then save the file as **bigj.css**.
    - d. Preview history.html in your browser.
    - e. Return to bigj.css in your text editor, insert a blank line above the closing curly brace for the #box style rule, then add a name-value pair styling the text with the font stack **tahoma, verdana, arial, helvetica, sans-serif**.
    - f. Open stylesheet.css in your text editor, copy all the code below the opening comment to the clipboard, then close stylesheet.css.
    - g. In bigj.css, paste the copied code into a blank line below the opening comment.
    - h. Create a style rule that styles the h1 and h2 elements with the font stack **MolengoRegular, arial, helvetica, sans-serif**.
    - i. Save your work then refresh history.html in your browser.

2. **Declare font sizes.**

   a. In bigj.css, add a name-value pair to the h1 style rule that sets the font size to **2em**.

   b. Add a name-value pair to the h2 style rule that sets the font size to **1.5em**.

   c. Save your work then refresh history.html in your browser.

3. **Implement bold and italic.**

   a. Return to history.html in your text editor, then create a span element with the id **title** containing the text **Toronto Times** in the second to last paragraph.

   b. Return to bigj.css in your text editor, then add a style rule to the bottom of the document that styles the text of the element with the id **title** in italics.

   c. Return to history.html in your text editor, then create a span element with the id **phone** containing the phone number near the bottom of the document.

   d. Save your work, return to bigj.css in your text editor, then add a style rule to the bottom of the document that styles the text of the element with the id **phone** in bold.

   e. Insert a blank line above the closing curly brace for the #words style rule, then add a name-value pair that styles the text in bold.

   f. Save your work then refresh history.html in your browser.

4. **Change font and background colors.**

   a. Return to bigj.css in your text editor, insert a blank line above the closing curly brace for the #words style rule, then add a name-value pair changing the font color to **red**.

   b. Save your work, then refresh history.html in your browser.

   c. Return to bigj.css in your text editor, insert a blank line above the closing curly brace for the #words style rule, then add a name-value pair changing the background color to **black**.

   d. Add name-value pairs changing the background colors of the h1, h2, and contact elements to **rgb(255,204,102)**.

   e. Save your work, then refresh history.html in your browser.

5. **Use special characters.**

   a. Return to history.html in your text editor.

   b. In the title element, replace the apostrophe in the name "Big J's Deep Dish Pizza" with the code **'**.

   c. Repeat Step b for the h1 element.

   d. Save your work, then refresh history.html in your browser. Compare your screen to Figure D-21.

   e. Use a validator to check your documents for conformance with the HTML5 and CSS3 specifications, then make any edits necessary to resolve issues and revalidate until both documents pass.

6. **Provide alternative style sheets.**

   a. Return to bigj.css in your text editor, then save a copy of the document as **bjprint.css**.

   b. Remove the name-value pairs that set the background color for the h1, h2, #contact, and #words elements.

   c. In the #box style rule, remove the border name-value pair, then in the #words style rule, remove the name-pair that styles the font color.

   d. Save your work, return to history.html in your text editor, then in the link element, add a media attribute with a value of **screen**.

   e. Below the existing link element, insert a new link element that duplicates the existing element, change the value for the href attribute to **bjprint.css**, then change the value of the media attribute to **print**.

   f. Save your work, then refresh history.html in your browser.

   g. If available in your browser, view a print preview of the current page. Compare your screen to Figure D-22.

FIGURE D-21

FIGURE D-22

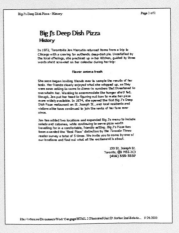

Skills Review (continued)

h. Close the print preview, use a validator to check bjprint.css for conformance with the CSS3 specification, then make any edits necessary to resolve issues and revalidate until the document passes.

i. If you have space on a Web server for publishing your documents, create a local root folder within the Review folder, move all the files in the Review folder to the local root folder, upload the files to your Web publishing location, then open history.html in your browser from the published location to verify that the upload was successful.

j. Close your browser, then close your text editor.

Independent Challenge 1

Sarah Nguyen, the owner and manager of the Spotted Wren Garden Center, is happy with your work so far on the company's Web site. She'd like you to begin to personalize the site by incorporating fonts and colors.

a. Open HTM D-5.html in your text editor from the Unit D/IC1 folder and save a copy as **hours.html**. Open HTM D-6.css in your text editor and save a copy as **spotwren.css**. Before the closing body tag in hours.html insert a paragraph element containing your first and last name and the text **HTML5 Unit D, Independent Challenge 1**. Add the same information as a new comment beneath the existing one in spotwren.css.

b. Copy both @font-face rules from stylesheet.css into spotwren.css. Add name-value pairs to style font families for the following elements:

- body: **verdana**, with **arial** and **helvetica** as backup font families, and **sans-serif** as the generic font family
- h1: **LatinModcrnSans10Bold**, with **arial** and **helvetica** as backup font families, and **sans-serif** as the generic font family
- h2 and tagline id: **LatinModernSans10Regular**, with **arial** and **helvetica** as backup font families, and **sans-serif** as the generic font family

c. Create a style rule to set the font size of the h1 element to **2em**. Create a second rule to set the font size of the h2 element to **1.5em**.

d. In hours.html, add a span element to contain each day of the week, for a total of seven new elements. Set the class of each element to "day". In spotwren.css, add a style rule that bolds the text of all elements that are part of the "day" class.

FIGURE D-23

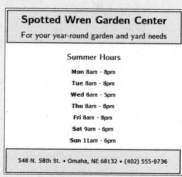

e. Set the font color of the h2 element to the color with the following rgb values: red: **51**, green: **102**, blue: **0**.

f. Set the background color of the box class to the color with the following rgb values: red: **255**, green: **238**, blue: **68**.

g. In the last p element, replace each occurrence of **::** with a bullet using the character code **•**.

h. Save your work then save a copy of your external style sheet with the name **swprint.css**. Remove the name-value pairs that style text color and background color. In the style rule for the box class, change the border color from **green** to **black**, then save your work.

i. In hours.html, add an attribute to the link element to specify its use for computer screens. Insert a second link element referencing swprint.css and specifying its use for printouts. Save your work.

FIGURE D-24

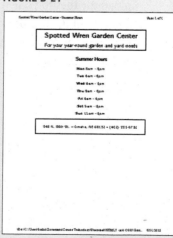

j. Preview your Web page in a browser and compare your screen to Figure D-23. Open a print preview if available and compare your screen to Figure D-24. Validate both your HTML and CSS documents.

k. If you have space on a Web server for publishing your documents, create a local root folder within the IC1 folder, move all the files in the IC1 folder to the local root folder, upload the files to your Web publishing location, then open hours.html in your browser from the published location to verify that the upload was successful.

l. Close your browser, then close your text editor.

Independent Challenge 2

As you continue developing the Web site for the Murfreesboro Regional Soccer League, you incorporate font styling and colors into the site.

a. Open HTM D-7.html in your text editor from the Unit D/IC2 folder and save a copy as **started.html**. Open HTM D-8.css in your text editor and save a copy as **mrsl.css**. Before the closing body tag in started.html, insert a paragraph element containing your first and last name and the text **HTML5 Unit D, Independent Challenge 2**. Add the same information as a new comment beneath the existing one in mrsl.css.

Advanced Challenge Exercise

- Create and implement a sans-serif font stack for the body text. Include at least two font families and one generic font family. (*Hint:* The sans-serif font family shown in Figure D-25 is Tahoma.)
- Create and implement a serif font stack for the h1 text and for the element with the id value "narsa". Include at least two font families and one generic font family. (*Hint:* The serif font family shown in Figure D-25 is Georgia.)

b. Set the font size of the h1 element to **2em**. Set the font size of the element with the id "narsa" to **1.25em**.

c. Use a span element with an id attribute to bold the text "MRSL" near the bottom of the Web page.

d. Set the font color of the element with the id "contact" to **white** and set the background color to **black**.

e. Set the background color of the element with the id "head" to the color with the following rgb values: red: **140**, green: **198**, blue: **63**.

f. Save your work, then save a copy of your external style sheet with the name **mrsprint.css**. Remove the name-value pairs that style text color, background color, and borders, then save your work.

g. In started.html, add an attribute to the link element to specify its use for computer screens. Insert a second link element referencing mrsprint.css and specifying its use for printouts. Save your work.

h. Preview your Web page in a browser and compare your screen to Figure D-25. Open a print preview if available and compare your screen to Figure D-26. Validate both your HTML and CSS documents.

i. If you have space on a Web server for publishing your documents, create a local root folder within the IC2 folder, move all the files in the IC2 folder to the local root folder, upload the files to your Web publishing location, then open started.html in your browser from the published location to verify that the upload was successful.

j. Close your browser, then close your text editor.

FIGURE D-25

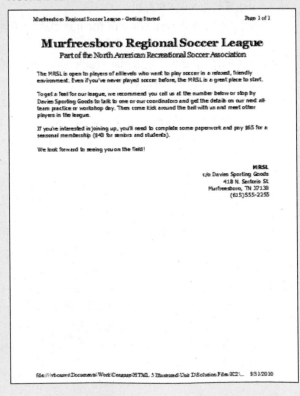

FIGURE D-26

Formatting Text with CSS

Independent Challenge 3

As you continue your work on the Web site for Hotel Natoma, you incorporate fonts and colors using CSS.

a. Open HTM D-9.html in your text editor from the Unit D/IC3 folder and save a copy as **nearby.html**. Open HTM D-10.css in your text editor and save a copy as **natoma.css**. Before the closing body tag in nearby.html, insert a paragraph element containing your first and last name and the text **HTML5 Unit D, Independent Challenge 3**. Add the same information as a new comment beneath the existing one in natoma.css.

b. Copy the @font-face rule from stylesheet.css and paste it into natoma.css. Add code to style the h1 element with the font face you imported, and supply at least one serif font family and a generic font family as fallback options. Add a name-value pair to style the h1 element as normal, rather than bold, text. Change the font color to **white** and the background color to the color with the following rgb values: red: **8**, green: **32**, blue: **8**.

c. Style text in the body element in a sans-serif font and supply at least one sans-serif font family and a generic font family as fallback options.

d. Style the element with the id "box" with the background color with the following rgb values: red: **147**, green: **173**, blue: **120**. Style the element with the id "contact" with a background color of white.

Advanced Challenge Exercise

This Advanced Challenge Exercise requires an Internet connection.

- Use your Web browser and a search engine to find a list of HTML character references.
- Explore the special characters available and find one that seems appropriate for separating sections of text, such as a bullet.
- Copy the numeric character reference to the clipboard, return to nearby.html in your browser, and replace each pipe character in the contact information at the bottom of the document with the character reference you chose. Be sure to include a space before and after each character reference.
- View the Web page in your browser. If the character does not appear as you expected, return to the list in your Web browser, select a different character, and repeat the previous step as necessary until you are satisfied with the result.

e. Save your work in natoma.css, then save a copy with another name and edit the new style sheet to remove font and background colors.

f. In nearby.html, specify that the referenced external style sheet is intended for use on a monitor. Add a reference to the new style sheet you created and specify that it is intended for printed use.

g. Open HTM D-11.html in your text editor and save a copy as **index.html**. Edit the existing style sheet reference and add a new one as described in Step f. If you completed the Advanced Challenge Exercise above, copy the contact information containing the character references you selected from nearby.html and paste it into index.html to replace the corresponding paragraph.

Independent Challenge 3 (continued)

h. Preview both Web pages in a browser. The appearance of nearby.html should resemble Figure D-27. For each document, open a print preview if available. Your preview of nearby.html should look similar to Figure D-28. Validate all of your HTML and CSS documents.

i. If you have space on a Web server for publishing your documents, create a local root folder within the IC3 folder, move all the files in the IC3 folder to the local root folder, upload the files to your Web publishing location, then open nearby.html and index.html in your browser from the published location to verify that the upload was successful.

j. Close your browser, then close your text editor.

FIGURE D-27

FIGURE D-28

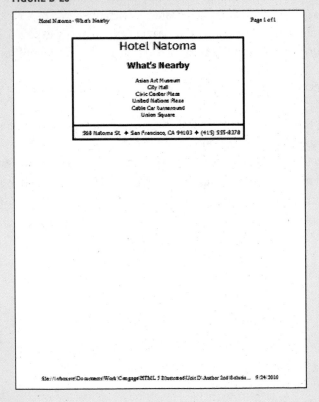

Real Life Independent Challenge

This assignment builds on the personal Web site you have worked on in previous units. You will add font styling and color to your Web site.

a. Copy your Web site files to the Unit D/RLIC folder on the drive and folder where you store your Data Files.

b. Referring to your storyboard and any other design documents, decide which sections of the page will use serif fonts and which will use sans-serif fonts. Decide which font families you'd like to use. If you'd like to use a downloadable font, enter a phrase such as "@font-face free download" in your search engine and explore the fonts you find.

c. In your external style sheet, add font stacks for the fonts you've chosen. Be sure to include at least one backup font family and one generic font family in each stack. If you're implementing a downloadable font, add the **@font-face** rule to the style sheet.

d. Using your design documents, decide which sections of text, if any, you'd like to style with font colors, and decide where you'd like to add background colors. Enter a phrase such as "HTML color picker" in your search engine to find a resource for picking colors that provides the associated rgb or hexadecimal value and use these colors to style your Web site. (*Hint*: If the borders of a background color don't appear as you expect, try setting the padding and margin for the element to **0**, or changing your existing values.)

e. If any of your Web pages need bold or italic formatting, add the necessary span elements and style rules to apply these styles.

f. Apply any character codes necessary to replace potentially confusing characters for browsers. If you want to implement other characters that aren't available on your keyboard, enter a phrase such as "HTML character references" in your Web browser and explore the results to find the code for the character(s) you need.

g. Save your style sheet document, create a copy with a different name, and customize it for printed output. Change the existing link elements in all of your Web pages to designated the original style sheet document for screen output. Add another link element to each Web page referencing your new style sheet and designating it for printed output.

h. Preview your Web pages in at least two browsers and make any edits necessary for them to appear as you expected. If available, open a print preview of each document and verify that the printed version is free of color. Validate all of your HTML and CSS documents and make any edits necessary to address any issues.

i. If you have space on a Web server for publishing your documents, create a local root folder within the RLIC folder, move all the files in the RLIC folder to the local root folder, upload the files to your Web publishing location, then open each Web page in your browser from the published location to verify that the upload was successful.

j. Close your browser, then close your text editor.

Visual Workshop

In your text editor, open the file HTM D-12.html from the Unit D/VW directory on the drive and folder where you store your Data Files. Save the file as **index.html**, then preview it in a browser. Use your text editor to style the Web page to match the one shown in Figure D-29. Specify a font stack starting with Verdana as the default font family for the body element. Use the downloadable font ChunkFiveRegular with a font stack for the main heading and for the contact information, copying the @font-face rule from the stylesheet.css file. For the main heading, use the rgb triplet **189,204,212** for the background, specify that the font should not appear in bold, and specify a font size. Add a paragraph element after the content shown that contains your first and last name and the text **HTML5 Unit D, Visual Workshop**. Validate your HTML and CSS code. If you have space on a Web server, create a local root folder within the VW folder, move **index.html** to the local root folder, upload the file to your Web publishing location, then open the Web page in your browser from the published location. Close your browser and text editor.

FIGURE D-29

Inserting and Working with Links

Files You Will Need:

To view a list of files needed for this unit, see the Data Files Grid in the back of the book.

While a Web site is made up of a collection of Web pages, another important element sets apart a Web site from a simple group of pages: linking. A **hyperlink**, more commonly known as a **link**, is text or another Web page element that users can select to open another document containing related content. Links let you widen the scope of a Web page from a standalone source of information to an integral part of a set of options available on a Web site. In turn, links enable you to integrate the contents of a Web site with anything available on the Web. Now that you have created a basic set of Web pages for Lakeland Reeds B&B, you integrate them into a Web site by creating links between the pages. You also include links to related documents and to relevant information available on other Web sites.

OBJECTIVES

Understand links

Create relative links

Create absolute links

Style links with CSS pseudo-classes

Open links in new windows or tabs

Link to anchors

Create a link to a document

Increase navigational accessibility

Understanding Links

The World Wide Web was initially built on the concept of **hypertext**, which refers to links in and between text-only documents. Today, you can create links on any visible Web page element, but the underlying power remains the same: the ability to present options for more information to users while displaying only a small subset on the screen at a time. ▰▰▱ As you prepare to incorporate links into the Lakeland Reeds B&B Web site, you review how to create and organize Web page links.

Use the following techniques to implement links effectively:

- ### Creating links

  To create a link, you enclose the text or other element you want to serve as a link within an **a element** using the <a></a> tag pair. You use the href attribute to specify the name of the Web page or other document to link to, which is known as the **target document**. Table E-1 explains the most common values for the href attribute. When a user agent encounters an a element, it enables users to interact with the element to open the linked document; for example, in a browser, users most commonly click linked text or images to follow links.

  Visual browsers apply colors to linked text to indicate that it is a link and to convey a user's interactions with the link at a glance. By convention, an unclicked link is blue, a link that a user is in the process of click-ing is red, and a link to a Web page or document that a user has already viewed is purple. Because CSS allows you to customize these colors, it's uncommon to see this color combination on the Web today.

- ### Organizing links

  Virtually every Web site includes a set of links for moving between Web pages in the site. This design element is known as a **navigation bar** or **nav bar**, and usually occurs near the top of a Web page, as shown in Figure E-1, or along one of the sides. A navigation bar should maintain the same location and appearance on every page in a Web site in order to give users a reliable way to move between pages. Some larger Web sites include a second set of links at the bottom of each page for information that most users may need only occasionally, such as the site's privacy policy or contact information for a company or organization.

  While the contents of a Web page should ideally not be much bigger than an average user's screen, longer Web pages make sense for some applications. In these situations, it can be useful to create an additional navi-gation bar that scrolls the user's screen to a section of the current page.

QUICK TIP

While several other protocols are in use on the Internet, the Web uses only http and https.

- ### Referencing Web resources

  Every Web page and other document available on the Web can be referred to using a **uniform resource identifier (URI)**, also known as a **Web address**, which is a standard format for specifying how and where to access a resource on the Internet. As shown in Figure E-2, a URI consists of three parts: the scheme, the server name, and the path. The **scheme** is the way that computers ask for and communicate about the requested document. Web servers make documents available using the **Hypertext Transfer Protocol (http)** or **Hypertext Transfer Protocol Secure (https)** schemes. The **server name**, such as course.com or mail.google.com, identifies the general location of the target document on the Web. The **path** is the sequence of folders in which the target document is stored on the server. A path may end with a filename such as index.html, which is the name of the document a user agent should open in response to a user selecting the link. However, some URIs, such as the one shown in Figure E-2, terminate instead with a series of variable names and values that a program on the Web server uses to generate content dynamically. For instance, a link to a specific location on a map Web site includes information in the URI that enables the Web site to show the desired spot.

FIGURE E-1: A navigation bar

Copyright © 2010 Cengage Learning

Navigation bar provides a consistent set of
links for moving around within the site

FIGURE E-2: A uniform resource identifier (URI)

https://mail.google.com/mail/?shva=1#inbox

Scheme   Server name   Path

TABLE E-1: Possible values for the href attribute

value	description	example
filename	the filename of a Web page or other document located in the same directory as the current page	`history.html`
	the path and filename of a Web page in a different location on the same server	`/docs/register.pdf`
URI	scheme, server name, and, optionally, path for a resource located on another server	`https://mail.google.com/ mail/?shva=1#inbox`
anchor	named location within the current Web document, preceded by a pound sign (#); can also be appended to a filename or URI	`#section3`

Creating Relative Links

You can link to other documents in an a element in two basic ways. When you enter a URI, you're creating an **absolute link**, which is the full and complete address for the target document on the Web. In some situations, however, it makes more sense to create a **relative link**, which gives only the path and filename information necessary to locate the target document based on the location of the current Web page. Because Web pages on a small Web site almost always share the same folder on a Web server, it's most efficient to create relative links when creating a nav bar. ▰▰▰ You start adding links to the Lakeland Reeds B&B Web site by creating a nav bar at the top of each Web page.

1. **In your text editor, open HTM E-1.html from the Unit E/Unit folder on the drive and folder where you store your Data Files, save it as index.html, then repeat to save HTM E-2.html as aboutus.html, HTM E-3.html as rooms.html, HTM E-4.html as reserve.html, and HTM E-5.css as lakeland.css**

2. **In index.html, create a new line beneath the h1 element, indent the same number of spaces and type <div>, press [Enter], indent two additional spaces, type <p id="mainnav">, then press [Enter]**

3. **Indent two additional spaces, type Home, press [Spacebar], type a pipe symbol (|), then press [Enter]**

4. **Repeat Step 3 to add the following lines of code at the same indent level:**

   About Us |

   Rooms |

   Reservations |

   Local Weather |

   Directions

   The pipe symbols create separations between the text for different links. Because only HTML elements and CSS code affect the appearance of text on the Web page, you can add line breaks to make the code easier to read without changing the layout in user agents.

5. **On a blank line, indent two fewer spaces than previously, type </p>, press [Enter], indent two fewer spaces than previously, then type </div>**

6. **Place the insertion point just to the left of the word Home, type <a href="index.html">, move the insertion point just after the word Home, then type </a>**
   The href value "index.html" is a relative link to the main page of the Web site.

7. **Repeat Step 6 to add a elements to the text for the following three links:**

   <a href="aboutus.html">About Us</a>

   <a href="rooms.html">Rooms</a>

   <a href="reserve.html">Reservations</a>

   Figure E-3 shows the completed code for the links.

8. **Save your work, then open index.html in your browser**
   Figure E-4 shows the main Web page containing the nav bar. The alignment and background color are styled by a rule in lakeland.css using the #mainnav selector.

9. **Click About Us in the nav bar**
   The "About Us" Web page opens.

```
<div id="box">
  <h1>Lakeland Reeds Bed &amp; Breakfast</h1>
  <div>
    <p id="mainnav">
      <a href="index.html">Home</a> |
      <a href="aboutus.html">About Us</a> |
      <a href="rooms.html">Rooms</a> |
      <a href="reserve.html">Reservations</a> |
      Local Weather |
      Directions
    </p>
  </div>
</div>
```

Code for
nav bar
with relative
links to
pages on the
same site

FIGURE E-4: Web page displaying nav bar

Navigation
bar

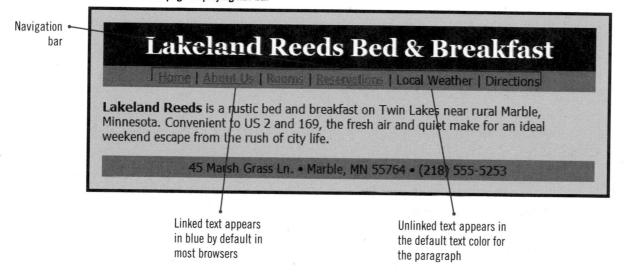

Linked text appears
in blue by default in
most browsers

Unlinked text appears in
the default text color for
the paragraph

Creating effective link text

You can create a link on any text on a Web page. However, keeping a few rules in mind can enhance your site's accessibility and usability. Above all, link text should describe the target document. In a nav bar, a word or two that summarizes the content is usually sufficient. When you're inserting a link within a paragraph, a few words or a phrase may make more sense. For instance, instead of linking a phrase like "click here," creating a link on text like "read more about your local watershed" helps users verify they're accessing the information they want. Users of screen readers may also check the link text on a Web page as a means of scanning the page; using descriptive text increases accessibility in this instance.

Creating Absolute Links

Providing entire URIs in a elements isn't necessary for links to other pages in a small Web site. However, when you want to link to information on another Web site, you must use absolute links. ███████ Philip Blaine, the owner of Lakeland Reeds B&B, wants to include a link to an online weather forecast for the town where the B&B is located. He'd also like the page to incorporate a link that enables users to easily generate customized driving directions to the establishment. You add absolute links targeting external Web sites to the last two items on the nav bar.

STEPS

1. **In your browser, open a site that provides current weather conditions, such as wunderground.com or weather.com, type Marble, MN in the location search box, then press [Enter]**

   The Web site displays current weather conditions in Marble, MN, along with a forecast.

2. **Click in the browser address box to select the address, then copy it to the Clipboard**

3. **Return to index.html in your text editor, place the insertion point just to the left of the phrase Local Weather, type <a href=", paste the contents of the Clipboard, type ">, place the insertion point just after the phrase Local Weather, type </a>, then save your work**

   The href value is an absolute link consisting of the entire URI for the target Web page.

4. **Return to your Web browser, open a site that provides driving directions, such as maps.google.com or mapquest.com, then click the Directions or Get Directions link**

5. **In the End or Destination section of the form that opens, enter Marble, MN, leaving any other fields blank, then click the Get Directions button**

   A Web page opens with a destination of Marble, MN, selected. If your home address doesn't appear automatically, you may be prompted to enter a starting point.

6. **Click in the browser address box to select the address, then copy it to the Clipboard**

7. **Return to index.html in your text editor, place the insertion point just to the left of the phrase Directions, type <a href=", paste the contents of the Clipboard, type ">, place the insertion point just after the phrase Directions, then type </a>**

   Figure E-5 shows the completed code for the two external links.

8. **Save your work, open index.html in your Web browser, then test the Local Weather and Directions links**

   Figure E-6 shows the completed nav bar.

9. **Return to index.html in your text editor, select the entire code for the nav bar, including the opening and closing div tags, copy the code to the Clipboard, paste it below the h1 element in aboutus.html, rooms.html, and reserve.html, then save your work on each document**

10. **In your Web browser, use the links on the index.html nav bar to open the other pages in the Web site, then verify that all the links work on each page**

QUICK TIP

If the URI you paste contains the & symbol, replace each occurrence with & to ensure your code validates.

QUICK TIP

If the URI in the address bar contains no text after the server name, explore the page for a way to create a link containing the information you've entered, such as the "link" link on maps.google.com, and verify that the link text begins with http.

QUICK TIP

If the URI you paste contains the & symbol, replace each occurrence with & to ensure your code validates.

FIGURE E-5: Navigation bar code with absolute links

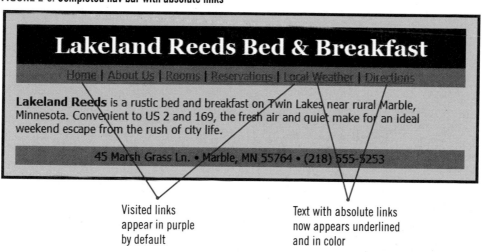

Code to create absolute links for weather and directions

```
index.html - Notepad
File  Edit  Format  View  Help
<!DOCTYPE html>
<html>
  <head>
    <meta charset="utf-8" />
    <title>Lakeland Reeds Bed &amp; Breakfast</title>
    <link rel="stylesheet" type="text/css" media="screen" href="lakeland.css" />
    <link rel="stylesheet" type="text/css" media="print" href="llprint.css" />
  </head>
  <body>
    <div id="box">
      <h1>Lakeland Reeds Bed &amp; Breakfast</h1>
      <div>
        <p id="mainnav">
          <a href="index.html">Home</a> |
          <a href="aboutus.html">About Us</a> |
          <a href="rooms.html">Rooms</a> |
          <a href="reserve.html">Reservations</a> |
          <a href="http://www.wunderground.com/cgi-bin/findweather/getForecast?query=marble,%20mn&amp;wuSelect=WEATHER">Local
          Weather</a> |
          <a href="http://maps.google.com/maps?f=q&amp;source=s_q&amp;hl=en&amp;geocode=&amp;q=marble,+mn&amp;sll=37.0625,-
          95.677068&amp;sspn=34.534108,55.634766&amp;ie=UTF8&amp;hq=&amp;hnear=Marble,+Itasca,+Minnesota&amp;z=13">Directions</a>
        </p>
      </div>
      <p><span class="callout">Lakeland Reeds</span> is a rustic bed and breakfast on Twin Lakes near rural Marble,
      Minnesota. Convenient to US 2 and 169, the fresh air and quiet make for an ideal weekend escape from the rush of city
      life.</p>
      <p id="footer">45 Marsh Grass Ln. &#8226; Marble, MN 55764 &#8226; (218) 555-5253</p>
    </div>
  </body>
</html>
```

Your URIs may be different

FIGURE E-6: Completed nav bar with absolute links

Lakeland Reeds Bed & Breakfast

Home | About Us | Rooms | Reservations | Local Weather | Directions

Lakeland Reeds is a rustic bed and breakfast on Twin Lakes near rural Marble, Minnesota. Convenient to US 2 and 169, the fresh air and quiet make for an ideal weekend escape from the rush of city life.

45 Marsh Grass Ln. • Marble, MN 55764 • (218) 555-5253

Visited links appear in purple by default

Text with absolute links now appears underlined and in color

Understanding mailto links

In addition to creating links that target Web pages and other documents, you can construct a link that creates a new email to a specified recipient. Instead of beginning with http://, these links start with mailto: and are often referred to as **mailto links**. Despite their usefulness, mailto links present both usability and security issues and are not widely used. When a mailto link is activated, it's up to the user agent to identify which program should complete the request. This program is known as the default mail client. On some systems, the default mail client is a program; other systems default to a Web-based email system. Especially on a shared computer, this situation can mean that accessing the link creates unpredictable results, including failure to create the email, accompanied by an error message. In addition, because a mailto link includes a real email address and is publicly available on the Internet, these links are prime targets for programs known as **email harvesters**, which continually explore Web pages looking for email addresses that in turn receive spam emails.

If communication from your users is important, a few alternatives have replaced mailto links. Using more advanced HTML elements, you can create a form where users can enter comments and contact information, and then submit it to you without your email address being exposed on the Web. You can also create a personal or organizational social network feed and make it available on your Web site, inviting users to direct feedback or questions to you through that network instead of via email.

Styling Links with CSS Pseudo-Classes

Just as with any other Web page element, you can use CSS to style links. However, unlike unlinked text and other Web page elements, linked elements have four different possible states, as detailed in Table E-2. Using CSS pseudo-classes, you can create CSS styles to change the format of a link depending on which state it is in. A **pseudo-class** is a categorization of a Web page element, but it is based on a relationship or condition of the element at a given moment, rather than on a static property value. ██████ You create pseudo-classes for the Lakeland Reeds B&B nav bar to maximize contrast within the site's color scheme.

STEPS

1. **Return to** lakeland.css **in your text editor, then insert a new line at the bottom**

2. **Type** #mainnav a:link {, **press [Enter], indent two spaces, type** color: black;, **press [Enter], indent two spaces, then type** }

   #mainnav is the id value for the p element that contains the nav bar text. The a:link pseudo-class applies only when the other three do not. The #mainnav a:link selector specifies any a element in the link pseudo-class that's within the element with the id "mainnav".

   QUICK TIP
   The a:active style rule must follow the a:hover style rule to be effective. Likewise, the a:hover style rule must follow both the a:link and a:visited style rules.

3. **Press [Enter], then add the code for the remaining three pseudo-classes shown in Figure E-7**

   Figure E-7 shows the completed code for the pseudo-classes in the style sheet. The a:visited and a:active rules style links in dark brown when they have been visited or are being clicked. The a:hover rule makes text white when a user's mouse pointer is over it but not clicking it; the resulting mouse interaction is known as a **rollover effect**.

4. **Save your work, return to your Web browser, then, if possible, clear your browsing history**

   The method for clearing browsing history varies among browsers but is commonly listed under privacy or safety settings.

5. **Reload** index.html **in your browser, then move your mouse pointer over the** About Us **link in the nav bar**

   As Figure E-8 shows, the link text appears white when the mouse pointer is over it.

6. **Press and hold the mouse button**

   The link text changes to dark brown.

   QUICK TIP
   While it's common to change font color for links using pseudo-classes, you can change other element styles as well, including background.

7. **Release the mouse button, then let the target page load**

   As Figure E-9 shows, the Home and About Us links appears dark brown, indicating that you've visited those pages.

TABLE E-2: pseudo-class states for linked elements

pseudo-class	applies to
a:link	link that has not been visited, does not currently have the mouse pointer over it, and is not being clicked
a:visited	link to a document that has already been viewed
a:hover	link that the mouse pointer is currently over
a:active	link that is currently being clicked

FIGURE E-7: Pseudo-class styles for nav bar

```
#mainnav a:link {
   color: black;
   }
#mainnav a:visited {
   color: #422100;
   }
#mainnav a:hover {
   color: white;
   }
#mainnav a:active {
   color: #422100;
   }
```

FIGURE E-8: Nav bar styled using pseudo-classes

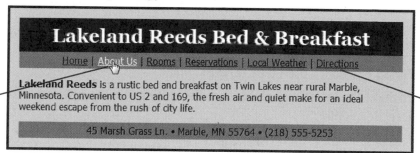

a:hover pseudo-class changes link text to white when mouse pointer is over it

Link text changed to black for unfollowed links

FIGURE E-9: Visited links styled using pseudo-classes

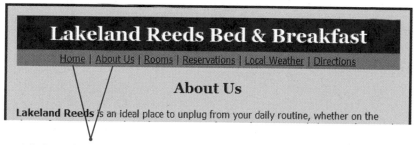

a:visited pseudo-class changes link text to dark brown for visited pages

Implementing descendant selectors

In addition to creating selectors based on element type, id, and class, you can combine multiple selectors to target elements based on their nesting. This type of selector, known as a **descendant selector**, can serve as a shorthand notation that in many cases lets you avoid adding additional class values to your HTML code. To create a descendant selector, you enter the parent element, followed by a space and the child element. For instance, a style rule starting with the selector `#box p` would apply to any p element within the element with the id "box". The parent or child in a descendant selector can be an element type, id, class, or pseudo-class.

Opening Links in New Windows or Tabs

By default, a link opens a new Web page in the same window and tab as the source page. This avoids overwhelming users with windows and tabs and enables users to revisit previous pages using the back buttons in their browsers. In certain situations, however, you want to be able to open a Web page in a new window or tab. For instance, some Web sites spawn target pages for links to external sites in new windows or tabs so users can have both sites open at once. Opening a link in a new window or tab from a Web page containing a lot of information allows a user to easily return to their place on the original page when they're done with the linked information. You can control where a link target opens by including the target attribute of the a element with a value of "_blank". ▰▰▰ In consultation with Philip and the designers in the art department, you've decided that the Local Weather and Directions link targets should open in new windows. You add the target attribute to these links.

STEPS

1. **Return to index.html in your text editor, then locate the code for the nav bar**

2. **Position the insertion point before the closing > in the opening <a> tag for the Local Weather link**

3. **Press [Spacebar], then type** target="_blank"

4. **Position the insertion point before the closing > in the opening <a> tag for the Directions link**

5. **Press [Spacebar], then type** target="_blank"

   Figure E-10 shows the Web page code with the target attributes added.

6. **Save your work, then refresh index.html in your Web browser**

7. **Click the Local Weather link**

   The Web page displaying the current weather opens in a new tab or new browser window, depending on the settings and capabilities of your browser.

Shortening links

Especially long external links can clutter your Web page code. To make your code easier to read, you can use a **link shortener** such as bit.ly or tinyurl.com, which are Web-based services that transform large, unwieldy links into manageable URIs. To use these services, you start by copying the full URI of the Web page you want to link to, then navigating to the Web site of whichever link shortener you choose. Next you paste your long link into the text box for that purpose, then click the associated button, which is often labeled "shorten" or something similar. The Web page processes your link and returns a new link that starts with the link shortener's name.

You then copy the new link to the Clipboard and paste it into your Web page.

One drawback of using shortened links in your Web site is that users are unable to tell from inspecting the URI what domain the link targets, which could be unsettling to some people. Shortened links make more sense on Web sites for large, well-established businesses and organizations and for Web sites that target people likely to have experience using such links. You may want to consider avoiding using shortened links on a Web site for a person or organization that's not well known, or on a site that targets more security-focused users.

FIGURE E-10: target attribute added

```
index.html - Notepad

File  Edit  Format  View  Help

<!DOCTYPE html>
<html>
    <head>
        <meta charset="utf-8" />
        <title>Lakeland Reeds Bed &amp; Breakfast</title>
        <link rel="stylesheet" type="text/css" media="screen" href="lakeland.css" />
        <link rel="stylesheet" type="text/css" media="print" href="llprint.css" />
    </head>
    <body>
        <div id="box">
            <h1>Lakeland Reeds Bed &amp; Breakfast</h1>
            <div>
                <p id="mainnav">
                    <a href="index.html">Home</a> |
                    <a href="aboutus.html">About Us</a> |
                    <a href="rooms.html">Rooms</a> |
                    <a href="reserve.html">Reservations</a> |
                    <a href="http://www.wunderground.com/cgi-bin/findweather/getForecast?query=marble,%20mn&amp;wuSelect=WEATHER"
target="_blank">Local
weather</a> |
                    <a href="http://maps.google.com/maps?f=q&amp;source=s_q&amp;hl=en&amp;geocode=&amp;q=marble,+mn&amp;sll=37.0625,-
95.677068&amp;sspn=34.534108,55.634766&amp;ie=UTF8&amp;hq=&amp;hnear=Marble,+Itasca,+Minnesota&amp;z=13"
target="_blank">Directions</a>
                </p>
            </div>
            <p><span class="callout">Lakeland Reeds</span> is a rustic bed and breakfast on Twin Lakes near rural Marble,
Minnesota. Convenient to US 2 and 169, the fresh air and quiet make for an ideal weekend escape from the rush of city
life.</p>
            <p id="footer">45 Marsh Grass Ln. &#8226; Marble, MN 55764 &#8226; (218) 555-5253</p>
        </div>
    </body>
</html>
```

target attribute set to _blank
for both links to external sites

Linking to Anchors

In addition to linking to other Web pages in your own Web site or an external one, sometimes it's useful to link to locations within the current Web page. These links use the same elements and attributes as other links you've created, but instead of linking to URIs or filenames, you link to named locations, known as **anchors**, within the current document. You create anchors by assigning unique names to elements in your Web page using the HTML id attribute. To reference an anchor with the href attribute of the a element, you simply precede it with a pound sign (#). 🔲🔳🔲 The Rooms Web page on the Lakeland Reeds B&B Web site contains descriptions of the four different rooms that guests can reserve. You add anchors to the room descriptions, then add a second nav bar containing a link to each description.

STEPS

1. **Return to rooms.html in your text editor**

2. **Locate the h3 element containing the text Sun Room, then add an id attribute with the value sun to the opening tag**

3. **Repeat Step 2 to add an id attribute with the value reed to the h3 element containing the text Reed Room, an id attribute with the value tree to the h3 element containing the text Treehouse, and an id attribute with the value garden to the h3 element containing the text Garden Room**

4. **Insert a blank line above the h3 element with the id reed, indent and enter the code <p class="toplink"><a href="#box">Back to top</a></p>, then repeat to add code above the h3 elements with the ids tree and garden and above the p element with the id footer**

   The topmost visible element on the Web page is the outline created by style rules applied to the div element with the id "box". Thus, you can use the target name #box to link to the top of the Web page. Figure E-11 shows the completed code for the anchor values and the Back to top links.

5. **Add a blank line before the h3 element containing the text Sun Room, indent and type <div>, press [Enter], indent two additional spaces, type <p id="pagenav">, then press [Enter]**

6. **Indent two additional spaces, type <a href="#sun">Sun Room</a> |, press [Enter], then enter the remaining three lines of code for the nav bar from Figure E-12**

7. **On a blank line, indent two fewer spaces than previously, type </p>, press [Enter], indent two fewer spaces than previously, then type </div>**

   Figure E-12 shows the completed code for the nav bar for links within the page.

8. **Save your work, then open lakeland.css in your text editor**

9. **Add a blank line above the style rules for the #mainnav pseudo-classes, then enter the code for the pseudo-classes shown in Figure E-13**

   As Figure E-13 shows, you enter two sets of pseudo-classes. The #pagenav style rules style the second nav bar you inserted, while the generic a: style rules apply to the Back to Top links, which are not covered by the other sets of style rules.

QUICK TIP

Most Web browsers attempt to scroll the page to place the target anchor at the top of the window. However, if the Web page is not long enough to make this possible, the target may remain in the middle or at the bottom of the window.

10. **Save your work, open rooms.html in your Web browser, then click each of the links in the new nav bar and each of the Back to top links**

    The alignment and background color for the new nav bar are styled by a rule in lakeland.css using the #pagenav selector.

```
        <h3 id="sun">Sun Room</h3>
        <p class="desc">With windows on three sides, the sunlight in this second-floor room supports a large selection of
houseplants.</p>
        <p class="beds">1 queen bed.</p>
        <p class="toplink"><a href="#box">Back to top</a></p>
        <h3 id="reed">Reed Room</h3>
        <p class="desc">This first-floor room looks out over the reeds on the edge of the lake and the water beyond.</p>
        <p class="beds">1 queen bed and 1 twin bed.</p>
        <p class="toplink"><a href="#box">Back to top</a></p>
        <h3 id="tree">Treehouse</h3>
        <p class="desc">A winding staircase takes you to your own private getaway at the top of the house, with view of the
surrounding trees and meadows and the lake.</p>
        <p class="beds">1 queen bed.</p>
        <p class="toplink"><a href="#box">Back to top</a></p>
        <h3 id="garden">Garden Room</h3>
        <p class="desc">This room's French doors open onto our stone patio and flower garden.</p>
        <p class="beds">1 queen bed and 2 twin beds.</p>
        <p class="toplink"><a href="#box">Back to top</a></p>
        <p id="footer">45 Marsh Grass Ln. &#8226; Marble, MN 55764 &#8226; (218) 555-5253<br /></p>
```

FIGURE E-12: Completed code for new nav bar

```
<div>
   <p id="pagenav">
      <a href="#sun">Sun Room</a> |
      <a href="#reed">Reed Room</a> |
      <a href="#tree">Treehouse</a> |
      <a href="#garden">Garden Room</a>
   </p>
</div>
```

FIGURE E-13: Style rules for generic link text and for new nav bar

```
a:link {
   color: #422100;
   }
a:visited {
   color: #422100;
   }
a:hover {
   color: black;
   }
a:active {
   color: #422100;
   }
```
← Style rules for links not covered by id-specific selectors

```
#pagenav a:link {
   color: white;
   }
#pagenav a:visited {
   color: #D7C39C;
   }
#pagenav a:hover {
   color: #C6A971;
   }
#pagenav a:active {
   color: white;
   }
```
← Style rules for links in new nav bar

Linking to anchors in other documents

You can combine a relative or absolute link with an anchor to link to a specific element in a different document. Simply enter the URI or filename for the target document, add a pound sign (#) to the end, then add the anchor name. When the target page opens in a user's browser, the page scrolls to the specified anchor.

Creating a Link to a Document

Most Web page links are to other Web pages. However, sometimes it's useful to create a link to another type of document, such as formatted text in a PDF file or data in CSV format. You can specify any type of computer-readable document as the value for an href attribute. ▄▄▄▄ Philip has created a form for reserving the entire grounds of Lakeland Reeds B&B for special events, and he's saved the form as a PDF file. You add a link to this file on the Reservations page. You also create an updated version of the version of the style sheet for printed output.

1. **Return to reserve.html in your text editor**

2. **Locate the text Read about reserving Lakeland Reeds for a wedding or other special event. below the h2 element, then position the insertion point to the left of the word Read**

3. **Type <a href="weddings.pdf">**

4. **Position the insertion point to the right of the period after the word event, type </a>, then save your work**

    Figure E-14 shows the completed code for the link.

5. **Open reserve.html in your Web browser, then click the link Read about reserving Lakeland Reeds for a wedding or other special event**

    If your computer has a PDF reader installed, the document opens, as shown in Figure E-15.

6. **If the PDF file opened in a program other than your Web browser, close the program displaying the file**

7. **Return to lakeland.css in your text editor, save your work, then save a copy as llprint.css**

8. **Remove all name-value pairs that specify color, including the border name-value pair in the #box rule, change all the colors in style rules based on pseudo-classes to black, then save your work**

    Because the background color for printed output will be white, changing all link colors to black increases legibility in printed formats.

Avoiding confusion in target documents

Although you can link to documents in most any format from your Web pages, it's important to keep in mind that HTML documents are the only ones that your users are guaranteed to be able to access. To be able to access documents in other formats, users' computers must have programs installed that interpret these files. The PDF format has become an unofficial Web standard for documents that require a specific printed format, such as forms that must be filled out by hand and/or signed, and you can rely on most of your users having the capability to view and print PDFs. Make documents in other formats available based on the likely computer configurations

of your target audience. For instance, on a Web site by and for users of a highly specialized type of software, you'd be safe in making files in that software format available; however, on a site for the general public, it's unlikely that most users would be able to access such files.

Keep in mind that Web-focused formats such as HTML and PDF minimize file sizes as much as possible, meaning that documents usually download quickly. If you are making a document available in another format, pay attention to the file size and take any steps available to reduce the size.

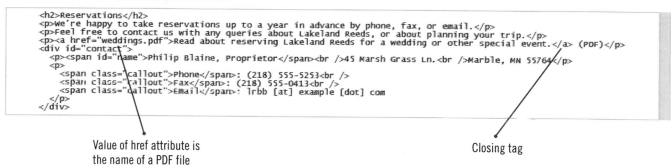

```
<h2>Reservations</h2>
<p>We're happy to take reservations up to a year in advance by phone, fax, or email.</p>
<p>Feel free to contact us with any queries about Lakeland Reeds, or about planning your trip.</p>
<p><a href="weddings.pdf">Read about reserving Lakeland Reeds for a wedding or other special event.</a> (PDF)</p>
<div id="contact">
    <p><span id="name">Philip Blaine, Proprietor</span><br />45 Marsh Grass Ln.<br />Marble, MN 55764</p>
    <p>
        <span class="callout">Phone</span>: (218) 555-5253<br />
        <span class="callout">Fax</span>: (218) 555-0413<br />
        <span class="callout">Email</span>: lrbb [at] example [dot] com
    </p>
</div>
```

Value of href attribute is
the name of a PDF file

Closing tag

FIGURE E-15: Target PDF file in PDF reader

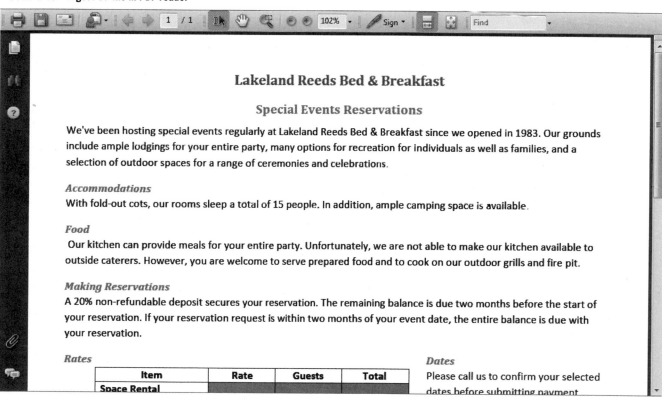

HTML5 and CSS3

Increasing Navigational Accessibility

Nav bars can present accessibility challenges for users with limited or no sight. Users of screen readers, for instance, often experience a Web page element-by-element in sequence from top to bottom, meaning that a screen reader would read the heading followed by each link in a nav bar before getting to the main content of the page. To provide more navigation options, it's good practice to include a **skip link** at the top of each Web page, which targets an anchor at the start of the main page content and allows users to bypass navigation. In addition, HTML5 introduced nav, a semantic element, to mark the main elements of site and page navigation. The nav element is expected to replace the need for skip links because assistive software will be able to offer users the option of bypassing it. For now, you can make your Web pages most accessible by incorporating both of these options. You add a skip link to each Web page in the Lakeland Reeds B&B site, and you make the site navigation and page navigation sections into nav elements.

STEPS

1. **Return to index.html in your text editor, locate the opening <p> tag for the first paragraph of Web page text, and add the attribute id="main"**

2. **Add a blank line beneath the opening <body> tag, indent to align with the div tag that follows, then type <p id="skipnav"><a href="#main">Skip navigation</a></p>**

   Figure E-16 shows the code for the target anchor and the skip link.

> **TROUBLE**
> Be sure not to delete the </div> tag at the end of the document just before the </body> tag, which is the closing tag for a different element.

3. **Below the h1 element, delete the tag <div>, type <nav>, then above the p element with the id value main, delete </div>, then type </nav>**

4. **Add a blank line above the closing tag for the head element near the top of the document, then enter the three lines of code shown in Figure E-16**

   Because recent versions of Internet Explorer interpret semantic elements in unexpected ways, you can ensure compatibility by including a **script**, which is more complex Web page code written in another programming language. This element is surrounded by comments and instructions so all user agents except the affected versions of Internet Explorer will ignore it.

> **TROUBLE**
> If your browser displays an error message about scripts, choose the appropriate option to allow the script on the current page to run.

5. **Save your work, then refresh index.html in your browser**

   As Figure E-17 shows, the skip link appears at the top of the browser window. Replacing the div element with the nav element does not change the page's appearance.

> **TROUBLE**
> If you do not see the main page content after clicking the skip link, double-check the code you entered in Steps 1 and 2 for errors.

6. **Drag the bottom border of your browser up so only the skip link and the h1 heading are visible, then click Skip navigation**

   The browser displays the beginning of the main page content.

7. **Repeat Steps 1–6 for aboutus.html and reserve.html, adding the id attribute in Step 1 to the h2 element in each document**

8. **Repeat Steps 1–7 for rooms.html, adding the id attribute in Step 1 to the h2 element, then replace the <div> and </div> tags for the internal page nav bar with <nav> and </nav>, then change the Back to top href values to #skipnav**

   Because the box element is no longer the first element on the page, you change the "Back to top" link targets to #skipnav so the links take users all the way to the top of the browser window.

9. **Validate the code for all your Web pages and style sheets, then make any necessary changes**

10. **If you have space on a Web server, publish your files to your Web publishing location, open index.html in your browser from the published location, then use the links to verify that all the pages display as expected**

FIGURE E-16: Skip link code

Script reference for compatibility with Internet Explorer

Code for skip link

div element replaced with nav to indicate content and function

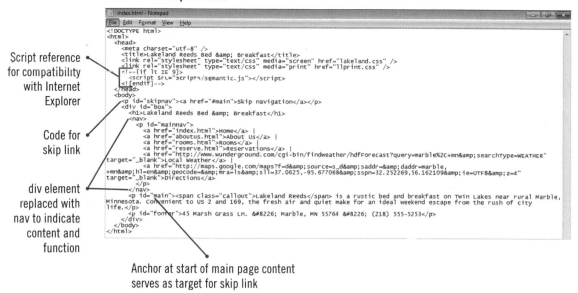

Anchor at start of main page content serves as target for skip link

FIGURE E-17: Web page with skip link

Skip navigation ———• Skip link to move to main page content

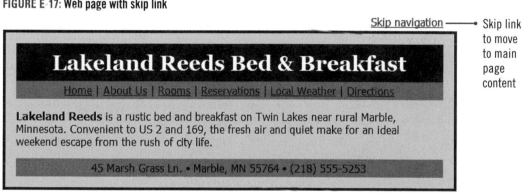

Implementing additional semantic elements

In addition to nav, HTML5 introduced several other semantic elements intended to indicate the contents and function of Web page elements that were previously created using div elements. The rich semantic information that all of these elements offer opens the door for Web pages that adapt more readily and creatively to different types of devices' user agents, from touch pads and smart phones to screen readers and other assistive devices. Table E-3 details several of these elements.

Like the nav element, these other semantic elements require the inclusion of a script to work properly with versions of Internet Explorer earlier than version 9. In addition, any CSS style rule for an HTML5 semantic element should include the name-value pair display: block; to maximize browser compatibility. It's unnecessary to specify this style for semantic elements without other associated CSS, however.

TABLE E-3: Additional HTML5 semantic elements

element	intended use
article	standalone piece of work, such as a single entry in a blog
aside	part of a page that's tangential to the main page content; in a book, this might lend itself to a sidebar or pull quote
footer	information about a section or document that usually appears at the end, such as attributions and/or footnotes
header	information about a section or document that usually appears at the beginning, such as a heading, logo, and/or table of contents
hgroup	group of related elements that include a heading; enables user agents to recognize content such as a tagline as related to a heading
section	section of content focused on a common theme, such as a chapter of a larger work

Practice

For current SAM information, including versions and content details, visit SAM Central (http://www.cengage.com/samcentral). If you have a SAM user profile, you may have access to hands-on instruction, practice, and assessment of the skills covered in this unit. Since various versions of SAM are supported throughout the life of this text, check with your instructor for the correct instructions and URL/Web site for accessing assignments.

Concepts Review

Refer to Figure E-18.

FIGURE E-18

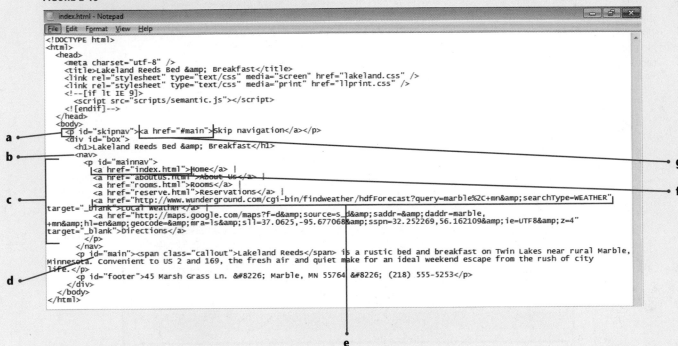

1. Which item is the code for a nav bar?
2. Which item is an absolute link?
3. Which item is a relative link?
4. Which item is an anchor?
5. Which item links to an anchor?
6. Which item is a semantic element for navigational content?
7. Which item creates a skip link?

Match each term with the statement that best describes it.

8. Uniform resource identifier (URI)
9. Relative link
10. Anchor
11. Nav bar
12. Absolute link
13. Skip link
14. Pseudo-class

a. A set of links for moving between Web pages in a Web site

b. A categorization of a Web page element based on a relationship or condition of the element at a given moment

c. A type of link that specifies the full and complete address for the target document on the Web

d. A standard format for specifying how and where to access a resource on the Internet

e. A link that targets an anchor at the start of the main page content and allows users to bypass navigation

f. A named location within a document

g. A link that gives only the path and filename information necessary to locate the target document based on the location of the current Web page

Select the best answer from the list of choices.

15. When creating a link, the Web page or other document you link to is known as the _____.
   - **a.** relative link
   - **b.** target
   - **c.** absolute link
   - **d.** hypertext

16. Which type of Web reference contains a scheme, a server name, and a path?
   - **a.** URI
   - **b.** relative link
   - **c.** anchor
   - **d.** nav element

17. Web servers make documents available using which protocol?
   - **a.** ftp
   - **b.** http
   - **c.** mailto
   - **d.** telnet

18. What does the value "#section3" for the href attribute target?
   - **a.** a URI
   - **b.** a PDF file
   - **c.** a filename
   - **d.** an anchor

19. When you enter a URI, which of the following are you creating?
   - **a.** an anchor
   - **b.** a skip link
   - **c.** an absolute link
   - **d.** a relative link

20. Because Web pages on a small Web site almost always share the same folder on a Web server, it's most efficient to create which type of links when creating a nav bar?
   - **a.** absolute
   - **b.** relative
   - **c.** anchor
   - **d.** skip

21. Which pseudo-class is active when a user's mouse pointer is over the affected link?
   - **a.** a:link
   - **b.** a:visited
   - **c.** a:hover
   - **d.** a:active

22. You create anchors by assigning unique names to elements in your Web page using which attribute?
   - **a.** id
   - **b.** class
   - **c.** href
   - **d.** target

Skills Review

1. **Create relative links.**
   a. In your text editor, open HTM E-6.html from the Unit E/Review folder on the drive and folder where you store your Data Files, save it as **index.html**, then repeat to save HTM E-7.html as **history.html**, HTM E-8.html as **location.html**, and HTM E-9.css as **bigj.css**.
   b. In index.html, enter an opening div tag beneath the h1 element, then below it, indent two additional spaces and add an opening p tag with an id value of **mainnav**.
   c. Insert a new line below the code you just added, indent two additional spaces, type **Home**, add a space, then type a pipe symbol.
   d. Repeat Step c to add the following lines of code at the same indent level:
   History |
   Menu |
   Locations
   e. Insert a new line below the code you just added, indent two fewer spaces than previously, insert a closing p tag, insert another new line, indent two fewer spaces than previously, then insert a closing div tag.
   f. Create a link on the word Home that opens the page index.html, then repeat to add links to the text History to open the page **history.html**, and Locations to open **location.html**.
   g. Save your work, open index.html in your browser, then click the **Locations** link to test it.

2. **Create absolute links.**
   a. Copy the full address of the first location from the Locations Web page to the Clipboard, open a Web site that provides maps, such as maps.google.com or mapquest.com, paste the contents of the Clipboard into the location box on the Web page, then press [Enter].

Skills Review (continued)

    b. Click in the browser address box to select the URI, then copy it to the Clipboard. If the URI in the address bar contains no text after the server name, explore the page for a way to create a link containing the information you've entered, such as the Link link on maps.google.com, verify that the link text begins with http, then copy it to the Clipboard.

    c. Return to location.html in your text editor, then add an absolute link on the word Map at the end of the first address, pasting the URI from the Clipboard as the href value. Be sure to add the closing tag for the a element. If the URI you paste contains the ampersand (&) symbol, replace each occurrence with & to ensure your code validates.

    d. Repeat Steps a–c for the remaining two locations, save your work, then open location.html in your Web browser and test each of the Map links.

3. Style links with CSS pseudo-classes.

    a. Return to bigj.css in your text editor, then insert a new line at the bottom.

    b. Add a style rule using a pseudo-class that formats the font color of a default link in the element with the id "mainnav" as **red**. Repeat to add rules to format the font colors of visited links within the element with the id "mainnav" as **#ffcc66**, links with the mouse pointer over them as **white**, and active links as **#ffcc66**. Ensure that the rules appear in your style sheet in the above order.

    c. Save your work, return to your Web browser, then if possible, clear your browsing history.

    d. Reload index.html in your browser, then verify that the font color changes for links in the nav bar when the mouse pointer is over them, when they are being clicked, and when the target pages have been viewed.

4. Open links in new windows or tabs.

    a. Return to location.html in your text editor, locate the end of the opening a tag for the first Map link, insert a space after the closing quote around the URI, then add an attribute-value pair that opens the link in a new browser window or tab. Repeat for the remaining two Map links.

    b. Save your work, reload location.html in your browser, then test each Map link.

5. Link to anchors.

    a. Return to location.html in your text editor.

    b. Locate the h3 element containing the text Queen's Park, then add an id attribute with the value **queen** to the opening tag.

    c. Repeat Step b to add an id attribute with the value **stclair** to the h3 element containing the text St. Clair, and an id attribute with the value **dundas** to the h3 element containing the text Dundas.

    d. Insert a blank line above the h3 element with the id stclair, then indent and insert a p element with the class **toplink**. Within the p element, insert the text **Back to top**, then link the text to the anchor with the id box.

    e. Repeat Step d to add the same code above the h3 element with the id dundas and above the p element with the id contact.

    f. Add a blank line before the h3 element containing the text Queen's Park, indent and enter an opening div tag, add another blank line beneath the code you just entered, indent two additional spaces, then add a p tag with the id **pagenav**.

    g. Add a blank line beneath the code you just entered, indent two additional spaces, insert the text Queen's Park followed by a space and a pipe symbol, then create a link on the text **Queen's Park** that moves to the element with the id queen. Repeat to add the text **St. Clair**, followed by a space and a pipe symbol. Link the text St. Clair to the element with the id stclair and add the text **Dundas** and link it to the element with the id dundas.

    h. Beneath the code you just entered, add closing tags for the p and div elements, reducing the indentation as necessary to match the opening tags.

    i. Save your work, then open bigj.css in your text editor.

    j. Add a blank line above the style rules for the #mainnav pseudo-classes, then enter a style rule using a pseudo-class that formats the font color of a default link as **#663300**. Repeat to add rules to format the font colors of visited links as **#754719**, links with the mouse pointer over them as **black**, and active links as **#754719**. Ensure that the rules appear in your style sheet in the above order.

Skills Review (continued)

k. Add a blank line above the style rules for the #mainnav pseudo-classes, then enter a style rule using a pseudo-class that formats the font color of a default link in the element with the id "pagenav" as **black**. Repeat to add rules to format the font colors of visited links within the element with the id "pagenav" as **#754719**, links with the mouse pointer over them as **#663300**, and active links as **#754719**. Ensure that the rules appear in your style sheet in the above order.

l. Save your work, open location.html in your Web browser, then click each of the links in the new nav bar and each of the Back to top links.

6. Create a link to a document.

a. Return to index.html in your text editor.

b. In the code for the nav bar, add a link on the text Menu that opens bigjmenu.pdf.

c. Open index.html in your Web browser, then click the Menu link to test it. If the PDF file opened in a program other than your Web browser, close the program displaying the file.

d. Return to index.html in your text editor, select the entire code for the nav bar including the opening and closing div tags, copy the code to the Clipboard, paste it below the h1 element in history.html and location.html, then save your work on each document.

e. In your Web browser, use the links on the index.html nav bar to open the other pages in the Web site, then verify that all the links work on each page.

f. Return to bigj.css in your text editor, save your work, then save a copy as **bjprint.css**.

g. Remove all name-value pairs that specify color, including any border name-value pairs, change all the colors in style rules based on pseudo-classes to **black**, then save your work.

7. Increase navigational accessibility.

a. Return to index.html in your text editor, locate the opening <p> tag for the first paragraph of the Web page text, and add an id attribute with the value "main".

b. Add a blank line beneath the opening <body> tag, add a p element with the id **skipnav** containing the text **Skip navigation**, then add a link to the text Skip navigation that moves to the anchor with the id **main**.

c. Below the h1 element, replace the opening div tag with an opening nav tag. Above the p element with the id value "main", replace the closing div tag with a closing nav tag.

d. Add a blank line above the closing tag for the head element near the top of the document, then enter the following three lines of code with appropriate indentation:

```
<!--[if lt IE 9]>
   <script src="scripts/semantic.js"></script>
<![endif]-->
```

FIGURE E-19

e. Save your work, then refresh index.html in your browser. If your browser displays an error message about scripts, choose the appropriate option to allow the script on the current page to run. Figure E-19 shows the final appearance of index.html.

f. Drag the bottom border of your browser up so only the skip link and the h1 heading are visible, then click Skip navigation.

g. Repeat Steps a–f for history.html, adding the id attribute in Step a to the h2 element.

Skip navigation

Big J's Deep Dish Pizza

Home | History | Menu | Locations

Authentic Chicago-style pies

Eat in, carry out, or call for delivery.

Voted "Best Pizza Joint" by the *Toronto Times!*

150 St. Joseph St.
Toronto, ON M5S 2C3
(416) 555-3337

Skills Review (continued)

    h. Repeat Steps a–f for location.html, adding the id attribute in Step a to the h2 element, then replace the opening and closing div tags for the internal page nav bar with opening and closing nav tags. Change the "Back to top" href values to **#skipnav**. Figure E-20 shows the final appearance of location.html.

    i. Validate the code for all your Web pages and style sheets.

Independent Challenge 1

As you continue your work on the Web site for the Spotted Wren Garden Center, you add a nav bar and links to gardening resources, along with navigational accessibility features.

    a. Open HTM E-10.html in your text editor from the Unit E/IC1 folder. Insert a blank line before the closing body tag, then insert a paragraph element containing your first and last name and the text **HTML5 Unit E, Independent Challenge 1**. Save the file as **index.html**, then repeat to save HTM E-11.html as **hours.html** and HTM E-12.html as **resource.html**. Open HTM E-13.css. Below the existing comment at the top of the document, add another comment containing your first and last name and the text **HTML5 Unit E, Independent Challenge 1**. Save the file as **spotwren.css**.

    b. In index.html, insert a div element beneath the opening tag for the "content" div element. Add a p element with the id **mainnav**, then add the text and separating characters for a nav bar, using the link text **Home**, **Hours**, **Location**, and **Gardening Resources**.

    c. Link the word Home to index.html, Hours to hours.html, and Gardening Resources to resource.html. Save your work, then open index.html in your browser and verify that the links you entered open the appropriate pages.

    d. Copy the business street address from the Web page, open the Web page for a map provider, such as maps.google.com or mapquest.com, then open a map showing the business location. Copy the URI in your browser's address box, or if the URI in the address bar contains no text after the server name, explore the page for a way to create a link containing the information you've entered, such as the Link link on maps.google.com, verify that the link text begins with http, then copy it.

    e. Return to index.html in your text editor, then add an absolute link to the word Location in the nav bar using the map URI you copied. Convert any occurrence of an ampersand symbol (&) to **&** and add code to specify that the target should open in a new window. Save your work. Reload index.html in your browser, then verify that the new link works correctly.

    f. Copy the code for the nav bar from index.html and paste it into the other two html documents at the top of the "content" div element.

    g. Return to spotwren.css in your text editor, then add four style rules using pseudo-classes to format the font color of a default link in the element with the id "mainnav" as **white**, a visited link as **#d6d6c2**, a link with the mouse pointer over it as **#ffff00**, and an active link as **#ffcc00**. Ensure that the rules appear in your style sheet in the order specified.

    h. Save your work, return to your browser and clear your browser history if possible, reload index.html, and verify that the default font color is white, that the font color changes on rollovers and clicks, and that links that have been followed appear in a different color than unfollowed links.

    i. Return to resource.html in your text editor. On the text Lawn and Garden Care Tip Sheet, add a link that opens tipsheet.pdf.

FIGURE E-20

Skip navigation

Big J's Deep Dish Pizza

Home | History | Menu | Locations

Locations

Queen's Park/UT | St. Clair | Dundas

Queen's Park/UT

150 St. Joseph St., Toronto, ON M5S 2C3 [Map]
(416) 555-3337

    Mon-Thu: 11am - 10pm
    Fri-Sat: 11am - 11pm
    Sun: Noon - 10pm

Back to top

St. Clair

783 St. Clair Ave. W, Toronto, ON M6G 3P7 [Map]
(416) 555-2047

    Mon-Thu: 11am - 9:30pm
    Fri-Sat: 11am - 11pm
    Sun: Noon - 9:30pm

Back to top

Dundas

360 Dundas St. W, Toronto, ON M5T 1G4 [Map]
(416) 555-1011

    Mon-Thu: 11am - 11pm
    Fri-Sat: 11am - Midnight
    Sun: Noon - 11pm

Back to top

150 St. Joseph St.
Toronto, ON M5S 2C3
(416) 555-3337

Independent Challenge 1 (continued)

j. Use a search engine to identify a site that provides weather forecasts for gardeners, using a search phrase such as **gardening weather forecast**. Navigate to the gardening forecast for Omaha, NE, copy the URI, then return to resource.html in your text editor and add a link to the URI you copied on the phrase Gardening weather forecast. Save your work.

k. Return to spotwren.css in your text editor, then above the existing pseudo-class rules, add four style rules using pseudo-classes to format the font color of a default link as **#993300**, a visited link as **#999966**, a link with the mouse pointer over it as **black**, and an active link as **#999966**. Ensure that the rules appear in your style sheet in the order specified. Open resource.html in your browser, verify that the link colors change in response to rollovers and clicks, then test all the links on the page.

l. Return to index.html in your text editor. Add an anchor with the name **main** to the first p element beneath the nav bar. Create a skip navigation link beneath the opening body tag that moves to the "main" anchor. Repeat for hours.html and resource. html, adding the anchor to the h2 element in each document. Save your work on each file, then reload each file in your browser and test the skip navigation link. Figure E-21 shows resource.html.

FIGURE E-21

m. Return to index.html in your text editor, replace the div element enclosing the nav bar with a nav element, then add the following three lines of code immediately before the closing head tag:

```
<!--[if lt IE 9]>
  <script src="scripts/semantic.js"></script>
<![endif]-->
```

n. Repeat Step m for resource.html and hours.html.

o. Return to spotwren.css in your text editor, remove all name-value pairs that reference colors, change all colors in rules based on pseudo-classes to black, then save a copy of the file as **swprint.css**.

p. Validate all your HTML and CSS documents.

q. If you have space on a Web server for publishing your documents, create a local root folder within the IC1 folder, move all the files and folders in the IC1 folder to the local root folder, upload the files to your Web publishing location, then open index.html in your browser from the published location and test the links.

r. Close your browser, then close your text editor.

Independent Challenge 2

As you continue developing the Web site for the Murfreesboro Regional Soccer League, you create links between pages as well as links to anchors. You also incorporate features to make the site navigation more accessible.

a. Open HTM E-14.html in your text editor from the Unit E/IC2 folder. Insert a blank line before the closing body tag, then insert a paragraph element containing your first and last name and the text **HTML5 Unit E, Independent Challenge 2**. Save the file as **index.html**, then repeat to save HTM E-15.html as **started.html** and HTM E-16. html as **schedule.html**. Open HTM E-17.css, then below the existing comment at the top of the document, add another comment containing your first and last name and the text **HTML5 Unit E, Independent Challenge 2**. Save the file as **mrsl.css**.

b. In index.html, insert a div element above the opening tag for the "maintext" div element. Add a p element with the id **mainnav**, then add the text and separating characters for a nav bar, using the link text **Home**, **Getting Started**, **Schedules**, and **Field Location**.

c. Link the word Home to index.html, Getting Started to started.html, and Schedules to schedule.html. Save your work, then open index.html in your browser and verify that the links you entered open the appropriate pages.

Independent Challenge 2 (continued)

d. In your browser, open a Web site that provides maps, such as maps.google.com or mapquest.com, then display a map that shows the address **515 Cherry Ln., Murfreesboro, TN**. Copy the URI in your browser's address box, or if the URI in the address bar contains no text after the server name, explore the page for a way to create a link containing the information you've entered, such as the Link link on maps.google.com, verify that the link text begins with http, then copy it.

e. Return to index.html in your text editor, then add an absolute link to the phrase Field Location in the nav bar using the URI you copied. Add code to specify that the target should open in a new window, then save your work. Reload index.html in your browser, then verify that the Field Location link works correctly.

f. Copy the code for the nav bar from index.html and paste it into the other two html documents above the opening tags for the "maintext" div elements.

g. Return to mrsl.css in your text editor, then add four style rules using pseudo-classes to format the font color of a default link in the element with the id "mainnav" as **white**, a visited link as **#8CC63F**, a link with the mouse pointer over it as **red**, and an active link as **#8CC63F**. Ensure that the rules appear in your style sheet in the order specified.

h. Save your work, return to your browser and clear your browser history if possible, reload index.html, and verify that the default font color is white, that the font color changes on rollovers and clicks, and that links that have been followed appear in a different color than unfollowed links.

i. Return to schedule.html in your text editor. Above the h3 element containing the text Red, add a p element with the id "**pagenav**", then add the text and separating characters for a nav bar, using the link text **Red**, **Blue**, **Green**, and **Yellow**.

j. Add an anchor to each of the four h3 elements on the page with an anchor name matching the displayed text. Link each of the four words on the page nav bar you created in the previous step to the anchor for the corresponding h3 element.

k. Beneath the paragraph containing schedule information for the Red team, add a p element with a class value of **toplink** containing the text **Back to top**. Link the text to the "maintext" anchor. Copy the code you created and paste it beneath the schedule paragraphs for the remaining three teams, then save your work.

l. Return to mrsl.css in your text editor, then add four style rules using pseudo-classes to format the font color of a default link in the element with the id "pagenav" as **black**, a visited link as **#754719**, a link with the mouse pointer over it as **red**, and an active link as **#754719**. Ensure that the rules appear in your style sheet in the order specified, save your work, open schedule.html in your browser, verify that the link colors change in response to rollovers and clicks, then test all the links on the page nav bar and all the Back to top links.

m. Return to index.html in your text editor. Add an anchor with the name **main** to the first p element beneath the nav bar. Create a skip navigation link beneath the opening body tag that moves to the "main" anchor. Repeat for started.html and schedule.html, adding the anchor to the h2 element in each document. In schedule.html, change the link targets for the four Back to top links to the skipnav anchor. Save your work on each file.

n. Return to mrsl.css in your text editor, then above the existing pseudo-class rules add four style rules using pseudo-classes to format the font color of a default link as **#663300**, a visited link as **#663300**, a link with the mouse pointer over it as **black**, and an active link as **#663300**. Ensure that the rules appear in your style sheet in the order specified. Save your work, then then reload each HTML file in your browser and test the skip navigation links. Figure E-22 shows schedule.html.

o. Return to index.html in your text editor, replace the div element enclosing the nav bar with a nav element, then add the following three lines of code immediately before the closing head tag:

```
<!--[if lt IE 9]>
  <script src="scripts/semantic.js"></script>
<![endif]-->
```

FIGURE E-22

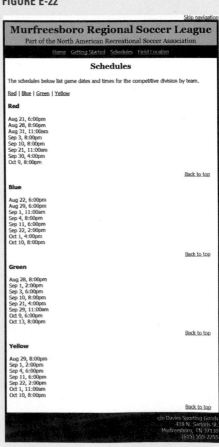

Independent Challenge 2 (continued)

p. Repeat Step o for started.html and schedule.html. In schedule.html, enclose the p element containing the page nav bar in a nav element, increasing the indentation for the existing code.

Advanced Challenge Exercise

- Return to index.html in your text editor. Replace the div element that has the id **headings** with the semantic **header** element, using the opening tag **<header>** with no attributes and the closing tag **</header>**.
- Near the bottom of the document, enclose the p element that has the id contact in a semantic footer element, using the opening tag **<footer>** with no attributes and the closing tag **</footer>**.
- Save your work, then repeat the previous two steps for started.html and schedule.html.
- Return to mrsl.css in your text editor. Locate the #headings style rule and change the selector to a type selector based on the "header" element. Add a name-value pair to the style rule that sets the display of the element to **block**. Save your work, open index.html in your browser, then verify that the appearance of all three Web pages is unchanged.

q. Return to mrsl.css in your text editor, remove all name-value pairs that reference colors, change the colors for all rules based on pseudo-classes to **black**, then save a copy of the file as **mrsprint.css**.

r. Validate all your HTML and CSS documents.

s. If you have space on a Web server for publishing your documents, create a local root folder within the IC2 folder, move all the files and folders in the IC2 folder to the local root folder, upload the files to your Web publishing location, then open index.html in your browser from the published location and test the links.

t. Close your browser, then close your text editor.

Independent Challenge 3

This Independent Challenge requires an Internet connection.

As you continue your work on the Web site for Hotel Natoma, you incorporate links between pages as well as to external Web sites, and incorporate navigational accessibility features.

a. Open HTM E-18.html in your text editor from the Unit E/IC3 folder. Insert a blank line before the closing body tag, then insert a paragraph element containing your first and last name and the text **HTML5 Unit E, Independent Challenge 3**. Save the file as **index.html**, then repeat to save HTM E-19.html as **nearby.html**. Open HTM E-20.css, then below the existing comment at the top of the document, add another comment containing your first and last name and the text **HTML5 Unit E, Independent Challenge 3**. Save the file as **natoma.css**.

b. In nearby.html, insert a nav bar beneath the h1 element. Enclose your code in a div element and lay out the navigation bar text using a paragraph element with with id **mainnav**. Add the link text **Home, What's Nearby**, and **Location**. Link the word Home to index.html and What's Nearby to nearby.html. Save your work, then open nearby.html in your browser and verify that the links you entered open the appropriate pages.

c. In your browser, open a Web site that provides maps, such as maps.google.com or mapquest.com, then display a map that shows the address **568 Natoma St., San Francisco, CA**. Copy the URI in your browser's address box, or if the URI in the address bar contains no text after the server name, explore the page for a way to create a link containing the information you've entered, such as the Link link on maps.google.com. Verify that the link text begins with http, then copy it.

d. Add an absolute link to the phrase "Location" in the nav bar using the URI you copied. If necessary, replace any occurences of ampersand (&) with the appropriate character reference. Add code to specify that the target should open in a new window, then save your work. Reload nearby.html in your browser.

e. Use a search engine to locate a Web page related to each of the topics in the What's Nearby list, then link the corresponding text to the site you identified. Save your work, then open nearby.html in your browser and check all the links.

Independent Challenge 3 (continued)

Advanced Challenge Exercise

- Open a Web site that provides a link shortening service, such as bit.ly or tinyurl.com. Paste the location URI you copied above into the appropriate box on the Web page, then click the associated button to generate the shortened URI.
- Copy the shortened URI, return to nearby.html in your text editor, then replace the href value for the link you created on the phrase "Location" in the nav bar with the shortened URI you copied. Save your work, reload nearby.html in your browser, then verify that the Location link works correctly.
- Repeat the process above to shorten the link on each topic in the What's Nearby list. Save your work, then open nearby.html in your browser and check all the links.

f. Copy the code for the nav bar from nearby.html, then paste it into index.html beneath the h1 element.

g. Return to natoma.css in your text editor, then add four style rules using pseudo-classes to format the font color of a default link in the element with the id "mainnav" as **#213621**, a visited link as **#394D39**, a link with the mouse pointer over it as **black**, and an active link as **#394D39**. Ensure that the rules appear in your style sheet in the order specified.

h. Above the pseudo-class rules you just entered, add four style rules using pseudo-classes to format the font color of a default link as **#213621**, a visited link as **#526352**, a link with the mouse pointer over it as **black**, and an active link as **#526352**. Ensure that the rules appear in your style sheet in the order specified.

i. Save your work, return to your browser and clear your browser history if possible, reload index.html, and verify that the default font color is **white**, that the font color changes on rollovers and clicks, and that links that have been followed appear in a different color than unfollowed links.

j. Return to index.html in your text editor. Add an anchor with the name **main** to the first p element beneath the nav bar. Create a skip navigation link beneath the opening body tag that moves to the "main" anchor. Repeat for nearby.html, adding the anchor to the h2 element. Save your work on each file.

k. Reload each HTML file in your browser and test the skip navigation links. Figure E-23 shows nearby.html.

l. Return to index.html in your text editor, replace the div element enclosing the nav bar with a nav element, then add the following three lines of code immediately before the closing head tag:

FIGURE E-23

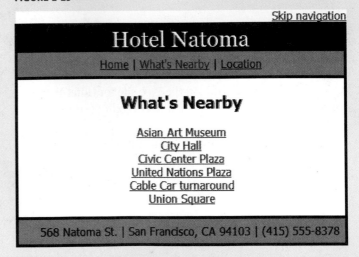

```
<!--[if lt IE 9]>
  <script src="scripts/semantic.js"></script>
<![endif]-->
```

m. Repeat the previous step for nearby.html.

n. Return to natoma.css in your text editor, remove all name-value pairs that reference colors, change the colors for all rules based on pseudo-classes to **black**, then save a copy of the file as **hnprint.css**.

o. Validate all your HTML and CSS documents.

p. If you have space on a Web server for publishing your documents, create a local root folder within the IC3 folder, move all the files and folders in the IC3 folder to the local root folder, upload the files to your Web publishing location, then open index.html in your browser from the published location and test the links.

q. Close your browser, then close your text editor.

Real Life Independent Challenge

This assignment builds on the personal Web site you have worked on in previous units. You will add links between the pages of your Web site, along with features to increase the accessibility of your navigation.

a. Copy your Web site files to the Unit E/RLIC folder on the drive and folder where you store your Data Files.

b. On your main Web page, create a nav bar including links to all the pages on your Web site, along with links to any relevant documents and external Web pages. If appropriate, designate one or more links to open in new windows or tabs. Copy the nav bar to the rest of the pages in your site.

c. Create pseudo-classes to set the font color of links in all four states.

d. For each of your Web pages that contains multiple sections, create a nav bar for moving within the page. Include a link at the end of each section that moves back to the top of the page. Add pseudo-classes for links in the page nav bar.

e. Add a skip link at the top of each page that moves to an anchor below the main nav bar. If you created page navigation anywhere on your site, update the links to move back to the top of the page to target the skip link. Add a third set of pseudo-classes to your style sheet above the ones you already created to format links that aren't children of the elements specified in the other pseudo-class rules.

f. Copy the scripts directory from the Unit E/Unit folder to the Unit E/RLIC folder, then add the script reference from Figure E-16 to the code of your all your Web pages. Enclose all your nav bars in nav elements.

g. Save changes to your style sheet document, save a copy using the name of your print style sheet, then take out name-value pairs that set color and change all colors in rules based on pseudo-classes to black.

h. Preview your Web pages in at least two browsers, then make any edits necessary for them to appear as you expected.

i. Validate all of your HTML and CSS documents and make any edits necessary to resolve any issues.

j. If you have space on a Web server for publishing your documents, create a local root folder within the RLIC folder, move all the files in the RLIC folder to the local root folder, upload the files to your Web publishing location, then open each Web page in your browser from the published location to verify that the upload was successful.

k. Close your browser, then close your text editor.

Visual Workshop

In your text editor, open the file HTM D-21.html from the Unit E/VW directory on the drive and folder where you store your Data Files and save it as **index.html**. Open HTM D-22.css, then save it as **revision.css**. Use your text editor to style the Web page to match the one shown in Figure E-24. Use the id **mainnav** for the nav bar. Link the text Location to a map showing the location listed at the bottom of the page. The target pages for the other links may be nonexistent pages. Use pseudo-classes to format all four states for the nav bar links and the skip link. Add the script reference from Figure E-16 to the head section of your Web page, then enclose the nav bar in a nav element. Add a paragraph element after the content shown that contains your first and last name and the text **HTML5 Unit E, Visual Workshop**. Validate your HTML and CSS code. If you have space on a Web server, create a local root folder within the VW folder, move both files to the local root folder, upload the file to your Web publishing location, then open the Web page in your browser from the published location. Close your browser and text editor.

FIGURE E-24

UNIT
F
HTML5 and CSS3

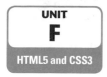

Inserting and Working with Images

Files You Will Need:

To view a list of files needed for this unit, see the Data Files Grid in the back of the book.

Just as in print media, images are integral in conveying information on the Web. You can use HTML to incorporate images into your Web pages and specify CSS properties to affect the way user agents display the images. Your design colleagues at Great Northern Sites have provided a logo image and several other graphics for the Lakeland Reeds B&B Web site. In this unit, you add the layout and presentational codes to add these images to the site.

OBJECTIVES

Evaluate image file types

Insert images

Align images

Control page flow

Insert a background image

Associate images with related text

Use images as links

Insert a favicon

Evaluating Image File Types

You can include many types of images, from company logos to photographs, on a Web page. Just as you can link to an external style sheet, you add an image to a Web page by linking to a separate file. While you may not be responsible for providing the image files themselves for inclusion on a Web page, designers who create the art may look to you as a Web developer for advice on aspects such as file format, size, and resolution. As you prepare to incorporate graphics into the Web site for Lakeland Reeds B&B, you review the basics of images in HTML documents.

To create optimal graphics for the Web, it's important to understand a few concepts:

- **File types**

  Images can currently be represented electronically in two ways: as bitmaps or as vectors. A **bitmap image** represents an image as a grid of dots and specifies the color of each dot. A **vector graphic** instead encodes the appearance of a graphic as geometric shapes. Many file formats are available that render bitmap or vector representations in different ways. The three most widely used formats on the Web are all different types of bitmap encoding. The **JPEG** or **JPG** format, named for the Joint Photographic Experts Group that created it, is optimized for images that contain many colors, such as photographs. **GIF**, an abbreviation for graphics interchange format, works best for art that contains limited numbers of colors and areas with defined borders between areas. As an added benefit, the GIF file type supports transparent pixels, allowing the page background or other elements to show through parts of an image.

  JPEG and GIF have been the standard Web formats for photos and drawn art, respectively, for years. Recently, though, user agent support has been increasing for two newer formats that offer their own advantages. **PNG**, short for Portable Network Graphics, was originally designed as a free alternative to GIF when GIF usage required licensing fees. While the patents on GIF have expired, PNG has won fans with its addition of an **alpha channel**, which allows graphics creators to specify the level of opacity for areas of a graphic, from totally transparent to totally opaque, or anywhere in between. More recently, the **Scalable Vector Graphics (SVG)** format has seen wider support in browsers. SVG is optimal for encoding line art; however, unlike the GIF or JPEG formats, which use bitmaps to encode graphics at specific dimensions, an SVG file can be displayed at different dimensions with no decrease in quality. Table F-1 summarizes support for the four main image formats in some of the most widely used Web browsers.

- **Resolution and size**

  When using any bitmap file formats, including JPEG, GIF, and PNG, it's important that an image is created and formatted with its use on the Web site in mind. All bitmap images are created to be displayed at a set resolution and size. **Resolution**, measured in **dots per inch (dpi)**, specifies how close the dots in the bitmap should appear on the output. While the standard for display on a monitor is 72 dpi, other media have different standards: for example, many home and office printers can print at 2400 dpi or greater. While a higher dpi image provides more detail, it also creates a file with a greater file size and takes up extra room on a Web page. Thus, it's important to save an image specifically for use on the Web to minimize download time and to ensure that the image fits in the page layout.

  The size of a bitmap image is measured in **pixels**, which are the individual dots that make up the image. Every bitmap image is created with a specific length and width. While a vector graphic can be scaled larger or smaller with no change in quality, bitmap graphics display optimally only at their original, or **native**, length and width, as shown in Figure F-1. Scaling an image to a smaller size than its native resolution negatively impacts the way the image is displayed; in addition, since a smaller bitmap is generally a smaller file size, displaying a file below its native resolution unnecessarily increases the amount of data users have to download. While scaling an image to a larger size than its native resolution decreases the amount of data that users have to download compared to the image's native size, it also results in markedly poor image quality. Thus, in addition to creating graphics with the correct resolution for the Web, it's important that designers generate them at the precise dimensions required for the layout.

FIGURE F-1: Scaling bitmaps

Image displayed larger than its native size

Image displayed smaller than its native size

Image displayed at its native size

Photo/Sasha Vodnik

TABLE F-1: Support for image formats in recent browser versions

format	Internet Explorer (IE)			Firefox	Chrome	Safari	Opera
	IE6 and earlier	IE7 and IE8	IE9 and later				
GIF	full	full	full	full	full	full	full	full
JPEG	full	full	full	full	full	full	full	full
PNG	limited; no alpha	limited	full	full	full	full	full	full
SVG	low	low	medium	medium	medium	high	high	high

Assessing the future of SVG

The most widely supported graphics formats—GIF, JPEG, and PNG—require external files created with image editors. SVG graphics, however, are written in a markup language similar to XML. As support for the format grows, you will be able to create simple graphics like you create style sheets: by creating external documents in a text editor and linking them to your Web pages. Browser makers are also beginning to incorporate support for SVG code within HTML documents, meaning that eventually you will have the option to embed graphics like you embed CSS.

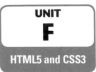
Inserting Images

You add an image to an HTML document using the one-sided img element. The element must include two attributes: src, whose value is the path and filename of the image file to display, and alt, which specifies text to display in case the image is unavailable or needs to be read in user agents by software such as screen readers. Table F-2 details all available attributes for the img element. Like span and br, img elements are inline elements by default. You can wrap an img element in its own block element, such as a div element, and align it horizontally using standard block-level alignment techniques. For an image occurring within a paragraph of text, the bottom of an image is aligned with the bottom of the text, which is known as the **baseline**. ▰▰▰▰ You add the Lakeland Reeds B&B logo in place of the heading at the top of the page in the Web site. You also replace the bullets separating the sections of the contact information with decorative graphics.

STEPS

1. **In your text editor, open HTM F-1.html from the Unit F/Unit folder on the drive and folder where you store your Data Files, insert a blank line before the closing body tag, insert a paragraph element containing your first and last name and the text HTML5 Unit F, save it as index.html, repeat to save HTM F-2.html as rooms.html then use a CSS comment to add the same information to HTM F-3.css and save it as lakeland.css**

QUICK TIP
Be sure to type a space before the closing /.

2. **In index.html, locate the h1 element, delete the text Lakeland Reeds Bed & Breakfast, leaving the <h1> and </h1> tags, move the </h1> tag to a separate line at the same indent level, then on a blank line between the h1 tags, indent two additional spaces and type <img src="images/lakeland.gif" width="664" height="180" alt="Lakeland Reeds Bed and Breakfast" />**

   While the width and height attributes are not required, it's highly recommended that you use them to specify the native dimensions of the image. This ensures that if a visual user agent is unable for any reason to display the referenced image, it can maintain a corresponding amount of blank space, preserving the layout of your Web page. Width and height attributes are always in pixels, so it's not necessary to specify units. Figure F-2 shows the code for the img element.

3. **In the paragraph element at the bottom of the page containing contact information, replace the first occurrence of the character code • with <img src="images/ flourish.gif" width="16" height="16" alt="" />, then repeat to replace the second occurrence of the character code with the same HTML code**

   Figure F-2 shows the completed code for adding images to the main Web page.

4. **Save your work, then return to lakeland.css in your text editor**

QUICK TIP
Don't make changes to the h1, h2, nav style rule.

5. **In the h1 style rule, remove all name–value pairs except font-size, then add the code margin: 0;**

6. **Save your work, then open index.html in your default browser**

   Figure F-3 shows index.html with images in a browser.

7. **Repeat Steps 2 through 4 to add the logo and decorative graphic to the corresponding elements in rooms.html, then preview your changes**

img element for the logo graphic

img elements replace special characters

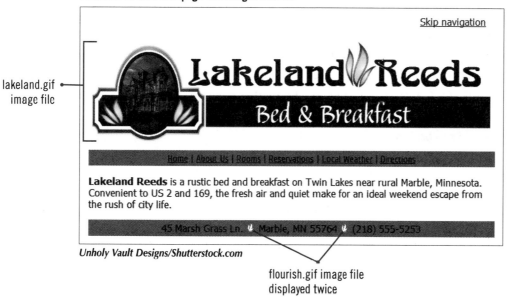

lakeland.gif image file

Unholy Vault Designs/Shutterstock.com

flourish.gif image file displayed twice

TABLE F-2: Attributes for the img element

attribute	value
src	path and filename for image file to display
alt	text to display or read in place of image
height width	native height and width of image file in pixels
longdesc	URI for a document that provides fuller alternative description of image

Creating useful alt text

The text you provide using the alt attribute for an image is an important accessibility element for your Web site. It's also significant from a usability perspective for users who are unable to download the image or who choose to browse without images. For graphics that include text, the text should be included in the value of the alt attribute, along with a description if it adds useful information. Photos and other graphics without text should include a description of the image in the alt value. Because there are many ways to describe any given image, it's important to identify what aspect or aspects of a graphic are relevant to the Web page, and focus on those aspects. Finally, if a graphic is merely presentational and doesn't add information to the Web page, include the alt attribute with nothing between the quotes. This lets screen readers know that the element isn't conveying information and that they can skip it, saving blind and visually impaired users from wasting time listening to text such as "stylized bullet" repeatedly while learning nothing about the page contents.

Aligning Images

HTML5 includes the semantic figure element to mark images that add information to a Web page. A user agent should be able to link the contents of a figure element and move them to another location (similar to an appendix in a book) without affecting the information conveyed by the Web page. Thus, a logo image would not be marked as a figure, because it's integral to stating the overall subject of each Web page. A picture, chart, or map illustrating the topic of a paragraph of text, however, would be marked as a figure. When integrating larger figures and other images with Web page contents, you can use the CSS float property to enable text or other Web page elements to flow around the figure. The left and right values of the float property align the top of the element with the top of the next element, and align the image horizontally with the left or right edge of the parent element, respectively. 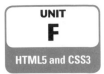 You add a photo of one of the rooms to complement the text on the main page and use the float property to flow the text around it. You also add figure elements containing images of each of the rooms on the Rooms page.

STEPS

1. **In index.html below the nav element for the main nav bar, insert a new line and indent to match the nav element, type <figure id="main">, press [Enter] twice, indent to match the opening tag, type </figure>, then delete the attribute–value pair id="main" from the following p element**

2. **Move the insertion point to the blank line between the figure tags, indent two spaces more than the figure tags, then type <img src="images/sun.jpg" width="369" height="268" alt=""/>**
   Because the image is decorative on this page rather than adding important information, you include an empty alt attribute to indicate that screen readers can ignore it, and that no substitute text needs to be displayed in a browser in case the image is unavailable.

3. **Save your changes, then reload the Web page in your browser**
   Because Web page elements are displayed sequentially from top to bottom by default, the browser displays sun.jpg aligned with the left side of the screen above the paragraph of text.

QUICK TIP

To make them easier to locate, the style rules in the style sheet have been grouped by selector type.

4. **Return to lakeland.css in your text editor, create a new style rule based on the figure selector, then add the name–value pairs display: block, float:right, margin: 0 0 0.5em 1em, and padding: 0**
   The value of "right" for the float property aligns the right edge of the image with the right edge of the parent element. Figure F-4 shows the completed code.

5. **Save your work, then reload the Web page in your browser**
   As Figure F-5 shows, the image is right-aligned, and the paragraph text flows around it, starting at the top of the image. Because the image is higher than the text of both elements that follow it, the contact information flows around the image as well.

6. **Return to rooms.html in your text editor, then insert the code for the four figure elements shown in Figure F-6 beneath the h3 headings**

TROUBLE

The Web page text may no longer match up with the images. You'll fix this in the next lesson.

7. **Save your work, open rooms.html in your browser, then scroll through the document to view the images**
   The style rule you created above based on the figure selector right-aligns these elements as well and flows the text that follows around them.

```
       font-family: tahoma, arial, helvetica, sans-serif;
       }
    figure {
       display: block;
       float: right;
       margin: 0 0 0.5em 1em;
       padding: 0;
       }
    footer {
```

float property takes element out of top-to-bottom flow of page and allows other page elements to appear next to it

FIGURE F-5: Web page with image aligned

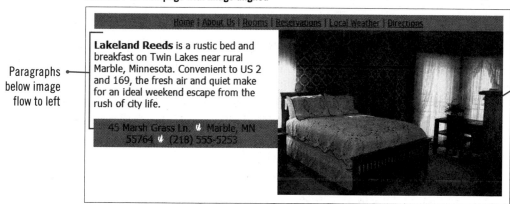

Paragraphs below image flow to left

float: right name–value pair aligns element with right side of parent element and lets elements below it flow around it

Faithe Wempen/sycamoreknoll.com

FIGURE F-6: Code for inserting images on Rooms Web page

```
      </nav>
  <h3 id="sun">Sun Room</h3>
  <figure>
      <img src="images/sun.jpg" width="369" height="268" alt="a bedroom with large windows and a desk, dresser, and queen bed" />
  </figure>
  <p class="desc">With windows on three sides, the sunlight in this second-floor room supports a large selection of houseplants.</p>
  <p class="beds">1 queen bed.</p>
  <p class="toplink"><a href="#skipnav">Back to top</a></p>
  <h3 id="reed">Reed Room</h3>
  <figure>
      <img src="images/reed.jpg" width="370" height="277" alt="a bedroom with a tall window, a dresser with mirror, and a queen bed" />
  </figure>
  <p class="desc">This first-floor room looks out over the reeds on the edge of the lake and the water beyond.</p>
  <p class="beds">1 queen bed and 1 twin bed.</p>
  <p class="toplink"><a href="#skipnav">Back to top</a></p>
  <h3 id="tree">Treehouse</h3>
  <figure>
      <img src="images/tree.jpg" width="370" height="277" alt="a low-ceilinged bedroom with a woodgrain wall and a queen bed" />
  </figure>
  <p class="desc">A winding staircase takes you to your own private getaway at the top of the house, with view of the surrounding trees and meadows and the lake.</p>
  <p class="beds">1 queen bed.</p>
  <p class="toplink"><a href="#skipnav">Back to top</a></p>
  <h3 id="garden">Garden Room</h3>
  <figure>
      <img src="images/garden.jpg" width="370" height="277" alt="a bedroom with ornate wood moldings and a magnifying lens perched above a fireplace" />
  </figure>
  <p class="desc">This room's French doors open onto our stone patio and flower garden.</p>
  <p class="beds">1 queen bed and 2 twin beds.</p>
  <p class="toplink"><a href="#skipnav">Back to top</a></p>
```

figure elements for four images

Floating figure elements in IE6

While recent versions of all major browsers can float elements without major issues, this is not the case for older browsers. Of particular note is Internet Explorer 6 (IE6), which is still in wide use in some large organizations and in some parts of the world. A bug in IE6 causes some floated elements to take up extra space on the page, changing the layout. It's important to know the browser preferences of the audience for any Web site you develop. If your audience included a large percentage of IE6 users, it would be important to understand this issue and implement methods that work around it. You can research this issue further by using a Web browser to search on "ie6 double margin bug".

Controlling Page Flow

The CSS float property enables a lot of possibilities for basic image alignment. However, in some situations, using float is not enough to create the layout you want. For instance, sometimes you want to ensure that text or another object follows a floated element, rather than running alongside it. You can control the flow of Web page elements more precisely with the CSS clear property, which prevents floated elements from being displayed to the left, right, or on either side of another element. ██████ You add the clear property to the paragraph containing contact information to make it appear beneath the image you added, as well as to the links that return users to the top of the page on the Rooms page.

1. **Return to lakeland.css in your text editor**

2. **Locate the footer style rule, insert a new line before the closing curly brace, indent two spaces, then type clear: right;**

   Specifying the value "right" for the clear property prevents a floated element from being displayed to the right of the current element. Because the bed.jpg image currently is displayed to the right, this name–value pair will move the contact information below the image. Figure F-7 shows the clear property inserted in the style sheet.

3. **Save your work, then reload index.html in your browser**

   As Figure F-8 shows, the contact information is displayed below the image.

4. **Return to lakeland.css in your text editor**

5. **Insert a blank line before the closing } for the .toplink style rule, indent two spaces, then type clear:right;**

   Elements with the "toplink" class are the final elements in the room descriptions on the Rooms Web page. Adding a clear value to them ensures that they are displayed consistently at the right edge of the page content, and that the room descriptions are spaced equally.

6. **Save your work, then reload rooms.html in your browser**

   As Figure F-9 shows, the Back to top links are displayed below the figure elements for the rooms.

Obtaining permission for image use

Although it's possible to find and copy images from the Web for use on your own Web pages, it's important to make sure you have permission to use a given image before incorporating it into your designs. In addition to avoiding potential legal action for unauthorized use of someone else's work, it's a show of respect to photographers and designers to ask for permission to use their work.

For small projects, a photographer or designer may allow use in return for credit and a link to their site; larger professional sites usually need to pay a use fee and agree on terms of use. If you're hiring a designer to create artwork for your Web site, make sure your agreement specifies how long and in what context you or your organization may use the work.

FIGURE F-7: Style sheet with page flow property

clear property added
to style rule for
footer element

```
footer {
    display: block;
    background: #B8944D;
    padding: 0.25em;
    margin: 0;
    clear: right;
}
```

FIGURE F-8: Web page with clear property added

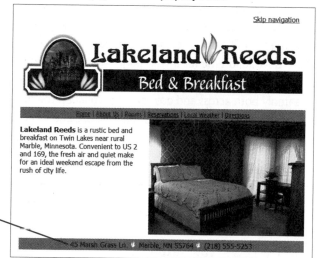

clear property causes footer
element to be displayed without
floated elements to its right

Unholy Vault Designs/Shutterstock.com
Faithe Wempen/sycamoreknoll.com

FIGURE F-9: Back to top links styled with clear property

Unholy Vault Designs/Shutterstock.com
Faithe Wempen/sycamoreknoll.com

Inserting a Background Image

In addition to specifying a color as the background for a Web page or Web page element, you can provide a path and filename for a background image using the background-image property. As with background colors, it's important to choose a background image that provides contrast with other Web page elements, especially text. Because user agents may display the same Web page in windows of different sizes, a given background image may not fill the entire window. In addition, it's best to minimize the sizes of background images to minimize download time for a Web page. User agents address both of these issues through the default behavior of **tiling** small background images, meaning that, like tiles on a floor or wall, the images are displayed repeatedly both across and down a page to fill up the browser window. ▨▨▨ The designers have provided you with a background image for the Lakeland Reeds B&B Web site. You will preserve a background color behind the current contents so the image shows only at the edges of the page, maintaining readability.

STEPS

1. **In your browser, open the file lake.jpg from the Unit F/Unit/images folder**

   The image is tall and narrow.

2. **Return to lakeland.css in your text editor**

3. **In the body style rule, insert a blank line before the closing }, indent two spaces, then type background: url("images/lake.jpg");**

   The value for the background property always starts with the text "url". The relative path, if necessary, and the filename for the background image are enclosed in parentheses and either single or double quotes.

4. **Insert a blank line above the code you just entered, indent two spaces, then type background: #6e93c8;**

   You specify a background color for user agents that don't display images, or for situations where the background image file is unavailable. The background color you specified matches the light blue at the top of the image, preserving both the contrast for the skip link and the overall color scheme of the Web site. When name–value pairs conflict, the one that occurs later in the rule takes precedence; you specify the background color first and the image second to ensure the image is displayed if it's available, and that the color value is present as a backup. Figure F-10 shows the code for the background color and image.

5. **Beneath the closing } for the a:active style rule, add style rules to change the colors for #skipnav a:link to white, #skipnav a:visited to white, #skipnav a:hover to #ff9, and #skipnav a:active to white**

   Because the background for the skip link is changing from a light to dark color, you change the text color to preserve contrast.

6. **Save your work, then reload index.html in your browser**

   As Figure F-11 shows, the background image appears as the background for the Web page. The image is repeated from left to right to fill the entire width of the browser window.

FIGURE F-10: Code for background color and image

```
/* Lakeland Reeds Bed and Breakfast */
@font-face {
  font-family: 'CuprumFFURegular';
  src: url('fonts/Cuprum-webfont.eot');
  src: local('☺'), url('fonts/Cuprum-webfont.woff') format('woff'), url('fonts/(
webfont.svg#webfontKLktnWy4') format('svg');
  font-weight: normal;
  font-style: normal;
  }
body {
  padding: 0;
  margin: 0;
  font-family: tahoma, arial, helvetica, sans-serif;
  background: #6e93c8;
  background: url("images/lake.jpg");
}
figure {
  display: block;
```

Background color and image
added using background property

FIGURE F-11: Main Web page with background image

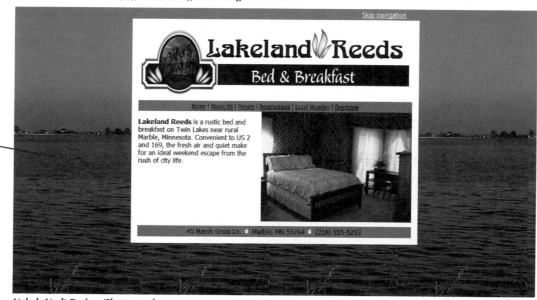

Tall, narrow
background
image is
tiled to fill
the entire
screen

Unholy Vault Designs/Shutterstock.com
Faithe Wempen/sycamoreknoll.com
Photo/Sasha Vodnik

Styling an image with opacity

Recent versions of all major browsers support opacity values for images. By changing the opacity of an image, you can increase its contrast with other page elements or make it more closely match a site's design. The standard CSS3 syntax uses the "opacity" property with a decimal value from 0 (fully transparent) to 1 (fully opaque). For instance, to set 50% opacity, you could use the code
```
opacity: 0.5;
```

Older versions of Internet Explorer don't support this syntax, however, and require an additional name–value pair using a Microsoft-specific property:
```
filter: alpha(opacity=number);
```
where *number* is a percentage from 0 (fully transparent) to 100 (fully opaque).

Associating Images with Related Text

In addition to specifying alternative text for an image with the alt attribute, you can associate other types of text with an image. Many images benefit from a text caption that provides context, explanation, or credit. To associate caption text with an img element, you place the text in a figcaption element that is nested within the figure element for the image. You can also specify additional information using the title attribute, which is supported by the img element as well as most other HTML elements. Most visual user agents display the value of this attribute as floating text when a user moves the mouse pointer over the associated element. When no title attribute is specified, some browsers display the alt text as a floating tooltip instead. 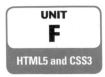 Because the images on the Rooms Web page are already explained by the surrounding content, you decide not to add captions to them. However, you add a caption to the image on the main page of the Web site. You also create title attributes with empty values for images with alt text to prevent the alt text from being displayed as tooltips.

STEPS

1. **Return to index.html in your text editor, insert a new line beneath the img tag for the file sun.jpg, indent the same number of spaces as the img element, then type**
   <figcaption>The Sun Room</figcaption>
   The figcaption element marks the text it contains as a caption for the associated image within the figure element.

2. **Save your work, return to lakeland.css in your text editor, then add a name–value pair to the figure style rule to set text-align to center**

QUICK TIP
The display property lets you change the behavior of an element from inline to block or vice versa.

3. **Create a new style rule using the figcaption selector that sets the margin and the padding to 0, then add the name–value pair display: block;**

4. **Save your work, then refresh index.html in your Web browser**
   The text "The Sun Room" is displayed beneath the image in the middle of the Web page.

5. **Return to index.html in your text editor, position the insertion point just before the word The in the caption you created, type <a href="rooms.html#sun">, position the insertion point just after the word Room, then type </a>**
   Because users who see the photo might want to know more about the room shown, you format the caption as a link to the description of the room on the rooms.html Web page. Figure F-12 shows the completed code for the figcaption element.

6. **Save your work, reload index.html in your Web browser, then click the text The Sun Room and verify that that Sun Room section of rooms.html opens**
   Figure F-13 shows the index.html page containing the caption.

7. **Return to index.html in your text editor, position the insertion point after the final " in the img element for lakeland.gif, press [Spacebar], type title="", then save your work**

8. **Repeat Step 7 in rooms.html for the logo and for the img elements for sun.jpg, reed.jpg, tree.jpg, and garden.jpg**
   Figure F-14 shows the completed code for each img element.

9. **Reload rooms.html in your Web browser, then verify that no floating text appears when you move your mouse pointer over the images**

FIGURE F-12: Code for the figure caption

figcaption element associates text with an image in a figure

```
<figure id="main">
   <img src="images/sun.jpg" width="369" height="268" alt="" />
<figcaption><a href="rooms.html#sun">The Sun Room</a></figcaption>
</figure>
```

FIGURE F-13: Figure caption in Web page

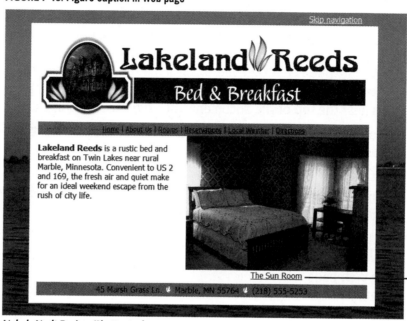

Unholy Vault Designs/Shutterstock.com
Faithe Wempen/sycamoreknoll.com
Photo/Sasha Vodnik

Figure caption is linked to Web page providing more details about the pictured room

FIGURE F-14: Code with title attributes added

logo image for all files

Rooms: sun.jpg, reed.jpg, tree. jpg, and garden.jpg

```
<h1>
   <img src="images/lakeland.gif" width="664" height="180" alt="Lakeland Reeds Bed and Breakfast" title="" />
</h1>
```

```
<h3 id="sun">Sun Room</h3>
<figure>
   <img src="images/sun.jpg" width="369" height="268" alt="a bedroom with large windows and a desk, dresser,
and queen bed" title="" />
</figure>
   <p class="desc">With windows on three sides, the sunlight in this second-floor room supports a large
selection of houseplants.</p>
   <p class="beds">1 queen bed.</p>
   <p class="toplink"><a href="#skipnav">Back to top</a></p>
   <h3 id="reed">Reed Room</h3>
   <figure>
      <img src="images/reed.jpg" width="370" height="277" alt="a bedroom with a tall window, a dresser with
mirror, and a queen bed" title="" />
   </figure>
   <p class="desc">This first-floor room looks out over the reeds on the edge of the lake and the water
beyond.</p>
   <p class="beds">1 queen bed and 1 twin bed.</p>
   <p class="toplink"><a href="#skipnav">Back to top</a></p>
   <h3 id="tree">Treehouse</h3>
   <figure>
      <img src="images/tree.jpg" width="370" height="277" alt="a low-ceilinged bedroom with a woodgrain wall and
a queen bed" title="" />
   </figure>
   <p class="desc">A winding staircase takes you to your own private getaway at the top of the house, with view
of the surrounding trees and meadows and the lake.</p>
   <p class="beds">1 queen bed.</p>
   <p class="toplink"><a href="#skipnav">Back to top</a></p>
   <h3 id="garden">Garden Room</h3>
   <figure>
      <img src="images/garden.jpg" width="370" height="277" alt="a bedroom with ornate wood moldings and a
magnifying lens perched above a fireplace" title="" />
   </figure>
   <p class="desc">This room's French doors open onto our stone patio and flower garden.</p>
   <p class="beds">1 queen bed and 2 twin beds.</p>
   <p class="toplink"><a href="#skipnav">Back to top</a></p>
```

Using Images as Links

UNIT F

HTML5 and CSS3

You can add a link to an image in an HTML document by enclosing the img element in an a element. By default, many visual user agents add a colored border around a linked image to display the color associated with its link state. As with text links, you can use pseudo-classes to modify the colors, or you can use CSS to remove the border altogether. Many Web sites add links to the logo image on each page to return to the main page of the site. You link the logo image on each page back to index.html to provide an extra shortcut for visitors to the site.

STEPS

1. **Return to rooms.html in your text editor**

2. **Position the insertion point before the opening < of the img tag for the lakeland.gif image near the top of the document, then type <a href="index.html">**

3. **Position the insertion point after the closing > of the img tag, type </a>, then save your work**

   Figure F-15 shows the final link code.

4. **Return to lakeland.css in your text editor, then insert a new style rule using the img selector that sets the border value to 0**

   This rule prevents a colored border from being displayed around linked images. Figure F-16 shows the style rule.

5. **Save your work, refresh rooms.html in your browser, then click the logo image at the top of the Web page**

   The main page of the Lakeland Reeds B&B Web site opens.

Inserting and Working with Images

```
<div id="box">
    <h1>
        <a href="index.html"><img src="images/lakeland.gif" width="664" height="180" alt="Lakeland Reeds Bed and
Breakfast" title="" /></a>
    </h1>
    <nav id="mainnav">
```

Opening and closing a tags
surround img element

FIGURE F-16: New style rule based on img selector

```
img {
    border: 0;
}
```

Inserting preformatted code for linked images

Many Web sites, such as social networks, make images containing their logos available for use on personal or organizational Web sites to facilitate linking. Often these sites provide HTML code that you can copy and paste directly into your Web page code. In many cases this code is nothing more than an img element with an href attribute referencing a publicly available graphic hosted on the target site, along with an a element linking to a specific page on the site. Thus, as long as the site's user agreement allows it, you can use any of the styles and techniques that you'd use for other images and links to style this code to fit your site.

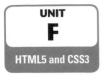
Inserting a Favicon

Many user agents allow Web page authors to specify the icon associated with a Web page in the address bar and on the bookmark or favorites menu and bar. This custom icon, known as a **favicon**, is a graphic file 16 pixels in width by 16 pixels in height, saved in the .ico format, and named favicon.ico. You can specify a favicon for all the pages on a Web site by placing the favicon.ico in the root folder for the Web site. You can also specify a different favicon on an individual page using the link element to reference the appropriate .ico file. Because user agents don't always recognize the file in the root folder, it's best to add link elements as well to ensure that your favicon is accessible to users of as many user agents as possible. The art department has created a favicon, which you add to the Lakeland Reeds B&B Web site.

STEPS

1. **In your file manager, navigate to the** Unit F/Unit folder **on the drive and folder where you store your Data Files**

2. **Make a copy of the file** HTM F-4.ico, **then rename the copy** favicon.ico

3. **Return to** index.html **in your text editor, then insert a blank line beneath the link element for the second external style sheet**

4. **Indent four spaces, type** <link rel="shortcut icon" href="favicon.ico" />, **then save your work**

   Figure F-17 shows the code for the link element inserted in the document.

5. **Reload** index.html **in your Web browser, then examine the address bar and the browser title bar or tab for the Lakeland Reeds favicon, which resembles the icon you inserted in the contact information at the bottom of the page**

   Figure F-18 shows the favicon in a browser. However, some browsers show favicons only for Web sites accessed over the Internet and don't look for the icons for local files.

6. **Repeat Steps 3 and 4 for** rooms.html

7. **Return to** lakeland.css **in your text editor, save your work, save a copy as** llprint.css, **remove all name–value pairs that specify color as well as the pair that specifies the background image, change all the colors in style rules based on pseudo-classes to black, then save your work**

8. **Validate the code for your Web pages and your style sheet, then make changes as necessary to fix any errors**

9. **If you have space on a Web server for publishing your documents, create a local root folder within the Unit folder, move all the files in the Unit folder to the local root folder, then upload the files to your Web publishing location**

10. **Open** index.html **in your browser from the published location to verify that the upload was successful, check the address bar and the browser title bar or tab for the Lakeland Reeds favicon, then navigate to the** rooms.html **to verify the upload and the favicon**

FIGURE F-17: Code for favicon added to Web page

```
index.html - Notepad
File  Edit  Format  View  Help
<!DOCTYPE html>
<html>
  <head>
    <meta charset="utf-8" />
    <title>Lakeland Reeds Bed &amp; Breakfast</title>
    <link rel="stylesheet" type="text/css" media="screen" href="lakeland.css" />
    <link rel="stylesheet" type="text/css" media="print" href="llprint.css" />
    <link rel="shortcut icon" href="favicon.ico" />
    <!--[if lt IE 9]>
      <script src="scripts/semantic.js"></script>
    <![endif]-->
  </head>
```

link element associates favicon with Web page in browsers that don't support the other method

FIGURE F-18:

Customized favicon for the Lakeland Reeds B&B Web site

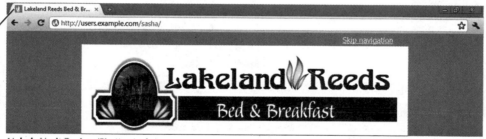

Unholy Vault Designs/Shutterstock.com
Photo/Sasha Vodnik

Labeling text appropriately

Optimizing your use of the figcaption element and the alt and title attributes of the image tag requires examining the purpose of any image-related text you want to add to your Web pages. As a general rule, alt text should describe an image without adding additional information, as this text is intended to be able to substitute for the image. A caption can add information not provided by surrounding page content. The title attribute is generally used to provide explanation or additional information if a user seeks it out. While increasing the resources available to your site's users is often helpful, remember that in some instances, excluding one or more of these types of associated text can actually increase your sites usability or accessibility.

Practice

For current SAM information, including versions and content details, visit SAM Central (http://www.cengage.com/samcentral). If you have a SAM user profile, you may have access to hands-on instruction, practice, and assessment of the skills covered in this unit. Since various versions of SAM are supported throughout the life of this text, check with your instructor for the correct instructions and URL/Web site for accessing assignments.

Concepts Review

Refer to Figure F-19.

FIGURE F-19

Unholy Vault Designs/Shutterstock.com
Faithe Wempen/sycamoreknoll.com
Photo/Sasha Vodnik

1. Which item is styled by providing a url value for the background property?
2. Which item is created using the figcaption element?
3. Which item is styled using the float property?
4. Which item is styled using the clear property?
5. Which item is an inline image?
6. Which item is created using the link element?

Match each term with the statement that best describes it.

7. **native**
8. **baseline**
9. **resolution**
10. **pixel**
11. **alpha channel**

a. specifies how close the dots in a bitmap should appear on the output
b. one of the dots that make up a bitmap image
c. another term for the original dimensions of a bitmap image
d. allows graphics creators to specify the level of opacity for areas of a graphic
e. the bottom of a line of text

Select the best answer from the list of choices.

12. Which type of image is represented as a grid of dots and their colors?

    a. SVG   **c.** vector

    b. bitmap   **d.** native

13. Which type of image encodes the appearance of a graphic as geometric shapes?

    a. bitmap   **c.** vector

    b. GIF   **d.** JPEG

14. Which image type is best for photographs?

    a. GIF   **c.** PNG

    b. JPEG   **d.** SVG

15. Which is the most widely supported format for images with limited colors and defined borders between areas?

    a. GIF   **c.** PNG

    b. JPEG   **d.** SVG

16. Which attribute do you use to specify text to display in case an image is unavailable or to be read in user agents by programs such as screen readers?

    a. figcaption   **c.** title

    b. href   **d.** alt

17. Which property enables text or other Web page elements to flow around an element?

    a. float   **c.** alt

    b. clear   **d.** title

18. Which property prevents floated elements from being displayed to the left, right, or on both sides of an element?

    a. float   **c.** alt

    b. clear   **d.** title

Skills Review

1. Insert images.

    a. In your text editor, open HTM F-5.html from the Unit F/Review folder on the drive and folder where you store your Data Files. Insert a blank line before the closing body tag, then insert a paragraph element containing your first and last name and the text **HTML5 Unit F, Skills Review**. Save the file as **index.html**, then repeat to save HTM F-6.html as **history.html** and HTM F-7.html as **location.html**. In HTM F-8.css add a comment containing your first and last name and the text **HTML5 Unit F, Skills Review**, then save the file as **bigj.css**.

    b. In index.html, insert opening and closing div tags with the id **logo** just before the h1 element at the same indent level on separate lines, then on a blank line between the div tags, indent two additional spaces and add an img element that references the file **images/bigjs.gif**. Specify a height and a width of **225**, then add **Big J's Deep Dish Pizza** as alt text.

    c. Save your work, then open index.html in your default browser.

    d. Repeat Step b to add the logo element and graphic to the corresponding location in history.html and location.html, then preview your changes.

Skills Review (continued)

2. Align images.

   a. Return to bigj.css in your text editor.

   b. Create a new style rule based on the logo id selector, then add the name–value pair **float: right;**.

   c. Save your work, then reload index.html in your browser.

   d. Return to history.html in your text editor, locate the p element that begins "Jan has added two locations"… then insert the following code above it:

```
<figure>
   <img src="images/slices.jpg" width="350" height="228" alt="A red banner reading Pizza next to a
neon sign with the words Fresh Hot Slices" />
</figure>
```

   e. Return to bigj.css in your text editor.

   f. Create a new style rule based on the figure selector, then set the display value to **block**, the float value to **left**, the padding to **0 0.5em 0.25em 0.5em**, the margin to **0**, and text-align to **center**.

   g. Create a new style rule for img elements within figure elements, then set the margin and padding to **0**.

   h. Save your work, reload history.html in your browser, then scroll down to verify that the figure you inserted is left-aligned with text flowing along the right side.

3. Control page flow.

   a. Return to bigj.css in your text editor.

   b. Locate the #awards style rule, then add the clear property with a value that prevents a floated element from being displayed to the right.

   c. Save your work, then reload index.html in your browser.

4. Insert a background image.

   a. In your browser, open the file brick.jpg from the Unit F/Review/images folder.

   b. Return to bigj.css in your text editor.

   c. In the body style rule, insert a name–value pair that sets **brick.jpg** as the background image for the site.

   d. Insert a blank line above the code you just entered, then add a name–value pair to set the background color to **white**.

   e. Using the #skiplink selector, add a new rule style rule that sets the background to **white** and adds **0.25em** of padding to all sides.

   f. Save your work, then reload index.html in your browser.

5. Associate images with related text.

   a. Return to history.html in your text editor, then beneath the img tag for the file slices.jpg, type **<figcaption> Big J's famous neon sign</figcaption>**.

   b. Save your work, then return to bigj.css in your text editor.

   c. Using the figcaption selector, create a new style rule that sets the margin and the padding to **0**, font-weight to **bold**, and display to **block**.

   d. Save your work, then refresh history.html in your Web browser.

   e. Return to index.html in your text editor, add the title attribute to the img tag for bigjs.gif with a null value (""), then save your work.

   f. Repeat Step e for the logo images in history.html and location.html, and for the slices.jpg image in history.html, then save your work.

   g. Reload index.html in your Web browser, verify that no tooltip appears when you move your mouse pointer over the logo image, then repeat to test the images in history.html and location.html.

Skills Review (continued)

6. Use images as links.

   a. Return to history.html in your text editor.

   b. Add a link to the bigjs.gif img element that opens index.html, then save your work.

   c. In bigj.css, add a style rule based on the img selector that sets the border property to 0.

   d. Refresh history.html in your browser, then click the logo image at the top of the Web page to test the link.

   e. Repeat Steps b and c to add a link to the img element for the logo graphic in location.html.

7. Insert a favicon.

   a. In your file manager, navigate to the Unit F/Review folder on the drive and folder where you store your Data Files, then rename the file HTM F-9.ico as **favicon.ico**.

FIGURE F-20

   b. Return to index.html in your text editor, then below the existing link elements add a new link element that links to favicon.ico as a shortcut icon.

   c. Reload index.html in your Web browser, then examine the address bar and the browser title bar or tab for the Big J's favicon, which resembles the red J in the logo graphic, as shown in Figure F-20. (You may not see the icon unless you view your Web site through an Internet connection.)

   d. Repeat Steps b and c for history.html and location.html. Figure F-21 shows history.html.

Xtremer/Shutterstock.com

FIGURE F-21

   e. Return to bigj.css in your text editor, save your work, save a copy as **bjprint.css**, remove all name–value pairs that specify color as well as the pair that specifies the background image, change all the colors in style rules based on pseudo-classes to black, then save your work.

   f. Validate the code for all your Web pages and your style sheet, then make changes as necessary to fix any errors.

   g. If you have space on a Web server for publishing your documents, create a local root folder within the Review folder, move all the files and folders in the Review folder to the local root folder, then upload the files and folders to your Web publishing location.

   h. Open index.html in your browser from the published location to verify that the upload was successful, check the address bar and the browser title bar or tab for the Big J's favicon, then navigate to the remaining pages to verify the uploads and the favicon.

Independent Challenge 1

Sarah Nguyen, the owner of the Spotted Wren Garden Center, has provided you with a version of the company logo for the Web site, as well as related photos and a favicon. You add these images to the company's Web site.

Xtremer/Shutterstock.com
Photo/Sasha Vodnik

   a. Open HTM F-10.html from the Unit F/IC1 folder in your text editor. Insert a blank line before the closing body tag, then insert a paragraph element containing your first and last name and the text **HTML5 Unit F, Independent Challenge 1**. Save the file as **index.html**, then repeat to save HTM F-11.html as **hours.html** and HTM F-12.html as **resource.html**. Open HTM F-13.css, below the existing comment at the top of the document, add another comment with your first and last name and the text **HTML5 Unit F, Independent Challenge 1**. Save the file as **spotwren.css**.

Independent Challenge 1 (continued)

b. In index.html, replace the contents of the h1 element with an img element referencing the file **images/spotwren.gif**. Specify a width of **864** and a height of **184**, and add **Spotted Wren Garden Center** as the alt text. Repeat for hours.html and resource.html, then save your work.

c. In spotwren.css, create a rule based on the "h1 img" selector that specifies the value **block** for the display property. Save your work, then preview all three Web pages in your browser.

d. In index.html, below the closing tag for the nav element, add a figure element. Add an id attribute with the value **main**, then delete the identical attribute–value pair from the p element below. Within the figure element, add an image element that references the file **images/quince.jpg**. Specify a width of **350** and a height of **233**, and enter a **small red flower** as alt text. Save your work, then refresh the page in your browser.

e. Return to spotwren.css, then add a style rule based on the figure selector that specifies a display value of block, and a margin and a padding of **0**. Add a second style rule based on the figure img selector that sets margin and padding to **0** and specifies a float value of right. Add a property to the footer style rule that prevents the element from being displayed with a floated element to its right.

f. Return to hours.html, then repeat Step d to add an img element that references **images/cone.jpg** and specifies a width of **232**, a height of **350**, and **a monarch butterfly perched on a purple coneflower** as alt text. Repeat for resource.html to reference **images/flowers.jpg**, specifying a width of **150**, a height of **225**, and **a cluster of purple coneflowers** as alt text.

g. Return to spotwren.css in your text editor, then add a background property to the body style rule that sets the image file located at **images/grass.jpg** as the background. Insert a name–value pair before the one you just inserted that sets the background color to **green** in case the background image is unavailable. Add a property to the #box style rule to set the background color of the element to **white**. Save your work, then refresh each Web page in your browser.

h. Return to spotwren.css in your text editor, then add the same name–value pairs you added to the body style rule in Step g to the #skipnav style rule. Add a name–value pair to the #skiplink style rule that sets the background to **white**. Save your work, then reload index.html in your browser to verify that the skip link is easily readable.

i. Add the title attribute with an empty value to the img elements on all three Web pages, then save your work.

j. In your file manager, navigate to the Unit F/IC1 folder, make a copy of the file HTM F-14.ico, then rename the copy **favicon.ico**. Return to index.html in your text editor, then add a link element that references favicon.ico as a favicon. Repeat for hours.html and resource.html. Save your work, then preview the files in your Web browser. Figure F-22 shows the main Web page.

k. Return to spotwren.css in your text editor, remove all name–value pairs that reference colors, change all colors in rules based on pseudo-classes to **black**, then save a copy of the file as **swprint.css**.

l. Validate all your HTML and CSS documents.

m. If you have space on a Web server for publishing your documents, create a local root folder within the IC1 folder, move all the files and folders in the IC1 folder to the local root folder, upload the files to your Web publishing location, then open all three Web pages in your browser from the published location.

n. Close your browser, then close your text editor.

FIGURE F-22

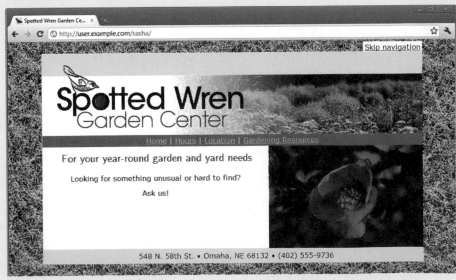

Weldon Schloneger/Shutterstock.com
Maxim Tupikov/Shutterstock.com
Xtremer/Shutterstock.com

Inserting and Working with Images

Independent Challenge 2

You incorporate the logo for the Murfreesboro Recreational Soccer League into the organizational Web site that you are creating. You also add images from some of the groups events.

a. Open HTM F-15.html from the Unit F/IC2 folder in your text editor. Insert a blank line before the closing body tag, then insert a paragraph element containing your first and last name and the text **HTML5 Unit F, Independent Challenge 2**. Save the file as **index.html**, then repeat to save HTM F-16.html as **started.html** and HTM F-17.html as **schedule.html**. Open HTM F-18.css, below the existing comment at the top of the document, add another comment your first and last name and the text **HTML5 Unit F, Independent Challenge 2**. Save the file as **mrsl.css**.

Advanced Challenge Exercise

- In your file manager, navigate to the Unit F/IC2/images folder. Click jump.jpg, then in a blank document in your text editor or on a sheet of paper, note the height and width displayed. If necessary, in Windows right-click the file and click Properties, or on a Mac, control-click the file and click Get Info to view the dimensions.
- Close the properties or info window if necessary, then double-click jump.jpg to open it in your default image viewer. Study the image, then write a description of less than 15 words in your text document or on your sheet of paper. Close the image.
- Repeat the previous two bullets for kick.jpg and mrsl.gif, being sure to include any text in an image in your description.

b. In index.html, beneath the nav element insert a div element with the id **logo** containing an img element that references the file **mrsl.gif** in the images folder. Specify height, width, and alt values based on the information you recorded above, or use the following values: height: **376**; width: **198**; and alt: **Murfreesboro Recreational Soccer League**.

c. In mrsl.css, create a rule based on the **#logo** img selector that specifies the value **block** for the **display** property and floats the image on the left side of the parent element. Save your work, then preview the Web page in your browser.

d. In started.html, beneath the h2 element insert a figure element containing an img element that references the file **kick.jpg** in the images folder. Specify height, width, and alt values based on the information you recorded above, or use the following values: height: **350**; width: **233**; and alt: **a soccer player about to kick a ball**. Repeat for schedule.html, placing the figure element above the element with id pagenav and referencing the file **jump.jpg.**, using the values you determined or the following: height: **350**; width: **526**; and alt: **two soccer players vying for control of a ball**.

e. Return to mrsl.css, then add a style rule based on the **figure** selector that sets display to **block**, floats the element on the right, and specifies margin of **0** and padding of **1em 0 0.25em 0.5em**. Create a second style rule based on the **footer** selector that prevents the element from being displayed with a floated element to its left. Save your work, then preview all three Web pages.

f. Return to mrsl.css in your text editor, then add a background property to the body style rule that sets the image file located at **images/grass.jpg** as the background. Insert a name–value pair before the one you just inserted that sets the background color to **green** in case the background image is unavailable. Add a property to the #box style rule to set the background color of the element to **white**. Save your work, then refresh each Web page in your browser.

g. Return to mrsl.css in your text editor, then add the same name–value pairs you added to the body style rule in Step f to the #skipnav style rule. Add a name–value pair to the #skiplink style rule that sets the background to **black**. At the bottom of the style sheet, create style rules for the #skipnav element based on the four link pseudo-classes, setting the link color to **white** in each state. Save your work, then reload index.html in your browser to verify that the skip link is easily readable.

h. Add the title attribute with an empty value to the img elements on all three Web pages, then save your work.

Independent Challenge 2 (continued)

i. In your file manager, navigate to the Unit F/IC2 folder, make a copy of the file HTM F-19.ico, then rename the copy **favicon.ico**. Return to index.html in your text editor, then add a link element that references favicon.ico as a favicon. Repeat for started.html and schedule.html. Save your work, then preview the files in your Web browser. Figure F-23 shows the main Web page, and Figure F-24 shows the Getting Started page.

j. Return to mrsl.css in your text editor, remove all name–value pairs that reference colors, change all colors in rules based on pseudo-classes to **black**, then save a copy of the file as **mrsprint.css**.

k. Validate all your HTML and CSS documents.

l. If you have space on a Web server for publishing your documents, create a local root folder within the IC2 folder, move all the files and folders in the IC2 folder to the local root folder, upload the files to your Web publishing location, then open all three Web pages in your browser from the published location.

m. Close your browser, then close your text editor.

FIGURE F-23

Xtremer/Shutterstock.com

FIGURE F-24

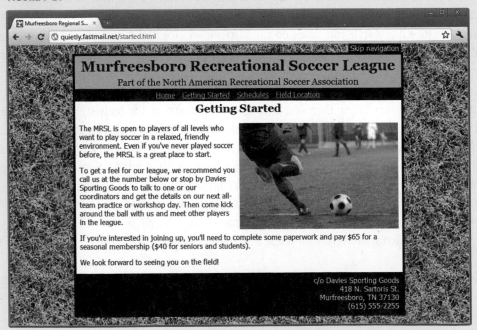

Lario Tus/Shutterstock.com
Xtremer/Shutterstock.com

Independent Challenge 3

Diego Merckx, the manager of Hotel Natoma, has provided you with a Web-ready version of the facility's logo as well as photos of a few local attractions. You incorporate these into the hotel's Web site.

a. Open HTM F-20.html from the Unit F/IC3 folder in your text editor. Insert a blank line before the closing body tag, then insert a paragraph element containing your first and last name and the text **HTML5 Unit F, Independent Challenge 3**. Save the file as **index.html**, then repeat to save HTM F-21.html as **nearby.html**. Open HTM F-22.css, below the existing comment at the top of the document, add another comment with your first and last name and the text **HTML5 Unit F, Independent Challenge 3**. Save the file as **natoma.css**.

b. In index.html, replace the contents of the h1 element with an img element that references **images/natoma.gif**. Specify a width of **368**, a height of **65**, and alt text of **Hotel Natoma**. Repeat for nearby.html. Add a style rule to the style sheet to style img elements within h1 elements, setting the display to **block**, the padding to **0**, and the margin to **0 auto**.

c. In index.html, above the p element containing contact information, add a figure element containing an img element referencing **images/bridge.jpg**. Specify a width of **350**, a height of **232**, and the **Golden Gate Bridge** as alt text. Add a property to make the figure part of the center class, then add a style rule for the center class to the style sheet, setting the padding to **0** and the margin to **0 auto**. Create a second rule to style any img element within an element in the center class, setting the padding to **0 0 2em 0** and the margin to **0**. Create a third rule for figure elements to set the display property to **block**.

Advanced Challenge Exercise

- In nearby.html, add a figure element containing an img element that references **images/asian_sm.jpg**, specifying a width of **150**, height of **89**, and **front facade of the Asian Art Museum** as alt text. Add a figcaption element before the closing figure tag containing the text **Asian Art Museum**. Repeat to create a second figure element referencing **images/cable_sm.jpg**, with the same dimensions, a cable car as alt text, and **Cable Cars** as the content of the figcaption element.

- Specify a class of **right** for both figure elements added in the previous step, then add a rule to the style sheet using the **right** class selector, setting the margin to **0 1em 0 0**, padding to **0**, float to **right**, and **clear** to right. Create another rule that applies to images within an element in the right class, setting the display to **block** and padding and margin to **0**. Create another rule based on the figcaption element that centers text and sets the margin and padding to **0**.

- Add a link to the asian_sm.jpg image with a target of **images/asian_lg.jpg**. Add the same link to the text within the figcaption element for this image. Repeat for the cable_sm.jpg image, linking the image and the figcaption text to **images/cable_lg.jpg**. (*Note*: the link to the text should go within the figcaption element, not outside of it.)

- Add a title attribute to each image with a value of **Click to enlarge**.

- Save your work, open nearby.html in your browser, move the pointer over one of the images you inserted to verify that the text **Click to enlarge** appears, then click the first image to verify a larger version of the image opens in the browser. Return to the nearby.html page, then repeat to test the link on the caption and both links for the second image.

d. Add the title attribute with an empty value to the logo img elements on both Web pages and to the bridge image on the main page, then save your work.

Independent Challenge 3 (continued)

e. In your file manager, navigate to the Unit F/IC3 folder, make a copy of the file HTM F-23.ico, then rename the copy **favicon.ico**. Return to index.html in your text editor, then add a link element that references favicon.ico as a favicon. Repeat for nearby.html. Save your work, then preview the files in your Web browser. Figure F-25 shows the main Web page, and Figure F-26 shows the What's Nearby page.

f. Return to natoma.css in your text editor, remove all name–value pairs that reference colors, change all colors in rules based on pseudo-classes to **black**, then save a copy of the file as **hnprint.css**.

g. Validate all your HTML and CSS documents.

h. If you have space on a Web server for publishing your documents, create a local root folder within the IC3 folder, move all the files and folders in the IC3 folder to the local root folder, upload the files to your Web publishing location, then open both Web pages in your browser from the published location.

i. Close your browser, then close your text editor.

FIGURE F-25

somchaij/Shutterstock.com

FIGURE F-26

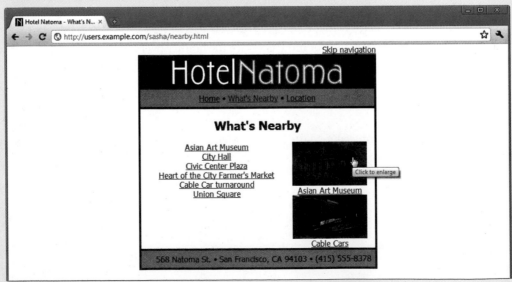

Photos/Sasha Vodnik

Real Life Independent Challenge

This assignment builds on the personal Web site you have worked on in previous units. You identify and add images to your Web site.

a. Copy your Web site files to the Unit F/RLIC folder on the drive and folder where you store your Data Files.

b. Review your storyboard and any other design documents to identify locations and sources for images on your Web pages. If your original designs did not include images, create a revised sketch that incorporates one or more images, including logos, photos, and/or background images.

c. Identify sources for your images—which may include a designer who works with your organization, your own photo collection, and/or friends with design skills—and collect them. Verify that you have permission to use the images you collect for your Web site.

d. Incorporate the images you collected into your Web site. Be sure to specify height, width, and alt attributes for each img element. Use the figure element where appropriate and add captions with the figcaption element. Specify values for padding and margin to create the desired amount of space between adjacent elements. Use the float and clear elements at least once each.

e. Save changes to your style sheet document, save a copy using the name of your print style sheet, then take out name–value pairs that set color and change all colors in rules based on pseudo-classes to **black**.

f. Preview your Web pages in at least two browsers and make any edits necessary for them to appear as you expected.

g. Validate all of your HTML and CSS documents and make any edits necessary to address any issues.

h. If you have space on a Web server for publishing your documents, create a local root folder within the RLIC folder, move all the files in the RLIC folder to the local root folder, upload the files to your Web publishing location, then open each Web page in your browser from the published location to verify that the upload was successful.

i. Close your browser, then close your text editor.

Visual Workshop

In your text editor, open the file HTM F-24.html from the Unit F/VW directory on the drive and folder where you store your Data Files, add a paragraph before the closing body tag that contains your first and last name and the text **HTML5 Unit F, Visual Workshop**, then save the file as **index.html**. Open HTM F-25.css, add a comment containing the same information, then save it as **revision.css**. Use your text editor along with the files in the images folder to style the Web page to match the one shown in Figure F-27. The logo graphic is revision.gif, and the background image is books.jpg. Save a copy of HTM F-26.ico as **favicon.ico** and specify this image as the favicon for the page. Save a copy of your style sheet with the name **revprint.css**, then make any necessary changes for print formatting. When you are finished, validate your HTML and CSS code. If you have space on a Web server, create a local root folder within the VW folder, move both files to the local root folder, upload the file to your Web publishing location, then open the Web page in your browser from the published location. Close your browser and text editor.

FIGURE F-27

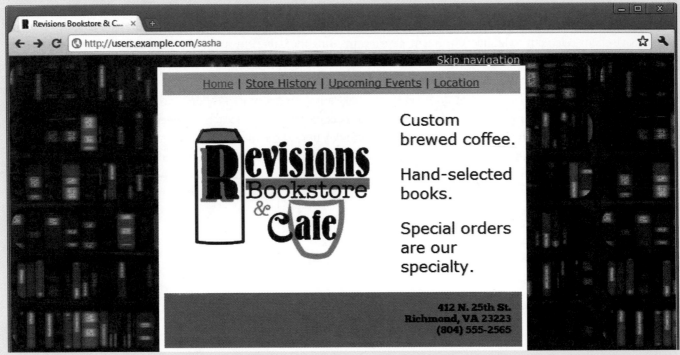

Kentoh/Shutterstock.com

Inserting and Working with Images

Organizing Content with Lists and Tables

Files You Will Need:

To view a list of files needed for this unit, see the Data Files Grid in the back of the book.

While standard paragraphs are appropriate for many types of Web page content, some information is easier to present and understand in more specific formats. HTML includes elements that enable you to present information as lists or tables. In addition to changing the display of information in a browser, these elements convey semantic data about their contents, facilitating access by many types of user agents. As you continue your work on the Web site for the Lakeland Reeds Bed & Breakfast, you add lists and tabular content. You also use list elements to add semantic value to existing Web site content.

OBJECTIVES

Create an ordered list

Create an unordered list

Create a description list

Create a navigation bar using a list

Insert a table

Span columns and rows

Format a table with CSS

Apply a table-like structure to other elements

Creating an Ordered List

You use the HTML ol element to create a list in which items are numbered or lettered sequentially. This type of list is known as an **ordered list**, because the order in which the items are listed is important. You create each item in an ordered list with the li element. All the li elements for a list are nested within the opening and closing ol tags. The default marker for each list item is determined by the user agent rendering the Web page but is most often an Arabic numeral (1, 2, 3, . . .). You can use the values of the CSS list-style-type property shown in Table G-1 to change the markers to letters or to a different numbering style. Philip Blaine, the owner of Lakeland Reeds B&B, has provided additional information that he'd like you to incorporate into the Reservations Web page. You start by adding a list of the most popular weekends at the B&B.

STEPS

1. **In your text editor, open HTM G-1.html from the Unit G/Unit folder on the drive and folder where you store your Data Files, insert a blank line before the closing body tag, insert a paragraph element containing your first and last name and the text HTML5 Unit G, save it as index.html, repeat to save HTM G-2.html as aboutus.html, HTM G-3.html as rooms.html, and HTM G-4.html as reserve.html, then use a CSS comment to add the same information to HTM G-5.css and save it as lakeland.css**

QUICK TIP
Each h3 heading is grouped with its related elements using the semantic section element, which helps user agents identify units of content that share a common theme.

2. **In reserve.html, insert a blank line beneath the paragraph Our most sought-after weekends, indent to the same level as the paragraph, type <ol>, add another blank line, indent to the same level, then type </ol>**
   All items in an ordered list are contained between the opening and closing tags for the ol element.

3. **Insert a blank line beneath <ol>, indent two additional spaces, then type <li>Independence Day</li>**
   The content of each list item is contained between the opening and closing tags for the li element.

4. **Insert a blank line beneath the code you just entered, indent to the same level, then type <li>Memorial Day</li>**

5. **Insert a blank line beneath the code you just entered, indent to the same level, then type <li>Labor Day</li>**
   Figure G-1 shows the completed code for the ordered list.

6. **Save your work, then open reserve.html in your browser**
   As Figure G-2 shows, the list is displayed using the default style, with each list item numbered sequentially starting at the number 1.

TABLE G-1: Widely supported values for the CSS list-style-type property for the ol element

value	result
decimal	1. first item 2. second item
lower-roman	i. first item ii. second item
upper-roman	I. first item II. second item
lower-alpha	a. first item b. second item
upper-alpha	A. first item B. second item
none	first item second item

FIGURE G-1: HTML code for ordered list

ol element
contains
list items

li elements mark
list item content

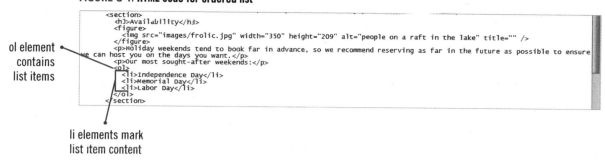

```
<section>
    <h3>Availability</h3>
    <figure>
        <img src="images/frolic.jpg" width="350" height="209" alt="people on a raft in the lake" title="" />
    </figure>
    <p>Holiday weekends tend to book far in advance, so we recommend reserving as far in the future as possible to ensure
we can host you on the days you want.</p>
    <p>Our most sought-after weekends:</p>
    <ol>
        <li>Independence Day</li>
        <li>Memorial Day</li>
        <li>Labor Day</li>
    </ol>
</section>
```

FIGURE G-2: Ordered list in Reservations Web page

Sequential
numbers
displayed
before
list items

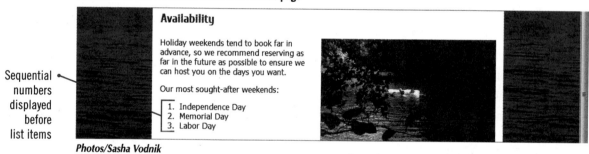

Photos/Sasha Vodnik

Specifying additional values for list-style-type

In addition to the widely supported values for list-style-type listed in Table G-1, browser support is growing for list enumerators in other numbering and lettering systems. With the exception of Internet Explorer 6, all commonly used browsers support the values "armenian", "georgian", and "lower-greek". Support for many other languages is increasing among user agents as well. To find the latest status on other languages, search on "list-style-type languages" in a search engine.

Creating an Unordered List

HTML also enables you to create a list in which the order of list items doesn't matter. You create this type of list, known as an **unordered list**, using the ul element. You mark list item content with the same li element that you use for an ordered list. List items are displayed with a bullet at the start of each line. The default bullet character is a solid circle, but you can use the CSS list-style-type property with the values shown in Table G-2 to specify a different bullet shape. ▓▓▓▓ Philip created a list of special events for which visitors might want to reserve the entire bed-and-breakfast facility. You add the list to the Reservations Web page as an unordered list.

STEPS

1. **In reserve.html, insert a blank line beneath the paragraph that begins** Lakeland Reeds is also available, **indent to the same level as the paragraph, type** <ul>, **add another blank line, indent to the same level, then type** </ul>

   All items in an ordered list are contained between the opening and closing tags for the ul element.

2. **Insert a blank line beneath** <ul>, **indent two additional spaces, then type** <li>Weddings</li>

   While the containing element is specific to the type of list you're creating, you use the li element for list items when creating either ordered or unordered lists.

3. **Insert a blank line beneath the code you just entered, indent to the same level, then type** <li>Birthdays</li>

4. **Insert a blank line beneath the code you just entered, indent to the same level, then type** <li>Family Reunions</li>

   Figure G-3 shows the completed code for the ordered list.

5. **Save your work, then reload** reserve.html **in your browser**

   As Figure G-4 shows, the unordered list is displayed using the default style with a solid circular bullet next to each list item.

6. **Return to** lakeland.css **in your text editor, create a style rule using the** ul **type selector, then add the name–value pair** list-style-type: square;

7. **Save your work, then reload** reserve.html **in your browser**

   As Figure G-5 shows, the bullet characters are now displayed as solid squares.

TABLE G-2: Values for the CSS list-style-type property for the ul element

property	description	example
circle	unfilled circle	O list item
disc	filled circle (default)	● list item
square	filled square	■ list item
none	no character	list item

Specifying custom bullets

In addition to choosing from the standard selection of bullet characters using the list-style-type property, you can instead choose to specify an image to display as the bullet character using the list-style-image property. The syntax is the same as that for specifying a background image: the text *url* followed by the path and filename of the image file, enclosed in quotes and parentheses. For instance, the code

```
ul {
    list-style-image:url("images/browntri.gif");
}
```

specifies the file browntri.gif, located in the images folder, as the bullet character for unordered lists.

FIGURE G-3: Code for unordered list

ul element contains list items

```
<section>
  <h3>Rates</h3>
</section>
<section>
  <h3>Special Events</h3>
  <p>Lakeland Reeds is also available for booking group special events, including</p>
  <ul>
    <li>Weddings</li>
    <li>Birthdays</li>
    <li>Family Reunions</li>
  </ul>
  <p><a href="weddings.pdf">Guidelines and reservation form for a special event at Lakeland Reeds.</a> (PDF)</p>
</section>
```

li elements mark list item content

FIGURE G-4: Unordered list in Web page

Default bullet character displayed before each list item

Special Events

Lakeland Reeds is also available for booking group special events, including

- Weddings
- Birthdays
- Family Reunions

Guidelines and reservation form for a special event at Lakeland Reeds. (PDF)

Photo/Sasha Vodnik

FIGURE G-5: Unordered list with customized bullets

Bullet character changed to square

Special Events

Lakeland Reeds is also available for booking group special events, including

- Weddings
- Birthdays
- Family Reunions

Guidelines and reservation form for a special event at Lakeland Reeds. (PDF)

Photo/Sasha Vodnik

Creating a Description List

In addition to ol and ul, HTML includes an element that marks content as a third type of list. The dl element creates a **description list**, which enables you to specify a name–value pair for each list item. A description list was known in previous versions of HTML as a **definition list**, because it was originally intended for listing terms and their definitions. However, in HTML5, dl is recommended as a semantic marker for any content that includes items and descriptions. Unlike ol and ul, dl does not use the li element to specify list items. Instead, each list item is composed of two elements: dt marks the term or item being described, and dd indicates the description. ▄▄▄▄ The contact information for Philip Blaine on the Reservations page is a set of name–value pairs. You change the markup for this section to a definition list to add semantic information to the data and to increase your options for visual presentation.

STEPS

QUICK TIP

Adding a class enables you to style this list and others like it in your Web site without specifying default formatting for every description list on your site.

1. **Return to reserve.html in your text editor, locate the \<p\> tag immediately before the span element containing the text Philip Blaine, Proprietor, then replace it with \<dl class="contact"\>**

2. **Delete the code \<span id="name"\>, type \<dt\>Proprietor\</dt\>, then press [Enter]**

3. **Indent to match the previous line, type \<dd\>, delete everything after the word Blaine, then at the end of the line type \</dd\>**

4. **On the next line, indent to match the previous line, replace the code \<span class="callout"\> with \<dt\>, replace \</span\> with \</dt\>, then press [Enter]**

5. **Indent to match the previous line, replace the colon and space with \<dd\>, then replace \<br /\> with \</dd\>**

TROUBLE

Because there's no \<br /\> element after the email informa-tion, just insert \</dd\> after the word **com**.

6. **Repeat Steps 4 and 5 to convert the fax and email information to list items**

7. **Beneath the final dd element, replace \</p\> with \</dl\>**
   Figure G-6 shows the completed code.

8. **Save your work, return to lakeland.css in your text editor, locate the style rule that sets the font-family value for a group of type selectors to a font stack starting with CuprumFFURegular, then add dt to the list of type selectors**

9. **Add a style rule that sets the font-weight to bold for each dt element within the contact class**
   Figure G-7 shows the completed style sheet code.

10. **Save your work, then reload reserve.html in your browser**
    As Figure G-8 shows, the list items are displayed in the default layout with the second line indented beneath the first and additional space between each item–description pair.

FIGURE G-6: Code for description list

dl element
marks start
and end of
description
list

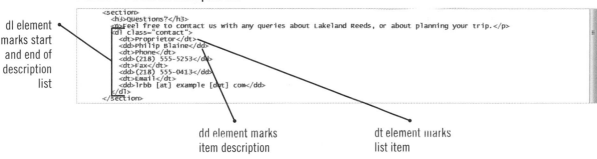

dd element marks
item description

dt element marks
list item

FIGURE G-7: Style sheet containing styles for dt elements

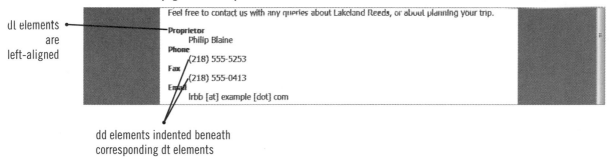

FIGURE G-8: Web page with description list

dl elements
are
left-aligned

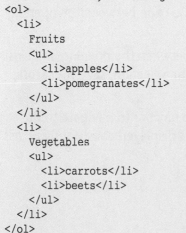

dd elements indented beneath
corresponding dt elements

Creating nested lists

Sometimes nesting a list within another list is the clearest way to present information. It's easy to nest lists in HTML: you simply insert valid code for a list within the content of an li element.

For instance, Figure G-9 shows the appearance in a browser of the nested lists created by the following code:

```
<ol>
  <li>
    Fruits
    <ul>
      <li>apples</li>
      <li>pomegranates</li>
    </ul>
  </li>
  <li>
    Vegetables
    <ul>
      <li>carrots</li>
      <li>beets</li>
    </ul>
  </li>
</ol>
```

FIGURE G-9

1. Fruits
   - apples
   - pomegranates
2. Vegetables
   - carrots
   - beets

Creating a Navigation Bar Using a List

Some common Web page content that at first glance may not appear to be a list may nevertheless benefit from being marked up using list elements. One common example is a navigation bar, which is fundamentally a list of related links. By marking up a navigation bar using the ul and li elements, you add semantic information that helps user agents more accurately render it. In addition, list elements give you greater layout flexibility using fewer HTML tags, making your code easier for yourself and other developers to read. ████ You convert the main navigation bar to an ordered list.

STEPS

1. Return to **reserve.html** in your text editor, locate the opening **<nav>** tag for the main nav bar, then in the line below it, replace the **p** with **ul**, leaving the id attribute–value pair unchanged

2. Position the insertion point just to the left of the opening **<a>** tag for the Home link, type **<li>**, position the insertion point at the end of the line, delete **|** and the **space** before it, then type **</li>**

3. Repeat Step 2 to enclose the remaining links in li elements

4. In the line beneath the **Directions** link, replace **</p>** with **</ul>**

   Your code should match Figure G-10.

5. Save your work, return to **lakeland.css** in your text editor, create a new style rule based on the **#mainnav li** selector, then add the following name–value pairs:

   ```
   display: inline;
   list-style-type: none;
   padding: 0.25em;
   ```

   Setting the value of display to inline keeps all the elements on the same line, rather than displaying them on separate lines, which is the default. Setting list-style-type to none prevents bullet characters from displaying next to each item. The padding value creates space between the links, as well as between the nav bar and the elements above and below it.

6. Save your work, then reload **reserve.html** in your browser

   As Figure G-11 shows, there is very little change in the appearance of the nav bar. However, the nav bar code now semantically indicates that it's a list of related items.

7. Return to **reserve.html** in your text editor, then copy all the code between the opening and closing nav tags to the Clipboard

8. Switch to **index.html** in your text editor, select the code between the opening and closing nav tags, paste the contents of the Clipboard to replace the selection, save your work, then repeat for **aboutus.html** and **rooms.html**

9. Return to **reserve.html** in your Web browser, then use the nav bar to navigate to the other pages in the Web site and ensure the new nav bar is displayed consistently across the pages

FIGURE G-10: Code for nav bar using ul and li elements

An li element contains each link in the nav bar

```
<nav>
    <ul id="mainnav">
        <li><a href="index.html">Home</a></li>
        <li><a href="aboutus.html">About Us</a></li>
        <li><a href="rooms.html">Rooms</a></li>
        <li><a href="reserve.html">Reservations</a></li>
        <li><a href="http://bit.ly/dl8xGc" target="_blank">Local weather</a></li>
        <li><a href="http://bit.ly/co7vcs" target="_blank">Directions</a></li>
    </ul>
</nav>
```

FIGURE G-11: Modified nav bar in browser

Extra space between links replaces pipe characters, but nav bar styling remains unchanged

Unholy Vault Designs/Shutterstock.com
Photo/Sasha Vodnik

Inserting a Table

In addition to a simple list of items or items and descriptions, HTML enables you to present a larger set of information as a table. As Figure G-14 shows, a table organizes data in horizontal **rows** and vertical **columns**. Each item of data in a table is displayed in a **cell**, which is the intersection of a row and a column. To create a table in HTML, you use four main elements: table marks the start and end of the table, th marks the content of a header cell, td marks the content of a data cell, and tr groups cells into rows. You can also add semantic information to a table by using the thead element to mark the header rows of the table, tbody to mark the rows that make up the body, and tfoot to mark footer rows. Table G-3 provides an overview of structuring elements for tables. ▬▬▬ Philip would like the Web site to include a breakdown of rates for rooms at Lakeland Reeds B&B during different times of the year. You add this information to the Reservations page as a table.

STEPS

1. **Return to reserve.html in your text editor, insert a blank line beneath the opening h3 tag for the heading Rates, indent to match the previous line, type <table>, press [Enter], indent to match the previous line, then type </table>**

2. **Insert a blank line beneath the <table> tag, indent two spaces more than the previous line, type <thead>, press [Enter], indent to match the previous line, then type </thead>**

3. **Press [Enter], indent to match the previous line, type <tbody>, press [Enter], indent to match the previous line, then type </tbody>**

   The basic structuring tags you've entered for the table should match Figure G-12.

4. **Insert a blank line beneath the <thead> tag, indent two spaces more than the previous line, type <tr>, press [Enter], indent to match the previous line, type </tr>, then repeat to add two tr elements in the tbody section**

5. **Insert a blank line beneath the first <tr> tag in the thead section, indent two spaces more than the previous line, type <th>Period</th>, press [Enter], then enter the remaining five lines of code shown in Figure G-13**

6. **Insert the two sets of td elements shown in Figure G-13**

   Your code should match Figure G-13.

7. **Insert a blank line beneath the closing table tag, indent to match the previous line, then type <p>* High Season includes Memorial Day weekend through Labor Day weekend</p>**

8. **Save your work, return to lakeland.css in your text editor, then add the following style rule:**

```
td, th {

   border: 1px solid black;

}
```

9. **Save your work, then reload reserve.html in your browser**

   As Figure G-14 shows, the table content you entered is displayed in a grid, with a border around each cell. The content of each th element and td element occupies an individual cell, and the cells are grouped in rows based on the tr elements you entered. The number of cells in each row is sufficient for a browser to calculate the number of columns; therefore, no element is required to specify the number or arrangement of columns.

FIGURE G-12: Basic table structuring tags

```
<table>
  <thead>
  </thead>
  <tbody>
  </tbody>
</table>
```

FIGURE G-13: Code for complete table

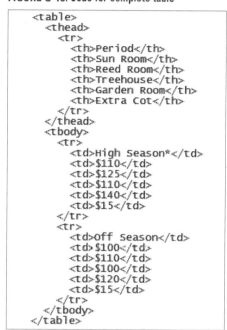

```
<table>
  <thead>
    <tr>
      <th>Period</th>
      <th>Sun Room</th>
      <th>Reed Room</th>
      <th>Treehouse</th>
      <th>Garden Room</th>
      <th>Extra Cot</th>
    </tr>
  </thead>
  <tbody>
    <tr>
      <td>High Season*</td>
      <td>$110</td>
      <td>$125</td>
      <td>$110</td>
      <td>$140</td>
      <td>$15</td>
    </tr>
    <tr>
      <td>Off Season</td>
      <td>$100</td>
      <td>$110</td>
      <td>$100</td>
      <td>$120</td>
      <td>$15</td>
    </tr>
  </tbody>
</table>
```

FIGURE G-14: Table in browser

Table column consists of a vertical series of cells

Header cell content is centered and displayed in bold

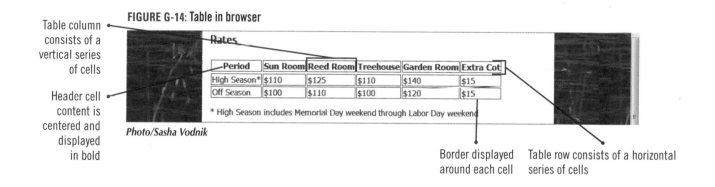

Photo/Sasha Vodnik

Border displayed around each cell

Table row consists of a horizontal series of cells

TABLE G-3: HTML Table Structuring Elements

element	marks
table	start and end of table content
thead	group of one or more rows that contain column headers; when a long table is printed, these are displayed at the top of each page
tbody	group of one or more rows that contain main body of table
tfoot	group of one or more rows that contain column footers; when a long table is printed, these are displayed at the bottom of each page
tr	start and end of a row
th	content of a table header cell; content is centered by default in most browsers
td	content of a standard table cell

Spanning Columns and Rows

When a table contains cells that repeat the same content across a row or down a column, you can improve usability by removing all but one occurrence of the content formatting the cell to be displayed across multiple columns or rows. To merge a cell across multiple columns in an HTML table, you use the colspan attribute in the opening th or td tag for the cell to specify the number of columns in which it should be displayed. Likewise, you use the rowspan attribute to specify the number of rows for cell content to span. You add colspan and rowspan attributes to make the Rates table easier to read.

STEPS

1. **Return to reserve.html in your text editor, insert a new line beneath the <thead> tag, indent two additional spaces, type <tr>, press [Enter], indent to match the previous line, then type </tr>**

2. **Between the opening and closing tr tags you just entered, indent two additional spaces and add the following code:**

   ```
   <th>Period</th>

   <th colspan="4">Room</th>

   <th>Extra Cot</th>
   ```

   Although the new header row includes only three cells, the colspan attribute marks the second cell to be displayed in the second, third, fourth, and fifth columns, meaning that the row occupies the same number of columns as the other rows in the table.

3. **Save your work, then reload reserve.html in your browser**

   As Figure G-15 shows, the text "Room" now appears just once in the table, and the cell that contains it spans four columns. However, the headings "Period" and "Extra Cot" are now duplicated in the two heading rows.

4. **Return to reserve.html in your text editor, in the code for the first table row, click before the closing > in the opening tag for the th element containing the text Period, press [Spacebar], then type rowspan="2"**

5. **In the code for the same row, click before the closing > in the opening tag for the th element containing the text Extra Cot, press [Spacebar], then type rowspan="2"**

6. **Delete the th element in the second heading row containing the text Period, then delete the th element in the second heading row containing the text Extra Cot**

   Even though the second heading row contains code for only four cells, the two cells that use the rowspan attribute in the previous row provide content for the two additional cells.

7. **In the first tr element in the tbody section, click before the closing > in the opening tag for the td element containing the text $15, press [Spacebar], then type rowspan="2"**

8. **In the second tr element in the tbody section, delete the td element containing the text $15**

   Figure G-16 shows the completed code for the table.

9. **Save your work, then refresh reserve.html in your browser**

   As Figure G-17 shows, the cells containing the text "Period", "Extra Cot", and "$15" all span two rows.

FIGURE G-15: Heading cell spanning multiple columns

colspan attribute causes cell contents to be displayed across four columns

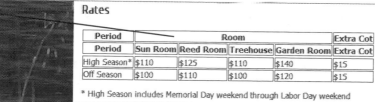

Photo/Sasha Vodnik

FIGURE G-16: Code containing colspan and rowspan attributes

colspan attribute added to display cell content in multiple columns

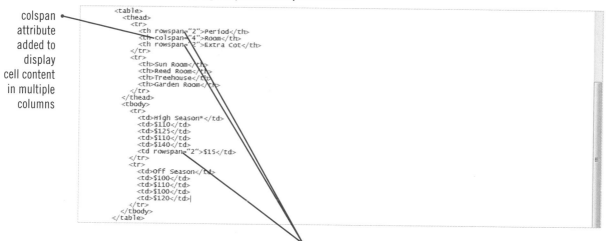

```
<table>
  <thead>
    <tr>
      <th rowspan="2">Period</th>
      <th colspan="4">Room</th>
      <th rowspan="2">Extra Cot</th>
    </tr>
    <tr>
      <th>Sun Room</th>
      <th>Reed Room</th>
      <th>Treehouse</th>
      <th>Garden Room</th>
    </tr>
  </thead>
  <tbody>
    <tr>
      <td>High Season*</td>
      <td>$110</td>
      <td>$125</td>
      <td>$110</td>
      <td>$140</td>
      <td rowspan="2">$15</td>
    </tr>
    <tr>
      <td>Off Season</td>
      <td>$100</td>
      <td>$110</td>
      <td>$100</td>
      <td>$120</td>
    </tr>
  </tbody>
</table>
```

rowspan attributes added to display cell content in multiple rows

FIGURE G-17: Table cells spanning multiple rows

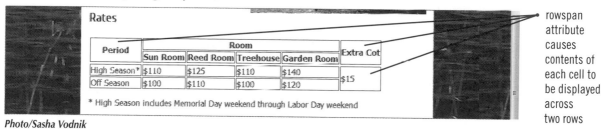

rowspan attribute causes contents of each cell to be displayed across two rows

Photo/Sasha Vodnik

Calculating table columns

In a table that doesn't use colspan or rowspan attributes, you can verify that each row includes content for every column by ensuring that each row contains the same number of th or td elements. When you use colspan and rowspan attributes, you still need to confirm that your content fits the table dimensions. To do so, start by adding the values for all colspan attributes used in the row. Next, add the number of th or td elements in the row without colspan attributes. Finally, add the number of th or td cells in earlier rows whose content is part of the current row due to rowspan values. In short:

current row colspan total + cells in current row without colspan + cells spanning from previous rows = total columns

Running this calculation on any row of your table should produce the same value.

If one or more rows appear to be shorter or longer than the surrounding rows, it can be helpful to preview your Web page in a browser and inspect the table to identify the cell where the contents of one row are no longer related to the contents in adjacent rows. You may simply need to adjust a rowspan or colspan value, or add or remove a cell.

Formatting a Table with CSS

CSS enables you to style many aspects of a Web page table. In addition to controlling font faces and font and background colors, you can style the borders between cells. Table G-4 describes the CSS properties and values that affect table borders. You can style an entire table, a table section (such as thead or tbody) or individual rows or cells. In addition, you can use the HTML colgroup and col elements to assign styles to a single column or to a group of columns. ▰▰▰▰ You style the borders and add background colors to different sections of your table to make it easier for users to read and understand.

STEPS

1. **Return to lakeland.css in your text editor, delete the style rule based on the td, th selector, then add the style rules shown in Figure G-18**

2. **Save your work, then reload reserve.html in your browser**

   As Figure G-19 shows, the border-collapse property merges adjacent borders into a single line. The width property for the table element controls the overall width of the table. Setting only the border-bottom value for th elements creates a single line rather than a grid for column headings.

QUICK TIP

Whenever you add col elements, they must cover all the columns in the table. Even if you don't need to style all the columns, if any col elements are present, your code won't validate unless all columns are included in col elements.

3. **Return to reserve.html in your text editor, insert a blank line beneath the opening table tag, indent two additional spaces, then add the following code:**

```
<colgroup>
    <col class="firstcol" />
    <col class="roomcols" span="4" />
    <col class="cotcol" />
</colgroup>
```

   By default, each col element applies to a single column, starting from the left side of the table. However, you can group consecutive columns into a single col element by specifying the number of columns to include as the value of the span attribute. The col elements you entered divide the six columns of your table into three units to which you can apply styles: the "firstcol" class applies to the first column; the "roomcols" group, with a span value of "4", includes the next four columns; and the "cotcol" class applies to the last column. All col elements must be contained in a colgroup element.

4. **In the tbody section, locate the td element containing the text High Season, add the code class="season" to the opening tag, locate the td element containing the text Off Season, then add the code class="season" to the opening tag**

   You can add a class or id attribute to any cell to style it specifically.

5. **In the opening tag for the p element below the closing table tag, click before the >, press [Spacebar], then type class="tablenote"**

6. **Save your work, return to lakeland.css in your text editor, then add the style rules shown in Figure G-20**

7. **In the th style rule, add the name–value pair background: #B8944D;**

QUICK TIP

The background color you specified for heading cells using the th element is a more specific level of styling than a col or colgroup; thus, the background color for the heading cells takes precedence over the background color for the col and col-group elements.

8. **Near the top of the style sheet, locate the style rule that sets the font-family value for a group of type selectors to a font stack starting with CuprumFFURegular, then add th to the list of type selectors**

   Figure G-20 shows the completed code for the style sheet.

9. **Save your work, then reload reserve.html in your browser**

   As Figure G-21 shows, different background colors are applied to the columns based on the styling of the corresponding col and colgroup elements.

FIGURE G-18: Code to style table elements

```
table {
  width: 90%;
  margin: 0 auto;
  padding: 0;
  border-collapse: collapse;
  }
td {
  border: 1px solid black;
  padding: 0.25em;
  }
th {
  border-bottom: 1px solid black;
  padding: 0.25em;
  }
```

FIGURE G-19: Table with styles applied

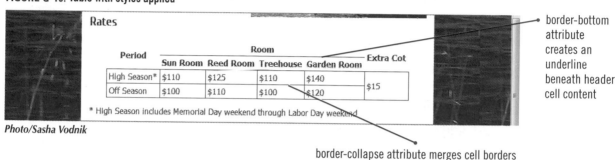

Photo/Sasha Vodnik

border-bottom attribute creates an underline beneath header cell content

border-collapse attribute merges cell borders of adjacent cells into a single line

FIGURE G-20: Completed style rules for table elements

```
dt, h1, h2, h3, nav, footer, th {
  font-family: CuprumFFURegular, georgia, "times new roman", times, serif;
  }
h1, h2, nav, footer {
```

th selector added to style rule for font family

```
th {
  border-bottom: 1px solid black;
  padding: 0.25em;
  background: #B8944D;
  }
h1 {
```

background attribute-value pair added to th style rule

Code to add in Step 6

```
.cotcol {
  background: #9daecd;
  width: 15%;
  }
.desc {
  padding: 0;
  margin: 1em 0 0 2em;
  }
.firstcol {
  background: #f1eace;
  width: 25%;
  }
.rates td {
  text-align: center;
  }
.rates td.season {
  text-align: left;
  }
.roomcols {
  background: #aecdf4;
  width: 15%;
  }
.tablenote {
  width: 90%;
  margin: 0.25em auto;
  }
.toplink {
```

FIGURE G-21: Table with background and font styling applied

Background color styling for th elements takes cascading precedence over styling for column groups

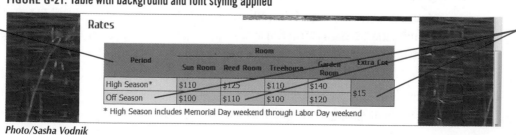

Photo/Sasha Vodnik

Background colors applied using style rules based on column groups

Organizing Content with Lists and Tables

Applying a Table-Like Structure to Other Elements

Sometimes you may be tempted to use HTML table markup to arrange Web page elements that don't otherwise belong in a table so they appear visually in a grid. While table and related elements should be used only to mark data whose relationships are best understood as a table, CSS lets you specify that you want elements treated as components of a table, but without marking them semantically as tabular data. To implement this layout, you use block-level elements, such as divs, to create a structure that parallels the arrangement of table, tr, and td elements in an HTML table. You convert the description list containing contact information for making reservations to a table-like layout using CSS.

1. Return to reserve.html in your text editor, scroll down to the Questions? section, then in the opening and closing tags for the description list, replace the dl with div, leaving the id attribute–value pair unchanged

2. Add a new line containing <div class="row"> before each dt element at the same indent level, add a new line containing </div> after each dd element, then increase the indentation for each dt and dd element by two spaces

   The div elements group content similar to the way a tr element does in an HTML table.

3. Replace each <dt> tag with <div class="category">, each <dd> tag with <div>, and each </dt> and </dd> tag with </div>

   The div elements that replace the dt and dd elements mark the contents of each cell. Figure G-22 shows the completed Web page code for approximating a table layout.

4. Save your work, return to lakeland.css in your text editor, change the selector for the .contact dt rule to .category, then enter the style rules shown in Figure G-23

   The .contact rule sets the display property to table for the description list. The .row rule styles the next level of div elements to behave as table rows. The .row div rule specifies that the next level of div elements behave as table cells, and specifies values for vertical and horizontal padding.

5. Save your work, refresh reserve.html in your browser, then scroll down to the Questions? section

   As Figure G-24 shows, the contact information is arranged in a grid without borders.

Do not delete the border name–value pairs for table elements because they make printed output easier to read.

6. Return to lakeland.css in your text editor, save your work, save a copy as llprint.css, remove all name–value pairs that specify color as well as the pair that specifies the background image, change all the colors in style rules based on pseudo-classes to black, then save your work

7. Validate the code for all your Web pages and your style sheets, and make changes as necessary to fix any errors

8. If you have space on a Web server for publishing your documents, create a local root folder within the Unit folder, move all the files in the Unit folder to the local root folder, upload the files to your Web publishing location, open index.html in your browser from the published location, then use the nav bar to open the remaining Web page and verify that the upload was successful

FIGURE G-22: Completed code for displaying contact information in a table-like layout

```
<div class="contact">
  <div class="row">
    <div class="category">Proprietor</div>
    <div>Philip Blaine</div>
  </div>
  <div class="row">
    <div class="category">Phone</div>
    <div>(218) 555-5253</div>
  </div>
  <div class="row">
    <div class="category">Fax</div>
    <div>(218) 555-0413</div>
  </div>
  <div class="row">
    <div class="category">Email</div>
    <div>lrbb [at] example [dot] com</div>
  </div>
</div>
```

FIGURE G-23: CSS code to display contact information in table-like layout

```
.contact {
  display: table;
}
```

```
.row {
  display: table-row;
}
.row div {
  display: table-cell;
  padding: 0.25em 0.5em;
}
```

FIGURE G-24: Contact information displayed in table-like layout

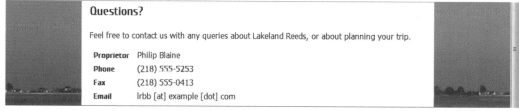

Questions?

Feel free to contact us with any queries about Lakeland Reeds, or about planning your trip.

Proprietor	Philip Blaine
Phone	(218) 555-5253
Fax	(218) 555-0413
Email	lrbb [at] example [dot] com

Photo/Sasha Vodnik

HTML5 and CSS3

Resisting the temptation to use tables for layout

You can style table borders with all the properties that are available for other Web page elements, including removing borders completely. In the early days of the Web, many developers combined spanned rows and columns with invisible borders to enable the positioning of text, images, and other elements side by side, and in specific areas of a Web page. However, as CSS grew and user agent support for it matured, CSS placement properties, which you'll learn in an upcoming unit, became the preferred method for positioning HTML elements. While you can place elements in arbitrary locations by manipulating the number and sizes of rows and columns in a table, doing so erroneously assigns semantic meaning to your Web page content; this suggests that user agents should attempt to understand it as a table of related data. In addition, this use of a table creates particularly strong challenges for non-visual user agents such as screen readers in conveying the relationships between Web page elements. For these reasons, you should restrict your use of tables only to data whose meaning can be better understood in a grid layout.

Practice

For current SAM information, including versions and content details, visit SAM Central (http://www.cengage.com/samcentral). If you have a SAM user profile, you may have access to hands-on instruction, practice, and assessment of the skills covered in this unit. Since various versions of SAM are supported throughout the life of this text, check with your instructor for the correct instructions and URL/Web site for accessing assignments.

Concepts Review

Refer to Figure G-25.

FIGURE G-25

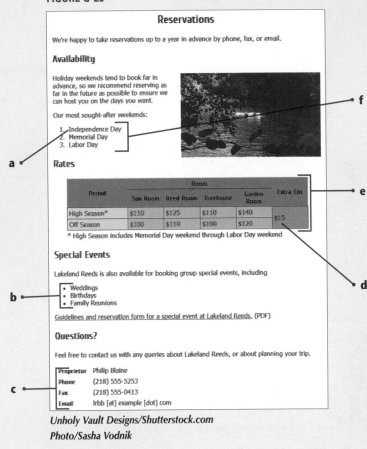

Unholy Vault Designs/Shutterstock.com
Photo/Sasha Vodnik

1. Which item is created using the table element?
2. Which item is created using the li element?
3. Which item is created using the td element?
4. Which item is created using the ul element?
5. Which item is created using the ol element?
6. Which item is created using only div elements?

Match each term with the statement that best describes it.

7. ordered list
8. unordered list
9. description list
10. row
11. column
12. cell

a. a group of table contents arranged vertically
b. a list that enables you to specify a name–value pair for each list item
c. a list in which the order of list items doesn't matter
d. a table component that displays a single item of data
e. a list in which items are numbered or lettered sequentially
f. a group of table contents arranged horizontally

Select the best answer from the list of choices.

13. Which element do you use to create a list in which items are numbered or lettered sequentially?

  a. ol   **c.** dl

  b. ul   **d.** dd

14. Which element do you use to create a list that is usually displayed with bullet characters?

  a. ol   **c.** dl

  b. ul   **d.** dd

15. Which element do you use to create a list that enables you to specify a name-value pair for each list item?

  a. li   **c.** ul

  b. ol   **d.** dl

16. Which element marks the term being described in a description list?

  a. li   **c.** dd

  b. dt   **d.** td

17. Which element marks the description of an item in a description list?

  a. li   **c.** dd

  b. dt   **d.** td

18. Which element marks the content of a table header cell?

  a. thead   **c.** th

  b. tbody   **d.** td

19. Which element marks the content of a table body cell?

  a. thead   **c.** th

  b. tbody   **d.** td

20. Which element marks the rows that make up the head section of a table?

  a. thead   **c.** th

  b. tbody   **d.** td

21. Which element marks the rows that make up the body section of a table?

  a. thead   **c.** th

  b. tbody   **d.** td

Skills Review

1. Create an ordered list.

  a. In your text editor, open HTM G-6.html from the Unit G/Review folder on the drive and folder where you store your Data Files, insert a blank line before the closing body tag, then insert a paragraph element containing your first and last name and the text **HTML5 Unit G, Skills Review**. Save it as **index.html**, then repeat to save HTM G-7.html as **history.html** and HTM G-8.html as **location.html**. Use a CSS comment to add the same information to HTM G-9.css and save it as **bigj.css**.

  b. In index.html, beneath the p element containing the text "Enjoy award winning pizza in your home in just three steps:", insert a blank line, then insert starting and ending tags for an ordered list on separate lines at the same indent level as the preceding p element.

  c. On a new line between the tags you just entered, indent two additional spaces, then add a list item element containing the text **Call the location nearest you**.

  d. Repeat Step c to insert two additional list items containing the text **Place your order and listen for your doorbell** and **Open the box and dig in!**

  e. Save your work, then open index.html in your browser.

2. Create an unordered list.

  a. In history.html, locate the p element with the id "words", then edit the opening and closing tags for the element to make it an unordered list with the same id.

  b. Move each of the words "flavor", "aroma", and "fresh" onto its own line, then mark each as a list item.

c. Save your work, return to bigj.css in your text editor, then create a style rule for list item elements within the element with the id words that makes the list items display without bullets. (*Hint*: Use the value **none** for the list-style-type property.)

d. Save your work, then open history.html in your browser.

3. **Create a description list.**

a. Return to index.html in your text editor, locate the p element with the id "contact", then edit the opening and closing tags for the element to make it a div element with the same id.

b. Insert a line beneath the opening contact div tag, indent two additional spaces, then add an opening tag for a description list. Repeat to add the closing description list tag above the closing div tag. Increase the indent by two spaces for each line of code within the description list element.

c. Mark the address "150 St. Joseph St." as a description list term, delete the colon and space that follow it, move the rest of the current line of code onto its own line at the same indent level, delete the line break tag at the end of the line, then mark the contents of the new line as a description list description. (*Hint*: Include the span element within the code for the description item.) Repeat for the contact information for the remaining two locations.

d. Save your work, then reload index.html in your browser.

4. **Create a navigation bar using a list.**

a. Return to index.html in your text editor, locate the p element with the id "mainnav", then edit the opening and closing tags for the element to make it an unordered list with the same id.

b. Delete the space and the pipe character following the code for the first nav bar link, mark the entire line of code as a list item, then repeat for the remaining three links.

c. Save your work, return to bigj.css in your text editor, create a new style rule based for list items within the element with the id mainnav, then add name–value pairs styling display as **inline**, making no bullet character appear before each item, and setting padding to **0.25em** on all sides.

d. Save your work, reload index.html in your browser, then verify that the nav bar appears as shown in Figure G-26 and that all links work correctly.

e. Return to index.html in your text editor, then copy all the code between the opening and closing nav tags to the Clipboard.

f. Switch to history.html in your text editor, select the code between the opening and closing nav tags, paste the contents of the Clipboard to replace the selection, save your work, then repeat for location.html.

g. Return to index.html in your Web browser, then use the nav bar to navigate to the other pages in the Web site and ensure the new nav bar is displayed consistently across all pages.

5. **Insert a table.**

a. Return to location.html in your text editor, locate the h3 heading containing the text "Queen's Park/UT", insert a blank line beneath the p element containing address information, indent to match the previous line, then insert opening and closing tags for a table element on separate lines at the same indent level.

FIGURE G-26

b. Between the opening and closing tags you just entered, add opening and closing tags for table head and table body sections with each tag on its own line and indented two spaces more than the table tags.

c. Within the table head tags, add opening and closing tags for a table row, with each tag on its own line and indented two spaces more than the thead tags. Repeat to add opening and closing tags for three table rows in the table body section.

d. Within the table row element for the table head section, add table head cell elements containing the text **Days**, **Open**, and **Close** on separate lines, indented two spaces more than the opening table row tag. Repeat to add the following contents to table data cell elements in the three table body rows:

Row 1: **Mon-Thu, 11am, 10pm**

Row 2: **Fri-Sat, 11am, 11pm**

Row 3: **Sun, Noon, 10pm**

e. Delete the p element with the class hours immediately beneath the table you just created.

f. Repeat Steps a–e to insert two more tables:

h3 heading "St. Clair":

Row 1: **Mon-Thu, 11am, 9:30pm**

Row 2: **Fri-Sat, 11am, 11pm**

Row 3: **Sun, Noon, 9:30pm**

h3 heading "Dundas":

Row 1: **Mon-Thu, 11am, 11pm**

Row 2: **Fri-Sat, 11am, Midnight**

Row 3: **Sun, Noon, 11pm**

g. Save your work, then return to bigj.css in your text editor. Add a style rule for table head cell and table data cell elements that sets borders to **1px solid black**.

h. Save your work, then reload location.html in your browser.

6. **Span columns and rows.**

a. Return to location.html in your text editor, locate the table you inserted beneath the h3 heading "Queen's Park/UT", then insert opening and closing tags for a new row element just beneath the opening tag for the table head section. Add a table head cell element that spans two rows containing the text **Day**. Add a second table head cell that spans two columns containing the text **Hours**.

b. In the code for the second table row in the table head section, delete the code for the cell containing the text "Days".

c. Repeat Steps a and b for the remaining two tables in the document. Save your work, then reload location.html in your browser.

7. **Format a table with CSS.**

a. Return to bigj.css in your text editor, then delete the style rule based on the td, th selector. Add a style rule that is based on the table type selector and sets margins to **1em**, padding to **0**, and collapses borders. Add a style rule that is based on the td type selector and sets borders to **1px solid black** and padding to **0.25em**. Add a style rule that is based on the th type selector and sets borders to **1px solid black**, padding to **0.25em**, and background to **#fc6**.

b. Save your work, then reload location.html in your browser.

c. Return to location.html in your text editor, insert a blank line beneath the opening table tag for the first table you created, indent two additional spaces, then add a container element for column groups. Within the container element, add an element that applies the class **daycol** to the first column, then add another element that is without a class value and spans the last two columns. Repeat for the other two tables.

d. In the table body section of each table, add the class **days** to the first table data element in each table row.

e. Save your work, then return to bigj.css in your text editor. Add a style rule for the class **days** that sets the font weight to **bold**. Add a style rule for the class **daycol** that sets the background to **#e0e0e0**.

f. Save your work, then reload location.html in your browser.

8. **Apply a table-like structure to other elements.**

a. Return to index.html in your text editor, then locate the dl element near the bottom of the document. Replace the opening `<dl>` tag with **`<div id="contact">`**. Replace the closing `</dl>` tag with **`</div>`**. Before each dt element, at the same indent level, add a new line containing an opening div tag with a class value of **row**. Add a new line containing a closing div tag after each dd element, then increase the indentation for each dt and dd element by two spaces.

Skills Review (continued)

b. Replace each \<dt\> and \<dd\> tag with **\<div\>** and each \</dt\> and \</dd\> tag with **\</div\>**.

c. Save your work, then return to bigj.css in your text editor. Create a style rule for the id **contact**, then add name–value pairs to set the display to **table** and the padding and margin to **0**. Create a style rule for the class **row**, then add an name–value pair to set the display to **table-row**. Create a style rule for div elements within elements with the class **row**, then add name–value pairs to set the display to **table-cell** and set the padding to **0.1em 0.5em**.

d. Save your work, copy the contact div element along with its contents to the Clipboard, then paste it into history.html and location.html to replace the existing contact element in each document. Save your work, refresh location.html in your browser, verify that the contact information at the bottom of the page matches that shown in Figure G-27, then use the nav bar to open the main page and the History page and verify that the contact information appears consistently across the site.

e. Return to bigj.css in your text editor, save your work, save a copy as **bjprint.css**, remove all name–value pairs that specify color as well as the pair that specifies the background image, change all the colors in style rules based on pseudo-classes to **black**, then save your work.

f. Validate the code for all your Web pages and your style sheets, and make changes as necessary to fix any errors.

g. If you have space on a Web server for publishing your documents, create a local root folder within the Review folder, move all the files in the Review folder to the local root folder, upload the files to your Web publishing location, open index.html in your browser from the published location, then use the nav bar to open the remaining Web page and verify that the upload was successful.

FIGURE G-27

Independent Challenge 1

Sarah Nguyen, the owner of the Spotted Wren Garden Center, has given you additional content to add to the Web site you've been creating for her. You add this information using lists and tables.

a. Open HTM G-10.html from the Unit G/IC1 folder in your text editor. Insert a blank line before the closing body tag, then insert a paragraph element containing your first and last name and the text **HTML5 Unit G, Independent Challenge 1**. Save the file as **index.html**, then repeat to save HTM G-11.html as **hours.html**, and HTM G-12.html as **resource.html**. Open HTM G-13.css, below the existing comment at the top of the document, add another comment with your first and last name and the text **HTML5 Unit G, Independent Challenge 1**. Save the file as **spotwren.css**.

b. In resource.html, change the four paragraph elements beneath the h2 heading "Resources" to an unordered list by replacing the opening and closing p tags with opening and closing **li** tags and then enclosing all four elements in a **ul** element. Save your work, then view resource.html in your Web browser to verify that the four paragraphs are displayed as an unordered list.

c. Return to resource.html in your text editor. Beneath the text "Omaha area plant hardiness zone information", insert the following table. (*Hint*: Use rowspan attributes for the cells containing the text **Zone**, **Last frost**, **First frost**, **May 1**, and **Oct 15**. Use a colspan attribute for the cell containing the text **Average annual minimum temp**. The HTML character code for the degree symbol is **\°**).

Independent Challenge 1 (continued)

Zone	Average annual minimum temp		Last frost	First frost
	Fahrenheit	**Celsius**		
4b	-25°F to -20°F	-28.9°C to -31.6°C		
5a	-20°F to -15°F	-26.2°C to -28.8°C	May 1	Oct 15
5b	-15°F to -10°F	-23.4°C to -26.1°C		

d. Delete the closing list item tag after the text "Omaha area plant hardiness zone information" above the table, add a blank line beneath the closing tag for the table, indent two fewer spaces, then add the closing list item tag. Save your work, then return to spotwren.css in your text editor. Add a style rule for table elements that sets the margin to **1em 0**, the padding to **0**, and collapses borders. Add a style rule for table data cell elements that sets borders to **1px solid black** and padding to **0.25em**. Add a style rule for table header cell elements that sets borders to **1px solid black**, padding to **0.25em**, and the background to **#e0e0e0**. Save your work, then reload resource.html in your browser and verify that the table appears as shown in Figure G-28.

e. Return to resource.html in your text editor. Mark up the list of plant names as a description list with the common names as terms and the Latin names that follow as descriptions. Delete the closing list item tag for the text "Recommended drought-tolerant perennials" above the list, then delete the closing unordered list tag below that line. Add a blank line beneath the closing tag for the description list, indent two fewer spaces, then type a closing list item tag for an unordered list. Add another blank line beneath the current line, indent two fewer spaces, then type a closing tag for an unordered list. Save your work, then return to spotwren.css in your text editor. Add a style rule to style the contents of all description elements in a description list in italic. Save your work, then reload resource.html in your browser. Verify that definition list matches the one shown in Figure G-28.

f. Return to resource.html in your text editor. Convert the code for the nav bar to an unordered list by changing the p element that encloses the links to a **ul** element, then enclosing the code for each link in an **li** element. Delete the space and pipe character (|) after each link. Save your work, then return to spotwren.css in your text editor. Create a style rule that applies only to list item elements within the element with the id "mainnav". Set the display property to **inline** and the padding to **0.25em**, then set the list to display without a bullet character. Save your work, reload resource.html in your browser, then verify that the appearance of the nav bar matches Figure G-28. Return to resource.html in your text editor, copy the new nav bar code to the Clipboard, then use it to replace the existing nav bar code in index.html and hours.html. Save your work, then view index.html and hours.html in your browser to verify that the nav bar is displayed as expected.

g. Return to hours.html in your text editor. Indent each line of code containing store hours information by four additional spaces. Beneath the h2 heading, insert a new line containing a div element with the class **table** at the same indent level as the previous line. Add a closing tag for the div element after the last line of store hours information. Enclose each line of code containing store hours information in a div element that belongs to the class **row**, then delete the opening and closing p tags from each line. Change the opening and closing span tags enclosing each day of the week to div tags. Click before the opening time on the first line, press **[Enter]**, indent to match the previous line, then enclose the hour information in a **div** element. Repeat for the remaining days.

FIGURE G-28

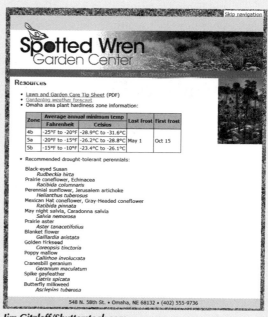

Jim Gitzlaff/Shutterstock.com
Maxim Tupikov/Shutterstock.com
Xtremer/Shutterstock.com

Independent Challenge 1 (continued)

h. Return to spotwren.css in your text editor. Add a style rule to style elements of the class row to display like table rows. Add a style rule to style div elements within elements of the class row to display like table cells with padding set to **0.1em 0.5em**. Add a style rule to style elements of the class table to display like tables with a margin and padding value of **0**. Save your work, then reload hours.html in your browser. Verify that the list of hours matches the one shown in Figure G-29.

i. Return to spotwren.css in your text editor, remove all name–value pairs that reference colors as well as the pair that specifies the background image, change all colors in rules based on pseudo-classes to **black**, then save a copy of the file as **swprint.css**.

j. Validate all your HTML and CSS documents.

k. If you have space on a Web server for publishing your documents, create a local root folder within the IC1 folder, move all the files and folders in the IC1 folder to the local root folder, upload the files to your Web publishing location, then open all three Web pages in your browser from the published location.

l. Close your browser, then close your text editor.

FIGURE G-29

Spotted Wren
Garden Center

Home   Hours   Location   Gardening Resources

Summer Hours
Mon 8am - 8pm
Tue 8am - 8pm
Wed 8am - 5pm
Thu 8am - 8pm
Fri 8am - 8pm
Sat 9am - 6pm
Sun 11am - 6pm

Skip navigation

548 N. 58th St. • Omaha, NE 68132 • (402) 555-9736

Jim Gitzlaff/Shutterstock.com
Maxim Tupikov/Shutterstock.com
Xtremer/Shutterstock.com

Independent Challenge 2

You incorporate the logo for the Murfreesboro Recreational Soccer League into the organizational Web site that you are creating. You also add images from some of the group's events.

a. Open HTM G-14.html from the Unit G/IC2 folder in your text editor. Insert a blank line before the closing body tag, then insert a paragraph element containing your first and last name and the text **HTML5 Unit G, Independent Challenge 2**. Save the file as **index.html**, then repeat to save HTM G-15.html as **started. html** and HTM G-16.html as **schedule.html**. Open HTM G-17.css, then below the existing comment at the top of the document, add another comment containing your first and last name and the text **HTML5 Unit G, Independent Challenge 2**. Save the file as **mrsl.css**.

b. In started.html, locate the paragraph that begins "If you're interested in joining up". Mark the text "complete some paperwork" as a list item for an unordered list. Delete the word "and" following the text you just marked, then mark the remainder of the sentence as a second list item. Enclose the two list items within an element that marks an unordered list and indent all elements appropriately. Move the closing paragraph tag after the word "to" just before the start of the list.

Advanced Challenge Exercise

■ Position the insertion point before the closing list item tag for the second list item, press **[Enter]** twice, then indent to match the first list item. On the blank line you created, insert opening and closing tags for a second unordered list, which will be nested within the first list. Add a list item containing the text **$65 (standard)** and a second list item containing the text **$40 (seniors and students)**. Edit the second list item in the previous list to read **pay for a seasonal membership**. Save your work.

■ In mrsl.css, add a style rule that applies to all unordered lists. Set the property list-style-image to **url("images/ soccer.gif")** to specify a soccer ball icon as the unordered list bullet. Save your work, open started.html in your browser, then verify the page matches Figure G-30.

Independent Challenge 2 (continued)

c. Return to started.html in your text editor. Convert the code for the nav bar to an unordered list by changing the p element that encloses the links to an element that marks an unordered list, then enclosing the code for each link in a list item element. Delete the space and pipe character (|) after each link. Save your work, then return to mrsl.css in your text editor. Create a style rule that applies only to list item elements within the element with the id "mainnav". Set the display property to **inline** and the padding to **0.25em**, and set the list to display without a bullet character. Save your work, reload started.html in your browser, then verify that the appearance of the nav bar matches Figure G-30. Return to started.html in your text editor, copy the new nav bar code to the Clipboard, then use it to replace the existing nav bar code in index.html and schedule. html. Save your work, then view index.html and schedule.html in your browser to verify that the nav bar is displayed as expected.

d. In schedule.html, convert the four lists of game dates and times into tables. Create a heading row for each table with heading cells containing the text **Date** and **Time**. Split the information for each game into two cells, the first containing the date and the second containing the start time. Save your work, then return to mrsl.css in your text editor. Add a style rule for table elements that sets the margin to **1em 0**, the padding to **0**, and collapses borders. Add a style rule for table data cell elements that sets borders to **1px solid black** and padding to **0.25em**. Add a style rule for table header cell elements that sets borders to **1px solid black**, padding to **0.25em**, and the background to **#e0e0e0**. Save your work, then preview schedule.html in your browser. Verify that all four tables are displayed correctly.

e. Using Figure G-31 as a guide, add a third column to each table that displays the field letter where each game will be played. (*Hint*: To add a column, add a new cell at the end of each row element.) Save your work, reload schedule. html in your browser, then verify that your tables match those shown in Figure G-31.

f. Return to mrsl.css in your text editor, remove all name–value pairs that reference colors as well as the pairs that specify background images, change all colors in rules based on pseudo-classes to black, then save a copy of the file as **mrsprint.css**.

g. Validate all your HTML and CSS documents.

h. If you have space on a Web server for publishing your documents, create a local root folder within the IC2 folder, move all the files and folders in the IC2 folder to the local root folder, upload the files to your Web publishing location, then open all three Web pages in your browser from the published location.

i. Close your browser, then close your text editor.

FIGURE G-30

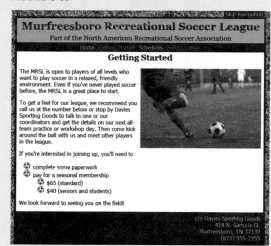

Lario Tus/Shutterstock.com
Xtremer/Shutterstock.com

FIGURE G-31

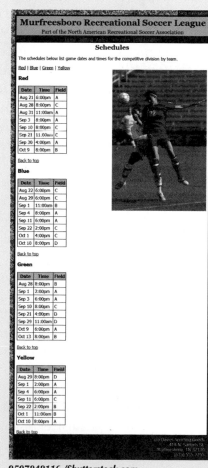

9507848116 /Shutterstock.com
Xtremer/Shutterstock.com

Independent Challenge 3

As you continue your work on the Web site for Hotel Natoma, you incorporate additional information about the hotel and local attractions using some of the techniques for organizing content that you learned in this unit.

a. Open HTM G-18.html from the Unit G/IC3 folder in your text editor. Insert a blank line before the closing body tag, then insert a paragraph element containing your first and last name and the text **HTML5 Unit G, Independent Challenge 3**. Save the file as **index.html**, then repeat to save HTM G-19.html as **nearby.html** and HTM G-20.html as **greensf.html**. Open HTM G-21.css, then below the existing comment at the top of the document, add another comment containing your first and last name and the text **HTML5 Unit G, Independent Challenge 3**. Save the file as **natoma.css**.

b. In nearby.html, mark the list of nearby locations as an unordered list. Save your work, then preview the page in your browser and compare it to Figure G-33.

c. In greensf.html, mark the list of green destinations as an ordered list. Save your work, then preview the page in your browser.

Advanced Challenge Exercise

■ In natoma.css, add a style rule to style ordered lists using lowercase Roman numerals. (*Hint*: Use the **lower-roman** value for the list-style-type property.) Save your work, then preview the page in your browser and compare it to Figure G-32.

d. In greensf.html, convert the markup for the main nav bar to use an unordered list and remove the bullets between links. Save your work, then add a style rule to natoma.css that sets the display of list items in the element with the id **mainnav** to **inline**, removes bullet characters, and sets padding to **0.25em**. Preview the Web page in your browser and compare it to Figure G-32. (*Note*: If you did not complete the Advanced Challenge Exercise, your ordered list will be displayed with standard numbers rather than Roman numerals.)

e. Copy the revised code for the nav bar to the Clipboard, then use it to replace the existing code for the nav bars in index.html and nearby.html. Save your work, then preview each file in your browser to ensure the nav bar is displayed consistently across the site.

f. Return to natoma.css in your text editor, change all border colors to black. remove all other name–value pairs that reference colors, change all colors in rules based on pseudo-classes to black, then save a copy of the file as **hnprint.css**.

g. Validate all your HTML and CSS documents.

h. If you have space on a Web server for publishing your documents, create a local root folder within the IC3 folder, move all the files and folders in the IC3 folder to the local root folder, upload the files to your Web publishing location, then open both Web pages in your browser from the published location.

i. Close your browser, then close your text editor.

FIGURE G-32

FIGURE G-33

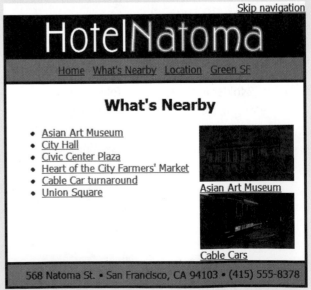

Photos/Sasha Vodnik

Real Life Independent Challenge

This assignment builds on the personal Web site you have worked on in previous units. As you continue to organize and add content to your Web site, you make use of the elements you learned in this unit.

   a. Copy your Web site files to the Unit G/RLIC folder on the drive and folder where you store your Data Files.

   b. Review your existing Web pages for any content that would be easier to read or would be better marked semantically as a list or as a table. Review your storyboard and any other design documents to identify any additional planned content that should be organized using one of these methods.

   c. For each list you are adding to your Web site, decide which list type makes the most sense. If you are adding an ordered or unordered list, choose a bullet character or ordering system as appropriate. Add the lists to your Web site on the appropriate Web pages. Save your work and preview all affected Web pages in a browser.

   d. Convert the code for the nav bar on your Web site to use an unordered list. Add appropriate styles to your style sheet to preserve the appearance of your nav bar. Copy the code you created to all the Web pages in your site. Save your work and preview all Web pages in a browser.

   e. For each table you are adding to your Web site, start by sketching the table on a sheet of paper. Decide which rows will be table head rows and which will be table body rows. Identify any cells that will span multiple columns or multiple rows. Count the total columns in the table. Add each table at the appropriate location in your Web site, then save each page and preview it in a browser. If a table does not display as expected, refer to your code and your sketch to identify discrepancies.

   f. Save changes to your style sheet document, save a copy using the name of your print style sheet, then take out name–value pairs that set color and background images and change all colors in rules based on pseudo-classes to black.

   g. Preview your Web pages in at least two browsers and make any edits necessary for them to appear as you expected.

   h. Validate all of your HTML and CSS documents and make any edits necessary to address any issues.

   i. If you have space on a Web server for publishing your documents, create a local root folder within the RLIC folder, move all the files in the RLIC folder to the local root folder, upload the files to your Web publishing location, then open each Web page in your browser from the published location to verify that the upload was successful.

   j. Close your browser, then close your text editor.

Visual Workshop

In your text editor, open the file HTM G-22.html from the /Unit G/VW directory on the drive and folder where you store your Data Files, before the closing body tag add a paragraph that contains your first and last name and the text **HTML5 Unit G, Visual Workshop**, then save the file as **upcoming.html**. Open HTM G-23.css, add a comment containing the same information, then save it as **revision.css**. Use your text editor to add the table shown in Figure G-34. (*Hint*: Use the **title** class to italicize the book title.) Convert the nav bar layout to use an unordered list. Save your work, save a copy of your style sheet with the name **revprint.css**, then make any necessary changes for print formatting. When you are finished, validate your HTML and CSS code. If you have space on a Web server, create a local root folder within the VW folder, move both files to the local root folder, upload the file to your Web publishing location, then open the Web page in your browser from the published location. Close your browser and text editor.

FIGURE G-34

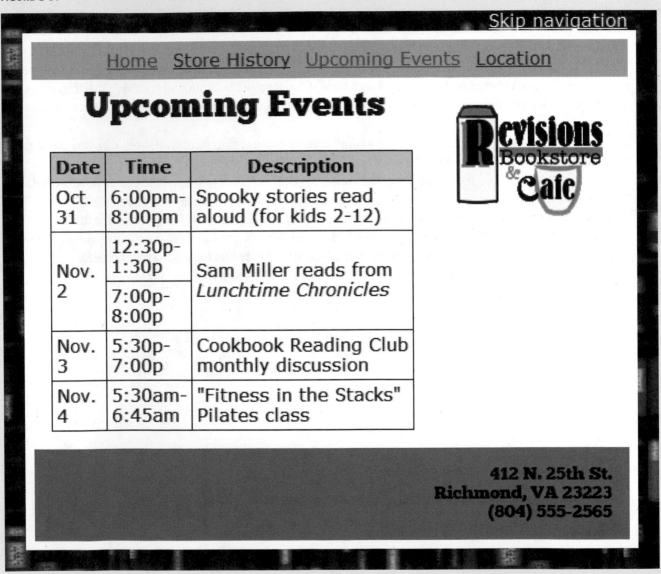

Kentoh/Shutterstock.com

Organizing Content with Lists and Tables

Implementing Page Layout with HTML and CSS

Combining HTML elements with basic CSS attributes offers some flexibility in the arrangement and appearance of Web page elements. You can use more advanced CSS to create even more complex layouts and to exercise more detailed control over the layout of your Web pages. You prepare to add new layout features to the Lakeland Reeds B&B Web site.

OBJECTIVES

Assess the CSS box model

Construct a multicolumn layout with float

Implement relative positioning

Implement absolute positioning

Stack elements

Create a multicolumn layout using positioning

Create a fluid layout

Control the visibility of elements

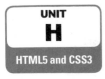
Assessing the CSS Box Model

Creating and modifying page layouts in CSS involves specifying size and position information for Web page elements. CSS represents the characteristics of every Web page element using the box model, which treats each element as a rectangular box having several global properties. Figure H-1 shows the relationship between the CSS padding, border, and margin properties in the box model. ▰▰▰▰▰ As you prepare to apply more complex layout features to the Web site for Lakeland Reeds B&B, you familiarize yourself with the CSS box model.

DETAILS

A few concepts are important for using box model properties effectively:

- ### Distinguishing between padding, border, and margin
  The padding, border, and margin properties all create space around the contents of a Web page element, but it's important to understand the relationship of these elements to each other in order to create the results you want. Of the three properties, border, formatted with the width, style, and color that you specify, is the only one that can be seen in a Web browser. However, a name-value pair of border: 0; means that the border for the affected element is not visible and takes up no space. Whether a border is visible or not, it serves as a reference point for the other two properties, as illustrated in Figure H-1. Padding is the space inside a border between the border and the element content, while margin is the space outside the border between the border and adjacent or parent elements.

QUICK TIP

You can set the CSS3 box-sizing property to "border-box" to change how box sizing is calculated, fitting the border and padding along with the content within the dimensions specified by "width" and "height"; however, the property is not globally supported.

- ### Calculating box size
  The size of the padding, border, and margin all increase the amount of space on a Web page that an element occupies or influences. However, the dimensions of these properties are generally not included in the calculated width or height of an element. By default, when you specify dimensions for an element using the width and height properties, the values you specify apply only to the element content. Any values you specify for padding, border, or margin are added to the height or width value you specify. Especially when you're fitting an element into a limited amount of space, you need to subtract the additional area occupied by padding, border, and margin to arrive at the appropriate width or height value, as Figure H-2 illustrates. For instance, when the width of an element must fit into a limited space, you have to subtract both the left and right values for padding, border, and margin to arrive at the appropriate width value for your style sheet. Similarly, to calculate a height value, you need to subtract all three values for the top and bottom of the element.
    There is one exception to this rule: when the bottom margin of one element is adjacent to the top margin of another element, the margins combine, or **collapse**, into a single margin equal to the greater of the two values.

- ### Combining properties
  As you create more complex layouts, setting specific widths for the padding and margin of specific sides of elements becomes more important. The box model supports a separate property for each side for both padding and margin, such as padding-top or margin-left. However, you can save time while coding and simplify your code by combining properties. When you want to set a common value for all four sides of an element, you can use generic properties with single values. For instance, padding: 0; sets padding on all four sides of an element to 0, while margin: 1em; sets the margin to 1 em all around an element. These properties also support more detailed shorthand values. As Table H-1 illustrates, if you provide four values for the margin or padding property, browsers apply the first value to the top and continue in a clockwise direction with the second value applied to the right, the third value to the bottom, and the final value to the left. For a name-value pair with three values, the first value applies to the top, the second to both the left and right, and the final value to the bottom. If you provide two values for either of these properties, browsers apply the first value to the top and bottom, and the second value to the left and right sides.

FIGURE H-1: The CSS box model

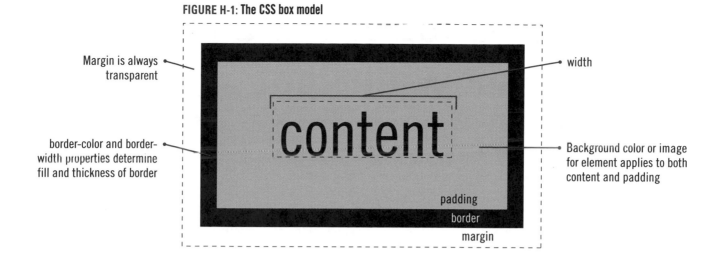

Margin is always transparent

width

border-color and border-width properties determine fill and thickness of border

Background color or image for element applies to both content and padding

content

padding
border
margin

FIGURE H-2: Calculating Web page space occupied by an element

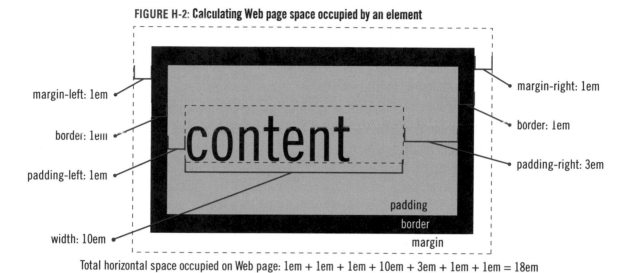

margin-left: 1em

margin-right: 1em

border: 1em

border: 1em

padding-left: 1em

padding-right: 3em

content

width: 10em

padding
border
margin

Total horizontal space occupied on Web page: 1em + 1em + 1em + 10em + 3em + 1em + 1em = 18em

TABLE H-1: Box model shorthand properties

property	# of values	values apply to	shorthand examples	equivalent to	
padding margin	four	top, right, bottom, left	margin: 0 1em 1em 0; padding: 0 1em 1em 0;	margin-top: 0; margin-right: 1em; margin-bottom: 1em; margin-left: 0;	padding-top: 0; padding-right: 1em; padding-bottom: 1em; padding-left: 0;
	three	top, left/right, bottom	margin: 0 2em 1em; padding: 0 2em 1em;	margin-top: 0; margin-right: 2em; margin-bottom: 1em; margin-left: 2em;	padding-top: 0; padding-right: 2em; padding-bottom: 1em; padding-left: 2em;
	two	top/bottom, left/right	margin: 0 1em; padding: 0 1em;	margin-top: 0; margin-right: 1em; margin-bottom: 0; margin-left: 1em;	padding-top: 0; padding-right: 1em; padding-bottom: 0; padding-left: 1em;
	one	top/left/bottom/right	margin: 1em; padding: 1em;	margin-top: 1em; margin-right: 1em; margin-bottom: 1em; margin-left: 1em;	padding-top: 1em; padding-right: 1em; padding-bottom: 1em; padding-left: 1em;
border	three	width, style, color	border: 3px solid red;	border-width: 3px; border-style: solid; border-color: red;	

Constructing a Multicolumn Layout with Float

Because user agents render HTML documents from top to bottom, it's relatively straightforward to create layouts that stack styled elements vertically. However, some of the most widely used layouts in print media involve columns of text and graphics running parallel to each other down the page. You can use the float and clear properties to create a basic version of this arrangement, known as a multicolumn layout, to unlock new possibilities for the arrangement of elements on your Web pages. ▰▰▰ The design modifications that you created with the art department involve transforming the nav bar into a stacked set of links running down the left side of the page, with the main body of the page displayed to the right. You add styles to create this layout.

STEPS

1. **In your text editor, open HTM H-1.html from the Unit H/Unit folder where you store your Data Files, insert a blank line before the closing body tag, insert a paragraph element containing your first and last name and the text HTML5 Unit H, save it as aboutus.html, then use a CSS comment to add the same information to HTM H-2.css and save it as lakeland.css**

QUICK TIP

The margin and padding settings for your other style rules have already been adjusted to account for this new style rule.

2. **In lakeland.css, beneath the @font-face rule, insert a style rule that is based on the selectors article, body, dd, div, dl, dt, figcaption, figure, footer, h1, h2, h3, li, nav, ol, p, section, table, th, td, and ul and that sets both margin and padding to 0**

   Setting the margin and padding to 0 for commonly used elements helps you ensure that you are specifying precise values for all of your page elements, rather than relying on default browser styles, which can vary between user agents.

3. **Examine the other rules in the style sheet, locate the #mainnav li style rule, then delete the name–value pair display: inline;**

   By removing the value *inline* for display, you cause the links to return to the default arrangement of list items: as block elements stacked one on top of the next.

QUICK TIP

While most current browsers enable users to resize text specified in pixels rather than em, IE6 does not. If IE6 support is not crucial for your target audience, using pixels can simplify sizing.

4. **Locate the #mainnav style rule, add the name–value pairs float:left; and width: 7em;, then remove the background name–value pair**

   Setting the float property styles the main content that follows the nav bar to be displayed next to it. Removing the background color emphasizes the space between the nav bar list items with whitespace, creating the appearance of a set of separate buttons.

5. **Below the #mainnav style rule, create a new style rule based on the #mainnav a selector, then set the text-decoration property to none**

   This rule removes the underline from the nav bar link text, reinforcing the appearance of buttons.

6. **In the #content style rule, set the float property to right, then set the width to 32em**

   The combination of float and width properties for both the mainnav and content elements creates the appearance of two columns. Figure H-3 shows the completed style sheet code.

7. **Save your work, then open aboutus.html in your browser**

   As Figure H-4 shows, the nav bar links are displayed in a vertical stack along the left side of the screen, and the remaining page content is displayed in a second column to the right.

FIGURE H-3: Style sheet code for multicolumn layout

margin and padding set to 0 for commonly used elements

Style rules for content and child elements

Style rules for mainnav and child elements

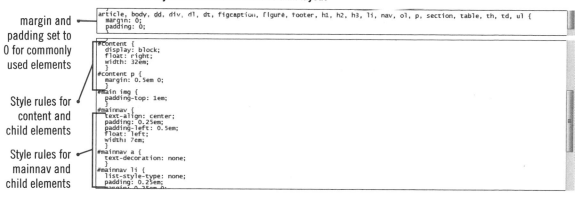

```
article, body, dd, div, dl, dt, figcaption, figure, footer, h1, h2, h3, li, nav, ol, p, section, table, th, td, ul {
    margin: 0;
    padding: 0;
}
#content {
    display: block;
    float: right;
    width: 32em;
}
#content p {
    margin: 0.5em 0;
}
#main img {
    padding-top: 1em;
}
#mainnav {
    text-align: center;
    padding: 0.25em;
    padding-left: 0.5em;
    float: left;
    width: 7em;
}
#mainnav a {
    text-decoration: none;
}
#mainnav li {
    list-style-type: none;
    padding: 0.25em;
    margin: 0.25em 0;
}
```

FIGURE H-4: Two-column layout in browser

Nav bar floated as left column

content element floated as right column

Unholy Vault Designs/Shutterstock.com
Jason Bucy

Adding additional columns

In addition to two-column layouts like the one shown in Figure H-4, multicolumn layouts including three columns are common on the Web. You can use the method outlined in this lesson to create a three-column layout by creating three content sections in your document and floating the first two on the left and the right. As long as the widths of the three sections (including padding, borders, and margins on both sides) total less than the total width of the parent element, the three sections are displayed side by side as columns when you open the page in a browser.

You'll explore advanced tools for creating layouts with more than three columns later in this unit.

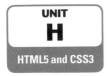

Implementing Relative Positioning

So far, your layouts have been limited to Web page elements being displayed based on the order they appear in your HTML documents, known as the **page flow**, or by moving elements outside the page flow to the left or right using the float property. CSS also lets you specify the exact position of an element on a Web page using the position property. You can make adjustments to the default position of an element while preserving the space allotted to the element in the default page flow. You implement this technique, known as **relative positioning**, by setting the position property to "relative". You style the exact location of the element using the top and left properties, as detailed in Table H-2. Figure H-5 illustrates how relative positioning affects the flow of elements in a Web page. ░░░░░ You'd like the top of the nav bar to be even with the first paragraph of text in the second column, rather than with the header, so you use relative positioning to move it down while maintaining its position on the left side of the Web page.

STEPS

QUICK TIP
You can determine top and left positioning values by calculating the amount of space you need to move an element, or by simple trial and error.

1. **Return to lakeland.css, in your text editor**

2. **At the bottom of the #mainnav ul selector, add the name–value pairs position: relative; and top: 2em;**
   This code moves the list containing the nav bar elements down the page 2em while preserving its position in the left column. Figure H-6 shows the inserted code.

3. **Save your work, then refresh aboutus.html in your browser**
   As Figure H-7 shows, the top of the nav bar is now below the h2 heading and even with the top of the main text in the right column.

TABLE H-2: CSS properties and values for relative positioning

property	value	note
position	**relative**	Moves the element relative to its original position but preserves the space reserved for the element in its original position
top	*value* in em, pixels, or another supported unit, or **percent** of the height of the parent element	Moves the element the specified distance from the top edge of the closest ancestor element that is also positioned; the default value, 0, leaves the element in its original vertical position
left	*value* in em, pixels, or another supported unit, or percent of the width of the **parent** element	Moves the element the specified distance from the left edge of the closest ancestor element that is also positioned; the default value, 0, leaves the element in its original horizontal position

Maintaining accessibility with positioning

When you alter the layout of your Web pages using positioning, it's important to plan for non-visual user agents, as well as devices with smaller screens, to make sure your page content still flows logically. User agents that don't process positioning continue to render all content from top to bottom in the document. Thus, your HTML code should contain elements in the order users will encounter them. In addition, you can help all user agents understand the content of your pages and present it appropriately by using semantic elements to indicate the content of different columns; for instance, nav for the nav bar, aside for a sidebar, and article for main page content.

FIGURE H-5: Relative positioning and page flow

Default flow of page elements   New layout with relative positioning applied

Other page elements do
not reflow into originally
occupied space after
relative positioning

FIGURE H-6: Code to relatively position nav bar

```
#mainnav ul {
    margin: 0;
    padding: 0;
    position: relative;
    top: 2em;
}
```

position and top properties
added to move nav bar down

FIGURE H-7: Nav bar relatively positioned

Nav bar moved
down 2em from
original location
in page flow

Unholy Vault Designs/Shutterstock.com
Jason Bucy

Implementing Absolute Positioning

An alternative to relative positioning is **absolute positioning**, which takes an element out of the page flow entirely and allows other elements to flow into the space it would have occupied. As with relative positioning, you can specify the new location of an absolutely positioned element relative to the closest ancestor element that is itself positioned. In addition to the top and left properties, you can use the right and bottom properties as well, causing the effects detailed in Table H-3. Figure H-8 illustrates how absolute positioning affects the flow of elements in a Web page. 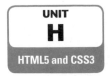 You want to add a decorative icon next to each nav bar button. You insert the images within the list items for the nav bar buttons and use absolute positioning to take them out of the list item block elements and specify their new locations.

1. **Return to aboutus.html in your text editor, then after the opening <li> tag for the list item containing the text About Us, enter the following tag:**

   ```
   <img src="images/fl_dark.gif" width="45" height="45" alt="" title="" />
   ```
   This code inserts a shaded icon to mark the current page in the nav bar.

QUICK TIP

When the remaining Web pages are modified for the vertical nav bar, the fl_dark.gif image will be inserted to the left of the link for the current page, and the fl_light.gif image will be added next to each of the other links.

2. **Insert the following after the opening <li> for each remaining nav bar button:**

   ```
   <img src="images/fl_light.gif" width="45" height="45" alt="" title="" />
   ```
   A matching icon with different shading marks each of the remaining nav bar icons.

3. **Save your work, then reload aboutus.html in your browser**

   An icon appears to the left of the text for each button and increases the button height.

4. **Return to lakeland.css in your text editor, then in the #mainnav style rule, change the value for the padding-left property to 1em, the value for the text-align property to left, and the value for the width property to 6em**

   This code narrows the nav bar buttons and inserts space for the icons to the left of the nav bar.

5. **Beneath the img style rule, add a style rule that is based on the li img selector and sets position to absolute, left to -40px, and top to -8px**

   A negative value for left moves the left border of the element to the left, rather than to the right. Similarly, a negative value for top moves the element up.

6. **In the #mainnav li style rule, add a name–value pair that sets position to relative**

   The location of an absolutely positioned element is calculated based on the closest ancestor element that has a position applied to it. You set the position of list items in the nav bar to relative without changing the position in order to simplify positioning the image for each nav bar button. Figure H-9 shows the style sheet containing your additions and changes.

QUICK TIP

Internet Explorer 6 renders some positioned elements inaccurately. If you need to position elements for a Web page that needs to be IE6 compatible, search on the phrase "ie6 positioning bug" for workaround tips.

7. **Save your work, then refresh aboutus.html in your browser**

   As Figure H-10 shows, the nav bar icons are displayed to the left of the buttons.

FIGURE H-8: Absolute positioning and page flow

Default flow of page elements

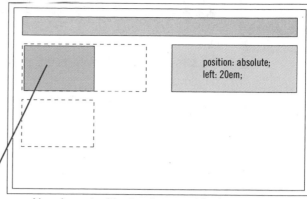

position: absolute;
left: 20em;

New layout with absolute positioning applied

Page elements following absolutely positioned
element reflow to occupy its space

FIGURE H-9: Code to absolutely position images

```
li img {
    position: absolute;
    left: -40px;
    top: -8px;
}
```

```
#mainnav {
    text-align: left;
    padding: 0.25em;
    padding-left: 1em;
    float: left;
    width: 6em;
}
#mainnav a {
    text-decoration: none;
}
#mainnav li {
    list-style-type: none;
    padding: 0.25em;
    margin: 0.25em 0;
    background: #B8944D;
    position: relative;
}
```

FIGURE H-10: Images absolutely positioned

Icon images
moved outside
of nav bar
buttons using
absolute
positioning

Unholy Vault Designs/Shutterstock.com
Jason Bucy

TABLE H-3: CSS properties and values for absolute positioning

property	value	result
position	**absolute**	Moves the element relative to its original position and allows other elements to flow into the space that the absolutely positioned element would have otherwise occupied
top	***value*** in em, pixels, or another supported unit, or ***percent*** of the height of the parent element	Moves the element the specified distance from the top, bottom, left, or right edge of the closest ancestor element that is also positioned
bottom		
left	***value*** in em, pixels, or another supported unit, or ***percent*** of the width of the parent element	
right		

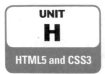

Stacking Elements

One of the additional effects of using positioning in your layouts is the possibility of two elements occupying the same space on a Web page. Both relatively and absolutely positioned elements can be moved to positions occupied by other elements, or two positioned elements can be moved to the same place. While it requires careful planning to ensure that a positioned element doesn't unintentionally obscure the view of another element, the ability to overlap, or **stack**, elements introduces additional possibilities for creative layouts. A positioned element is placed in a new **layer**, which is a new level displayed on top of the basic flow of elements on the Web page. As Figure H-11 illustrates, the arrangement of layers is similar to placing clear sheets of plastic over a page in a book. You can control the stacking order of positioned elements by assigning values for the z-index property to each element. Numbers can be positive or negative, and an element with a larger z-index value is displayed on top of an element with a smaller value. ▓▓▓▓ You want to modify the nav bar so the icon for each button overlaps the edge of the button. You also want to incorporate a green bar into the background of the nav bar for contrast. You reposition the nav bar icons, and you add the background box using the z-image property to set the stacking order.

STEPS

1. Return to **lakeland.css** in your text editor, then in the **#mainnav** style rule, change the value for **padding-left** to **0.5em** and the value for **width** to **7em**

QUICK TIP
You can apply a z-index value only to an element for which you've declared a value for the position property.

2. In the **#mainnav li** style rule, change the value for **padding** to **0.25em 0.25em 0.25em 1em**

3. In the **li img** style rule, change the value for **left** to **-22px**

4. Save your work, then reload **aboutus.html** in your browser
   Each icon now overlaps the end of its corresponding button.

5. Return to **aboutus.html** in your text editor, then below the closing **</ul>** tag for the list containing the nav bar buttons, insert opening and closing tags for a **div** element with no content and the id **navaccent**

6. Save your work, return to **lakeland.css** in your text editor, then above the **#pagenav** style rule, add a style rule the for the element with the id **navaccent** that sets the **width** to **1.5em**, the **height** to **12.25em**, the **background** to **#4D8103**, the **position** to **relative**, **top** to **-10em**, and **left** to **-0.75em**

QUICK TIP
Values for the z-index property can be any number, including a negative number. Stacking order is based solely on which element has a larger z-index value, not on the actual value.

7. Save your work, then reload **aboutus.html** in your browser
   The green box you created is positioned in front of the buttons and icons instead of behind them.

8. Return to **lakeland.css** in your text editor, in the **#navaccent** style rule add the name–value pair **z-index: 1**, then in the **#mainnav ul** style rule, add the name–value pair **z-index: 2**
   Figure H-12 shows the completed code for the style sheet.

9. Save your work, then reload **aboutus.html** in your browser
   As Figure H-13 shows, the green bar is now displayed behind the nav bar buttons.

Implementing fixed position

In addition to relative and absolute, the position property supports a third value: fixed. An element with **fixed positioning** behaves just like an element with absolute positioning except that it is displayed at the top of the stacking order and it is positioned relative to the browser window rather than to a Web page element. As a result, fixed positioning causes an element to remain in the same location in a browser window as a user scrolls through the Web page. This styling can be useful for information or tools that users may need at any point on a long Web page. However, keep in mind that Internet Explorer 6 and browsers on most mobile devices don't support this value.

FIGURE H-11: Stacking positioned elements

Element with the lowest z-index value is stacked below other positioned elements

z-index: 10

z-index: 30

z-index: 20

Element with the highest z-index value is stacked on top of other positioned elements

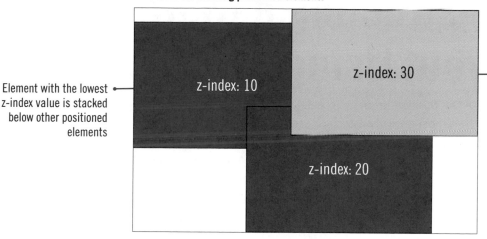

FIGURE H-12: Style sheet code for stacked items in nav bar

```
li img {
    position: absolute;
    left: -22px;
    top: -8px;
}
```

```
#mainnav {
    text-align: left;
    padding: 0.25em;
    padding-left: 0.5em;
    float: left;
    width: 7em;
}
#mainnav a {
    text-decoration: none;
}
#mainnav li {
    list-style-type: none;
    padding: 0.25em 0.25em 0.25em 1em;
    margin: 0.25em 0;
    background: #B8944D;
    position: relative;
}
#mainnav ul {
    margin: 0;
    padding: 0;
    position: relative;
    top: 2em;
    z-index: 2;
}
#name {
    font-weight: bold;
}
#navaccent {
    width: 1.5em;
    height: 12.25em;
    background: #4D8103;
    position: relative;
    top: -10em;
    left: -0.75em;
    z-index: 1;
}
```

FIGURE H-13: Nav bar elements ordered using z-index values

z-index values used to reorder nav accent div behind list element containing buttons

Unholy Vault Designs/Shutterstock.com

Jason Bucy

Constructing a Multicolumn Layout Using Positioning

You can use the position property to create multicolumn layouts that look and behave just like those created with the float property. However, each method can be useful in specific situations. Positioning can enable you to create three-column layouts with more flexibility and allows for four-column layouts as well. Figure H-14 illustrates different methods for creating a multicolumn layout. 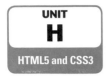 In the new Lakeland Reeds B&B Web site layout, the width of the main page content can widen and narrow depending on the size of the browser window. To start the process of making this change, you switch from float-based to position-based columns.

STEPS

1. **Return to lakeland.css in your text editor, then in the #mainnav style rule, delete the name–value pair** float: left;

2. **At the end of the #mainnav style rule, add the name-value pairs** position: absolute; **and** left: 15px;

   Instead of floating the nav bar on the left side of the page, you give it an absolute position.

3. **In the #box style rule, add the code** position: relative;

   Giving the box element a relative position without left or top values leaves it in the same place on the page while positioning the mainnav element relative to it.

4. **In the #content style rule, delete the name–value pairs** float: right; **and** width: 32em;

5. **At the end of the #content style rule, add the code** margin-left: 10em;

   You remove the float property from the main page content. If you were creating a fixed-width page using positioning, you could position this element as well. However, because you want the element width to change based on the width of the browser window, you leave the content in the page flow and add a left margin that leaves space for the nav bar. Figure H-15 shows the updated code for the style sheet.

6. **Save your work, then reload aboutus.html in your browser.**

   As Figure H-16 shows that, even though you changed the styling of the nav bar and the main page content, the page layout is unchanged.

Understanding IE6 and positioning

Internet Explorer 6 includes a few bugs in the way it renders positioned elements. While this unit focuses on positioning techniques for browsers without such bugs, you may find yourself designing or maintaining Web pages for an audience with significant IE6 use. In this case, it's important to continually test your pages in IE6 as your design them. Because the IE6 bugs have been around for several years, many workarounds have been developed for these bugs. To research a particular rendering error you may be encountering, search on the terms "ie6 positioning bug" in a Web search engine.

FIGURE H-14: Comparing multicolumn layout methods

float: left;

Both columns floated

float: right;

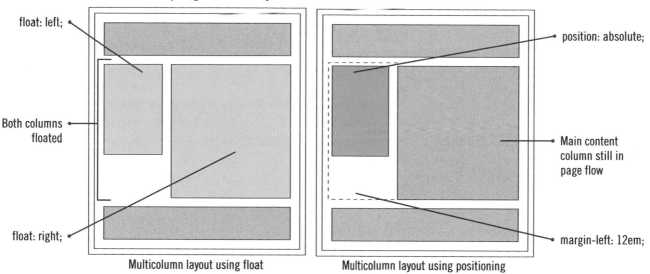

position: absolute;

Main content column still in page flow

margin-left: 12em;

Multicolumn layout using float

Multicolumn layout using positioning

FIGURE H-15: Style sheet code for positioned column layout

margin-left value increased to create space for nav bar

Nav bar removed from page flow with absolute positioning

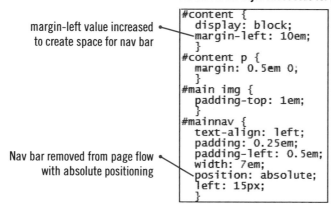

```
#content {
  display: block;
  margin-left: 10em;
}
#content p {
  margin: 0.5em 0;
}
#main img {
  padding-top: 1em;
}
#mainnav {
  text-align: left;
  padding: 0.25em;
  padding-left: 0.5em;
  width: 7em;
  position: absolute;
  left: 15px;
}
```

FIGURE H-16: Multicolumn layout using positioning

Unholy Vault Designs/Shutterstock.com
Jason Bucy

HTML5 and CSS3

Creating a Fluid Layout

By default, Web page content occupies the entire width of a user's browser window. One simple technique for ensuring consistency of the visual design in different window sizes and monitor resolutions is to specify a fixed width for the content of a Web page, creating what's commonly known as a **fixed layout**. However, some designers prefer to take advantage of the additional space on larger screens. By creating a **fluid layout**, which is also known as a **liquid layout**, you give your Web page the flexibility to adjust its width based on the width of a user's browser window while still maintaining your intended layout. 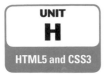 You've worked with the art department at Great Northern Web Services to adapt the design for the Lakeland Reeds B&B Web site so that it adjusts to different screen sizes. You apply those changes now.

1. **Return to lakeland.css in your text editor**

2. **In the body style rule, change the width property name to min-width, then insert a new line and add the name–value pair max-width: 60em;**

   Figure H-17 shows the changed code. The min-width property sets the minimum width for an element. By changing the width property for body to min-width, you're keeping the Web page at least as wide as its previous fixed width. The max-width property sets the maximum width of an element, allowing your Web page content to widen a limited amount to fit a larger browser window.

3. **Save your changes, then reload aboutus.html in your browser**

   Depending on the size of your browser window, the Web page may be displayed wider than before, or may look exactly the same.

4. **If your browser window is maximized, click the Restore Down button ▣, then drag the right side of your browser window to the left and the right and notice any changes in the locations of text and other elements on the page**

   As Figure H-18 shows, the browser changes the locations of elements on the Web page to occupy the additional space, a process known as **reflowing**.

Determining page widths

When planning the design of a Web site, it's important to start by understanding the screen resolution of most of your expected users. While the numbers of pixels that different monitors can display varies widely, 1024 pixels in width by 768 pixels in height is a widely accepted lowest common denominator for computers. However, even a Web site that's 1024 pixels wide would be cut off on such displays because a few other factors are involved. Most importantly, browsers themselves use some pixels on both sides for the scroll bar and window borders. As a result, many designers use a standard width of 960 pixels for Web sites created with a general audience in mind.

Designing Web pages for mobile devices such as phones and tablets requires planning for much smaller displays. When designing for mobile users, some Web designers create a second Web site that's optimized for small screens, while other designers create a single Web site that looks good on small devices and scales up to large screens as well. Creating a Web site that's usable for mobile users requires careful planning and testing.

min-width
property sets
the minimum
width for the
element

max-width
property sets
the maximum
width for the
element

```
body {
  min-width: 44em;
  max-width: 60em;
  margin: 0 auto;
  font-family: tahoma, arial, helvetica, sans-serif;
  background: #6e93c8;
  background: url("images/lake.jpg");
}
```

FIGURE H-18: Web page at minimum and maximum widths

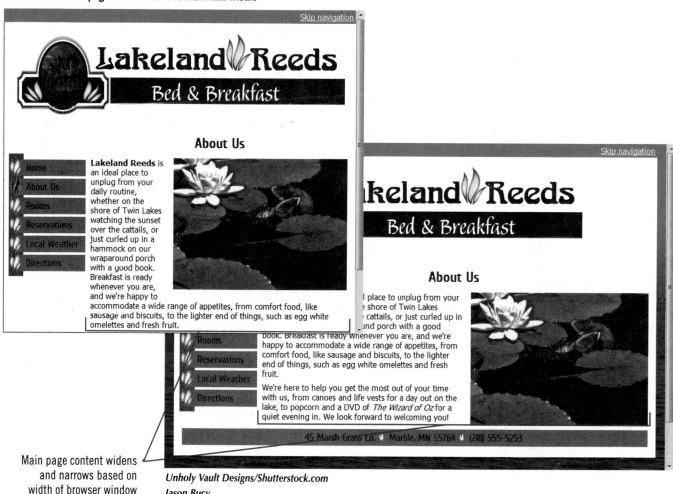

Main page content widens
and narrows based on
width of browser window

Unholy Vault Designs/Shutterstock.com
Jason Bucy
Photo/Sasha Vodnik

Controlling the Visibility of Elements

In addition to specifying where elements should be displayed in a Web page, you can use CSS properties to style whether an element is displayed at all. CSS includes two properties for this purpose. When you set the visibility property to "hidden", the contents of an element are no longer visible on the Web page. However, the element is still part of the page flow, meaning that it still takes up space on the page. As an alternative, you can set the display property to "none". In addition to not being visible, an element styled with this value is removed from the page flow, allowing other elements to occupy the space where it would have been displayed. Figure H-19 illustrates the difference between these two styles. ▓▓▓▓ The vertical nav bar takes up space on the Web page but is not necessary for printed output. You update the print style sheet for the Web site and use the display style to remove the nav bar when the page is printed.

STEPS

1. Return to lakeland.css in your text editor, save a copy as llprint.css, remove all name–value pairs that specify color as well as the pair that specifies the background image, then change all the colors in style rules based on pseudo-classes to black

2. At the end of the #mainnav style rule, add the name–value pair display: none;

3. In the #content style rule, delete the code margin-left: 10em;

   QUICK TIP
   Removing the margin and the width settings allows the main content to reflow across the entire printed page.

4. In the body style rule, remove the name–value pairs for the min-width and max-width properties

   Figure H-20 shows the final code for your style sheet.

5. Save your work, reload aboutus.html in your browser, then display a print preview if available in your browser

   As Figure H-21 shows, the nav bar is removed from the print layout.

6. Close the print preview, validate the code for aboutus.html and your style sheets, then make changes as necessary to fix any errors

7. If you have space on a Web server, publish your Web site, then open aboutus.html in your browser from the published location

FIGURE H-19: Alternatives for hiding Web page elements

Element content is hidden but element is still part of page flow

Element content is hidden and removed from page flow, allowing other elements to reflow

visibility: hidden;

display: none;

FIGURE H-20: Style sheet code to hide nav bar in printed output

Margin property removed from #content style rule

```
#content {
  display: block;
  }
#content p {
  margin: 0.5em 0;
  }
#main img {
  padding-top: 1em;
  }
#mainnav {
  text-align: left;
  padding: 0.25em;
  padding-left: 0.5em;
  width: 7em;
  position: absolute;
  left: 15px;
  display: none;
  }
```

display: none hides the #mainnav element and removes it from the page flow

FIGURE H-21: Nav bar removed from printed output

Nav bar hidden and removed from page flow, allowing main content to occupy entire width of printed page

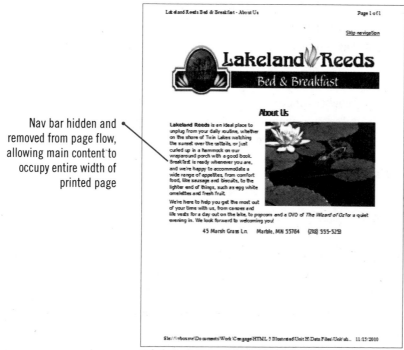

Unholy Vault Designs/Shutterstock.com
Jason Bucy

Practice

For current SAM information, including versions and content details, visit SAM Central (http://www.cengage.com/samcentral). If you have a SAM user profile, you may have access to hands-on instruction, practice, and assessment of the skills covered in this unit. Since various versions of SAM are supported throughout the life of this text, check with your instructor for the correct instructions and URL/Web site for accessing assignments.

Concepts Review

Refer to Figure H-22.

FIGURE H-22

1. Which item represents the element margin?
2. Which item represents the element padding?
3. Which item represents the element content?
4. Which item represents the element border?
5. Which item represents the element width?

Match each term with the statement that best describes it.

6. **multicolumn layout**
7. **relative positioning**
8. **absolute positioning**
9. **fixed layout**
10. **fluid layout**
11. **layer**

    a. a new level of content displayed on top of the basic flow of elements on the Web page

    b. a layout that specifies a fixed width for the content of a Web page

    c. a layout involving columns of text and graphics running parallel to each other down the page

    d. lets you make adjustments to the default position of an element while preserving the space allotted to the element in the default page flow

    e. a layout with the flexibility to adjust its width based on the width of a user's browser window

    f. takes an element out of the page flow entirely and allows other elements to flow into the space it would have occupied

Select the best answer from the list of choices.

12. **Which does CSS use to represent the characteristics of every Web page element?**
    a. absolute positioning
    b. multicolumn layout
    c. box model
    d. fluid layout
13. **Which property is NOT useful in creating a multicolumn layout?**
    a. width
    b. background
    c. float
    d. position
14. **Which name-value pair takes an element out of the page flow entirely and allows other elements to flow into the space it would have occupied?**
    a. display: none
    b. position: relative
    c. position: absolute
    d. visibility: hidden

15. **Which name-value pair makes the contents of an element no longer visible on the Web page but leaves the element in the page flow?**
   a. position: relative
   b. display: none
   c. position: none
   d. visibility: hidden

16. **Which property enables you to change the stacking order of layers?**
   a. visibility
   b. z-index
   c. display
   d. position

Skills Review

1. **Construct a multicolumn layout with float.**
   a. In your text editor, open HTM H-3.html from the Unit H/Review folder where you store your Data Files, insert a blank line before the closing body tag, insert a paragraph element containing your first and last name and the text **HTML5 Unit H, Skills Review**, save it as **index.html**, then use a CSS comment to add the same information to HTM H-4.css and save it as **bigj.css**.
   b. Open index.html in your browser, then examine the Web page elements for the redesigned page.
   c. Return to index.html in your text editor, locate the footer element, then add the id values **foot1**, **foot2**, and **foot3** to the three div elements within the footer. Save your work.
   d. In bigj.css, beneath the @font-face rule, insert a style rule based on the selectors article, body, dd, div, dl, dt, figcaption, figure, footer, h1, h2, h3, li, nav, ol, p, section, table, th, td, and ul that sets both **margin** and **padding** to 0.
   e. Create a style rule based on the foot1 id selector that floats the element to the **left** and sets its width to **320px**, a rule based on the **foot2** id selector that floats the element to the **right** and sets its width to **320px**, and a style rule based on the **foot3** id selector that sets the margins of the element to **0 auto** and sets its width to **320px**.
   f. Save your work, reload index.html in your browser, then verify that the addresses in the footer are displayed in three columns.

2. **Implement relative and absolute positioning.**
   a. Return to index.html in your text editor. In the li elements within the unordered list containing the nav bar links, add the id values **navlink1**, **navlink2**, **navlink3**, and **navlink4**. Save your work.
   b. In bigj.css, create a style rule for the id values you just created. Set background to **red**, then specify a background image of **images/redflag.png**. Also specify position as **absolute**, and width and height values of **150px**.
   c. In the "#mainnav li a" style rule, delete the name-value pair **background: red**.
   d. Create a style rule based just on the navlink1 id selector and specify a left value of **0**. Repeat for navlink2 to set a left value of **150px**, navlink3 to set a right value of **150px**, and navlink4 to set a right value of **0**.
   e. In the "#mainnav li a" style rule, delete **display: block**. Set position to **relative** and top to **20px**.
   f. In the #box style rule, set the position to **relative**.
   g. Save your work, refresh index.htm, then verify that the navigation bar links are displayed on red triangles along the top.

3. **Stack elements.**
   a. In index.html above the footer element, insert an empty div element with a class value of **center**. Save your work.
   b. In bigj.css, add a style rule based on the center class selector. Set the background to **white**, the width to **100%**, the height to **80px**, font-size to **1.5em**, padding to **2em**, position to **absolute**, and top to **200px**.
   c. Save your work, then reload index.html in your browser and observe the stacking order of the logo image and the box.
   d. Return to bigj.css in your text editor, then in the .center style rule, add code to set the z-index to **1**.
   e. Create a style rule based on the **logo** id selector, then set the position to **relative** and the z-index to **2**.
   f. In the "#mainnav li" style rule, set the z-index to **3**.
   g. Save your work, reload index.html in your browser, then verify that the white rectangle is displayed behind the logo.

4. **Construct a multicolumn layout using positioning.**
   a. Return to index.html in your text editor, locate the two aside elements above the div element you added earlier, add the class value **right** to the first aside element, then add the class value **left** to the second. Save your work.
   b. In bigj.css, create a style rule that applies to both of the classes you just applied. Add code to set width to **200px**, height to **80px**, font-size to **1.5em**, text-align to **center**, padding to **2em**, position to **absolute**, top to **200px**, z-index to **2**, and background to **none**.

Skills Review (continued)

c. Create a style rule based just on the left class selector and specify a border-left value of **5px solid black**. Repeat for right to set a right value of **0px** and a border-right value of **5px solid black**.

d. Save your work, then reload index.html in your browser and verify that a column of text appears on either side of the logo image, as shown in Figure H-23.

5. **Create a fluid layout.**

a. Return to bigj.css in your text editor.

b. In the #box style rule, change the width property name to **min-width**, then add code to set the max-width to **1060px**. Repeat for the #skipnav style rule.

c. Save your changes, then reload index.html in your browser.

d. If your browser window is maximized, click the Restore Down button.

e. Drag the right side of your browser window to the left and to the right and observe any reflowing.

6. **Control the visibility of elements.**

a. Return to bigj.css in your text editor, then save a copy as **bjprint.css**. Remove the name-value pairs that set color in the article, footer, and .strong style rules. Remove the name-value pairs that set borders for the .left and .right style rules.

b. At the end of the "#mainnav li a" style rule, add code to set display to **none**. Repeat for the #skipnav style rule.

c. In the #box style rule, remove the name-value pairs for the min-width and max-width properties. Repeat for the #skipnav style rule.

FIGURE H-24

d. Save your work, reload index.html in your browser, then display a print preview if available in your browser. Verify that the "Skip navigation" link and the nav bar links are not displayed, as shown in Figure H-24.

e. Close the print preview, validate the code for index.html and your style sheets, then make changes as necessary to fix any errors.

f. If you have space on a Web server, publish your Web site, then open index.html in your browser from the published location.

Independent Challenge 1

Sarah Nguyen, the owner of the Spotted Wren Garden Center, has asked you to make a few layout changes to the store's Web site. She also had a graphic designer split the logo into two separate images in order to reduce the total size of the files: the text is a gif file, while the photo is a jpg. You implement the new features on the home page.

a. In your text editor, open HTM H-5.html from the Unit H/IC1 folder. Insert a blank line before the closing body tag, then insert a paragraph element containing your first and last name and the text **HTML5 Unit H, Independent Challenge 1**. Save the file as **index.html**, then repeat to add the same information as a CSS comment in HTM H-6.css, saving the file as **spotwren.css**.

b. In index.html, locate the img element containing the logo image within the h1 element near the top of the page. Change the value for the src attribute to **images/swlogo_l.gif** and the width to **468**.

c. Just above the h1 element, insert a div element with an id of **logobg**. Within the div element, add an img element with a src value of **images/swlogo_r.jpg**, width of **578**, height of **184**, and an alt value of **grasses and flowers in bloom**. Save your work.

d. Return to spotwren.css in your text editor, then in the #box style rule, set position to **relative**. Create a style rule based on the "#logo img" selector. Set display to **block** and position to **relative**. Add another style rule based on the "#logobg img" selector. Set position to **absolute** and specify a right value that keeps the element in its original location. Set z-index values for the "#logo img" and the "#logobg img" elements so "#logo img" is stacked on top of "#logobg img". Save your work, then open index.html in your browser and verify that the appearance of the two stacked images for the logo graphic matches the appearance of the original logo graphic.

e. Return to spotwren.css in your text editor, then delete the #skiplink style rule. In the #skipnav style rule, delete the two background name-value pairs. Set position to **absolute**, specify a value for right that aligns the right edge of the element with the right edge of the parent element, and specify a z-index value that stacks the element on top of the "#logo img" element. Save your work.

Independent Challenge 1 (continued)

f. Return to index.html in your text editor. Delete the opening and closing span tags enclosing the text "Skip navigation", but leave the text. Save your work, then reload index.html in your browser and verify that the text "Skip navigation" is now displayed over the yellow border of the logo graphic and that the graphic is flush with the top of the browser window.

g. Return to spotwren.css in your text editor. In the aside style rule, set position to **relative**, width to **250px**, and create a right border that's **10px** wide, solid, and the same color as the background of the nav bar. In the article style rule, set position to **absolute**; a left value that leaves room for the aside element, including margin, padding, and border; and a width value that occupies the remaining width specified in the #box element. Save your work, reload index.html in your browser, then verify that the specials are displayed on the left side of the page and the main page content on the right side of the page, with a border the same color as the nav bar between them. See Figure H-25.

FIGURE H-25

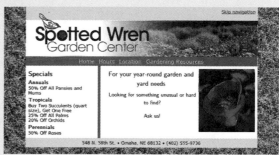

h. Return to spotwren.css in your text editor, change the border color for the aside element to **black**, remove the name-value pairs that specify the background image and background color for the body element, remove all non-border name-value pairs that specify color, change all colors in rules based on pseudo-classes to **black**, then save a copy of the file as **swprint.css**.

i. Validate your HTML and CSS documents.

j. If you have space on a Web server, publish your Web site, then open **index.html** in your browser from the published location.

k. Close your browser, then close your text editor.

Weldon Schloneger/Shutterstock.com, Maxim Tupikov/Shutterstock.com, Xtremer/Shutterstock.com

Independent Challenge 2

You incorporate the logo for the Murfreesboro Recreational Soccer League into the organizational Web site that you are creating. You also add images from some of the group's events.

a. In your text editor, open HTM H-7.html from the Unit H/IC2 folder. Insert a blank line before the closing body tag, then insert a paragraph element containing your first and last name and the text **HTML5 Unit H, Independent Challenge 2**. Save the file as **index.html**, then repeat to add the same information as a CSS comment in HTM H-8.css, saving the file as **mrsl.css**.

b. In index.html, locate the two img elements near the top of the page. Assign a unique id value to the div element containing each img, then save your work. Return to mrsl.css, then add code to the #box style rule to set the position to **relative**. Create a style rule that is based on the id selector you specified for the first img element and that takes it out of the flow of the page and positions its left margin flush with the left margin of the parent element. Repeat for the second img element, positioning its right margin flush with the right margin of the parent element. Save your work, open index.html in your browser, then verify that the images appear at both edges of the top of the body section.

c. Return to index.html in your text editor. In the h1 element below the images you styled, add a line break element after each word except the last. Enclose each word within a span element and assign each a unique id. Save your work. Return to mrsl.css, then add style rules that position all four word elements while retaining their space in the page flow. Using calculations and/or trial and error, position the first word so its left edge is just to the left of the first logo image. Position each remaining word farther to the right so the words are staggered, as shown in Figure H-26. Save your work and refresh index.html in your browser as many times as necessary until you are satisfied with the appearance of the words.

FIGURE H-26

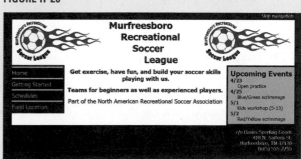

Independent Challenge 2 (continued)

d. Return to mrsl.css in your text editor. Edit the "#mainnav li" style rule to change the display of the unordered list containing the nav bar links from inline to the default layout. Change the background of the #mainnav element from black to **#8CC63F**. Delete the #mainnav name–value pairs for padding. Set the alignment of all text within the nav bar to **left**. Set the width of the nav bar to **175px** and float it to the left of the page content that follows it. Set top, right, and bottom borders that are **5px solid black**. Add a right margin of **10px**. In the "#mainnav li" style rule, add padding of **0.25em** to the top and bottom and a top margin of **0.25em**. Save your work, reload index.html in your browser, then verify that the nav bar links are stacked vertically and that the nav bar is displayed on the left edge of the page.

e. Create a style rule based on the aside selector. Set the element to float to the right of content that follows it, set padding to **8px**, top, left, and bottom borders that are **5px solid black**, a background of **#8CC63F**, and a left margin of **10px**. Save your work, reload **index.html** in your browser, then verify that the "Upcoming Events" list is displayed on the right edge of the page.

Advanced Challenge Exercise

- Return to mrsl.css in your text editor, then for the #mainnav and aside elements set the height to **250px**.
- Add bottom padding of **16px** to the #mainnav element. Remove the bottom borders from the #mainnav and aside elements.
- Save your work, reload index.html in your browser, then verify that the bottoms of the nav bar and sidebar are flush with the footer box at the bottom of the page.

f. Return to mrsl.css in your text editor, remove all name–value pairs that reference colors and background images, then change all colors in rules based on pseudo-classes to **black**. Add code to the #mainnav and #skipnav style rules to prevent the elements from displaying and to remove them from the page flow. Save a copy of the file as **mrsprint.css**.

g. Reload index.html in your browser, then display a print preview if available in your browser. Verify that the "Skip navigation" link and the nav bar are not displayed, as shown in Figure H-27.

h. Validate your HTML and CSS documents.

i. If you have space on a Web server, publish your Web site, then open index.html in your browser from the published location.

j. Close your browser, then close your text editor.

FIGURE H-27

> **Murfreesboro Recreational Soccer League**
>
> Get exercise, have fun, and build your soccer skills playing with us.
>
> Teams for beginners as well as experienced players.
>
> Part of the North American Recreational Soccer Association
>
> **Upcoming Events**
> 4/23
> Open practice
> 4/25
> Blue/Green scrimmage
> 5/1
> Kids workshop (5-13)
> 5/2
> Red/Yellow scrimmage
>
> c/o Davies Sporting Goods
> 418 N. Sartoris St.
> Murfreesboro, TN 37130
> (615) 555-2255

Independent Challenge 3

You've been working with Diego Merckx, the manager of Hotel Natoma, to develop a new multicolumn layout for the Web site. You style a page of museum listings with the new layout.

a. In your text editor, open HTM H-9.html from the Unit H/IC3 folder. Insert a blank line before the closing body tag, then insert a paragraph element containing your first and last name and the text **HTML5 Unit H, Independent Challenge 3**. Save the file as **museums.html**, then repeat to add the same information to HTM H-10.css, saving the file as **natoma.css**.

b. In natoma.css, set the position for the element with the id box to **relative**. Set the position for the element with the id skipnav to remove it from the page flow, then place it **10px** from the right edge of the parent element and **5px** from the top of the parent element. Save your work, open museums.html in your browser, then verify that the "Skip navigation" link is displayed in front of the green block surrounding the logo image.

Independent Challenge 3 (continued)

c. In natoma.css, modify the style rule for the #mainnav element and its child elements to convert it from a horizontal to a vertical navigation bar. Set the position for the #mainnav element to remove it from the page flow and position it as shown in Figure H-28. Add a margin to the article element in order to create adequate room for the nav bar along the left side of the page. Save your work and reload museums.html in your browser.

FIGURE H-28

Advanced Challenge Exercise

- In natoma.css, style the footer element with a position value of **fixed** and a bottom value of **0** to keep the footer always visible at the bottom of the Web page. Save your work, then reload museums.html in your browser.
- Add sufficient padding to the bottom of the box element so the last list item, "Zeum," is visible above the footer when you scroll to the bottom of the page in your browser.
- If necessary, add the width property to the style rule for the footer element so the footer width matches the width of the rest of the page content, then save your work and reload the page in your browser.
- If necessary, expand the border property for the footer element to cover all sides of the element, then save your work and reload the page in your browser.

d. Return to natoma.css in your text editor, change all border colors to **black**, remove all other name-value pairs that reference colors, then change all colors in rules based on pseudo-classes to **black**. Add code to the #mainnav style rule to prevent the element from displaying and to remove it from the page flow. Repeat for the #skipnav style rule. Save a copy of the file as **hnprint.css**.

e. Reload museums.html in your browser, then display a print preview if available in your browser. Verify that the "Skip navigation" link and the nav bar are not displayed, as shown in Figure H-29.

f. Validate all your HTML and CSS documents.

g. If you have space on a Web server, publish your Web site, then open museums.html in your browser from the published location.

FIGURE H-29

h. Close your browser, then close your text editor.

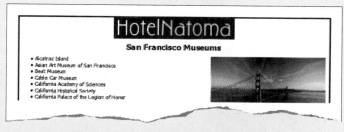

Real Life Independent Challenge

This assignment builds on the personal Web site you have worked on in previous units. You'll implement positioning and layout features that you learned in this unit.

a. Copy your Web site files to the Unit H/RLIC folder on the drive and folder where you store your Data Files.

b. Navigate through the pages of your Web site. Sketch the basic site layout on a sheet of paper, then create one or more sketches of an alternative layout using features you learned in this unit. Incorporate at least three features from the following list: multicolumn layout, relative positioning, absolute positioning, stacked elements, fluid layout.

c. Implement the new features from your sketch, saving and reloading your Web pages regularly during the process to ensure your code is creating the desired effects.

d. When your new layout is complete, save changes to your style sheet document, save a copy using the name of your print style sheet, then make the necessary alterations to the style sheet code for a print style sheet. If appropriate, add code to suppress the display of specific page elements in printed output.

e. Preview your Web pages in at least two browsers and make any edits necessary for them to appear as you expected.

f. Validate all of your HTML and CSS documents and make any edits necessary to address any issues.

g. If you have space on a Web server, publish your Web site, then open each page from the published location.

h. Close your browser, then close your text editor.

Visual Workshop

In your text editor, open the file HTM H-11.html from the Unit H/VW directory on the drive and folder where you store your Data Files, add a paragraph before the closing body tag that contains your first and last name and the text **HTML5 Unit H, Visual Workshop**, then save the file as **upcoming.html**. Open HTM H-12.css, add a comment containing the same information, then save it as **revision.css**. Use your text editor to create the layout shown in Figure H-30. Save your work, save a copy of your style sheet with the name **revprint.css**, then make any necessary changes for print formatting. When you are finished, validate your HTML and CSS code. If you have space on a Web server, publish your files, then open the Web page in your browser from the published location. Close your browser and text editor.

FIGURE H-30

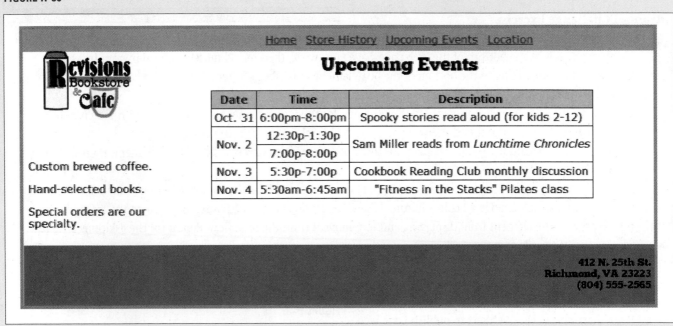

Implementing Page Layout with HTML and CSS

HTML Elements

This table includes all HTML elements covered in this text, along with selected attributes.

element	content/function	new in HTML5
global attributes that apply to all HTML elements		
id="*id*"	a unique identifier for the current element	
title="*title*"	information about an element; displayed in many browsers as floating text when the mouse pointer is over the element	
lang="*keyword*"	the primary language of the element contents, from a standard list of abbreviations	
dir="ltr | rtl | auto"	the direction of text in the element; "ltr" specifies left to right, while "rtl" indicates right to left	
class="*class*"	one or more classes that the element is part of, separated by spaces	
style="*style*"	one or more CSS name-value pairs that apply only to the current element	
!	contains comment text within the <!-- --> tag pair	
a	links enclosed text or elements to another Web page or other resource	
href="*filename* | *uri*"	address of Web page or other resource that opens when the link is clicked or activated	
target="*name* | _blank | _self"	the name or a keyword for the window or tab in which the linked resource opens	
rel="*keyword*"	keyword describing the relationship between the linked resource and the current Web page	
media="*media*"	media for which the linked resource is intended (default: "all")	
type="*type*"	MIME type of the linked resource	
article	contains a standalone piece of work, such as a single entry in a blog	✔
aside	contains a part of a page that's tangential to the main page content	✔
body	contains the contents visible in the main window of a Web browser	
br	inserts a line break	
caption	contains the title of a table	
col	encloses one or more table columns to treat as a unit	
span="*value*"	specifies the number of columns to include in the element	
colgroup	encloses the col elements for a table	
span="*value*"	specifies the number of columns to include in the element when no col elements are specified	
dd	marks a description associated with a dt element in a description list	
div	marks block-level content with no specific semantic meaning	
dl	marks a list in which each item is comprised of a name-value pair (a description list)	
dt	marks a term or item being described in a description list	
figure	contains an image that adds information to a Web page; a user agent should be able to link the contents of a figure element and move them to another location without affecting the information conveyed by the Web page	✔
figcaption	mark caption text associated with an img element; always enclosed within a figure element	✔
footer	contains information about a section or document that usually appears at the end of a Web page, such as attributions and/or footnotes	✔
h1, h2, h3, h4, h5, h6	mark heading text; h1 is the highest level heading on a Web page, and h6 is the lowest	
head	contains information about a Web page, including elements that are not visible within the browser window	
header	contains information about a section or document that usually appears at the beginning, such as a heading, logo, and/or table of contents	✔

element	content/function	new in HTML5
hgroup	contains a group of related elements that include a heading; enables user agents to recognize content such as a tagline as related to a heading	✔
html	encloses all the code for a Web page	

img
  alt="*text*"
  src="*uri | filename*"
  width="*value*"
  height="*value*"
	inserts an image
	text to display or be read aloud in place of the image
	path and filename for the image file to display
	native width of the image in pixels
	native height of the image in pixels	

li
  link
  href="*filename | uri*"
  rel="**keyword**"
  media="*media*"
  type="*type*"
	marks list item content in an ordered list or unordered list
	makes the contents of an external file available in an HTML document
	specifies the destination
	keyword specifying the type of link
	media for which the linked resource is intended (default: "all")
	MIME type of the linked resource	

meta
  name="*name*"
  http-equiv="*keyword*"
  content="*content*"
  charset="*charset*"
	enables you to pass information about a Web page to user agents that open it
	the type of metadata being provided, from list of standard metadata names
	directions to the user agent on handling the Web page
	the content of the metadata described by the "name" value
	the character encoding that the document uses	

nav	contains site or page navigation elements	✔
ol	marks a list in which items are numbered or lettered sequentially (an ordered list)	
p	marks a paragraph of text	

script
  src="*filename*"
  type="*type*"
	contains script code or a link to an external file containing script code
	path and filename for the external script file
	the script language or data format	

section	encloses a section of content focused on a common theme, such as a chapter of a larger work	✔
span	contains inline text or elements; enables you to style inline elements	
style type="*type*"	encloses style sheet code the styling language	
table	marks content to present as a table	
tbody	encloses table body rows	

td
  colspan="*value*"
  rowspan="*value*"
	marks the content of a table data cell
	the number of columns that the cell spans
	the number of rows that the cell spans	

tfoot	encloses table footer rows	

th
  colspan="*value*"
  rowspan="*value*"
	marks the content of a table header cell
	the number of columns that the cell spans
	the number of rows that the cell spans	

thead	encloses table header rows	
title	specifies text that appears in the title bar or tab of a Web browser opening the page	
tr	encloses table cell elements that make up a single table row	
ul	marks a list in which the order of items doesn't matter (an unordered list)	

HTML Elements

CSS Properties

This table includes all CSS properties covered in this text, along with selected values.

property	values	affects
background	*color* as a name from cross-browser compatibility list; *rgb triplet* in the format rgb(*rrr,ggg,bbb*); *hexadecimal triplet* in the format #rrggbb; *url('path/filename')*; **transparent**; **inherit**	the background color or image for an element
border	*width style color*	combined attribute for all settings for the border around an element
border-color border-top-color border-right-color border-bottom-color border-left-color	*color* as a name from cross-browser compatibility list; *rgb triplet* in the format rgb(*rrr,ggg,bbb*); *hexadecimal triplet* in the format #*rrggbb*; **transparent**; **inherit**	the color of an element border on one or more sides
border-style border-top-style border-right-style border-bottom-style border-left-style	**dotted**; **dashed**; **solid**; **double**; **groove**; **ridge**; **inset**; **outset**	the style of an element border on one or more sides
border-width border-top-width border-right-width border-bottom-width border-left-width	**thin**; **medium**; **thick**; *value* in em, pixels, or another supported unit	the thickness of an element border on one or more sides
border-collapse	**separate**; **collapse**	whether adjacent table cell borders are displayed separately or merged
bottom	*value* in em, pixels, or another supported unit; *percent* of the height of the parent element	amount the bottom edge of an element is offset from the bottom edge of the closest ancestor element that is also positioned
clear	**left**; **right**; **both**	element position, preventing a floated element from being displayed to the left, right, or either side of an element
color	*color* as a name from cross-browser compatibility list; *rgb triplet* in the format rgb(*rrr,ggg,bbb*); *hexadecimal triplet* in the format #*rrggbb*; **transparent**; **inherit**	the foreground color of an element, most often affecting text
display	**block**; **inline**; **table**; **table-row**; **table-cell**; **none**; **inherit**	the type of box that user agents create for an element; "none" removes an element from the page flow
float	**left**; **right**	element position, aligning the top of an element with the top of the next element, and horizontally with the specified edge of the parent element
font-family	*family-name*	the font family in which the text of an element is displayed
font-size	*size* in em, pixels, or another supported unit	the relative or absolute size of text
font-style	**normal**; **italic**; **oblique**	whether characters are displayed slanted or in standard orientation

property	values	affects
font-weight	**normal**; **bold**; **100**; **200**; **300**; **400**; **500**; **600**; **700**; **800**; **900**	whether text is displayed in boldface, normal, or somewhere in between
height	*value* in em, pixels, or another supported unit; *percent* of the parent element; **inherit**; **auto**	the height of an element, excluding, padding, border, and margin
left	*value* in em, pixels, or another supported unit; *percent* of the width of the parent element	amount the left edge of an element is offset from the left edge of the closest ancestor element that is also positioned
list-style-image	**url('*path*/*filename*')**	specifies an image to be used as a list item marker
list-style-type	ordered list: **decimal**; **lower-roman**; **upper-roman**; **lower-alpha**; **upper-alpha**; **none** unordered list: **circle**; **disc**; **square**; **none**	the list item marker for an ordered or unordered list
margin margin-top margin-right margin-bottom margin-left	*value* in em, pixels, or another supported unit; *percent* of the enclosing element; **auto**	buffer space outside of the element border
max-height	*value* in em, pixels, or another supported unit; *percent* of the parent element; **inherit**; **auto**	the maximum height of an element, excluding, padding, border, and margin
max-width	*value* in em, pixels, or another supported unit; *percent* of the parent element; **inherit**; **auto**	the maximum width of an element, excluding, padding, border, and margin
min-height	*value* in em; pixels, or another supported unit; *percent* of the parent element; **inherit**; **auto**	the minimum height of an element, excluding, padding, border, and margin
min-width	*value* in em, pixels, or another supported unit; *percent* of the parent element; **inherit**; **auto**	the minimum width of an element, excluding, padding, border, and margin
padding padding-top padding-right padding-bottom padding-left	*value* in em; pixels, or another supported unit; *percent* of the enclosing element	the space between element contents and border
position	**absolute**; **relative**; **fixed**	the way the position of an element is determined on the page
right	*value* in em, pixels, or another supported unit; *percent* of the width of the parent element	amount the right edge of an element is offset from the right edge of the closest ancestor element that is also positioned
text-align	**left**; **right**; **center**; **justify**; **inherit**	the horizontal alignment of text
top	*value* in em; pixels, or another supported unit; *percent* of the height of the parent element	amount the top edge of an element is offset from the top edge of the closest ancestor element that is also positioned
vertical-align	**top**; **middle**; **bottom**	the vertical alignment of table cell content
visibility	**hidden**; **visible**	whether element contents are visible on a Web page; "hidden" makes contents invisible while leaving the element as part of the page flow
width	*value* in em; pixels, or another supported unit; *percent* of the parent element; **inherit**; **auto**	the width of an element, excluding, padding, border, and margin
z-index	*integer*	the position of an element in the stacking order

Glossary

@font-face rule A variation of a style rule that indicates the font name and the location of the files necessary for implementing a downloadable font.

Absolute link The full and complete address for a target document on the Web.

Absolute positioning A positioning technique that takes an element out of the page flow entirely and allows other elements to flow into the space it would have occupied.

a element The element that creates a link on any element that it encloses.

Alpha channel An aspect of a graphic file that allows creators to specify the level of opacity for areas of a graphic, from totally transparent to totally opaque, or anywhere in between.

Anchors Named locations within the current document to which you can link.

Attribute HTML code that follows the element name in the opening tag, which you can use to provide additional information about the element.

Attribute-value pair The two pieces of information you provide to use an attribute: the attribute name and the value you are assigning to the attribute.

Baseline The bottom of text.

Bitmap image An electronic file that represents an image as a grid of dots and specifies the color of each dot.

Block-level element One of the larger chunks that structure a Web page, such as a heading or a paragraph.

Body section Web page section whose contents include elements that are visible in the main window of a Web browser, such as paragraphs and headings.

Box model The way CSS represents the characteristics of Web page elements, treating each element as a rectangular box with several global properties.

Cascading The process of determining precedence among inline styles, embedded styles, external styles, and/or browser settings, which results in all available styles coalescing into a single virtual style sheet for the user agent's reference in rendering content

Cascading Style Sheets (CSS) A companion language to HTML designed for describing the appearance of Web page elements.

Cell The intersection of a row and a column in a table, in which each item of data is displayed.

Character encoding The system user agents should employ to translate the electronic information representing a Web page into human-recognizable symbols, such as letters and numbers.

Character references Specially formatted codes that represent characters in the HTML document character set.

Child element An element nested within another element.

class selector A selector that creates a style rule based on values assigned to elements using the HTML class attribute.

Closing tag The tag you place at the end of an element you are marking.

Collapse What happens in the box model when adjacent top and bottom margins combine into a single margin equal to the greater of the two values.

Column A vertical set of cells in a table.

Comments Text elements in your Web page code that are not rendered by user agents and are viewable only by people who examine the HTML code of your Web pages.

CSS *See* Cascading Style Sheets.

Deprecated Describes HTML features that can still be used, but whose use is no longer recommended.

Descendant selector A compound selector made up of multiple individual selectors, which targets elements based on their nesting.

Description list A list that enables you to specify a name–value pair for each list item.

Design document *See* project plan.

DOCTYPE declaration An element that lets user agents know the language in which document contents are written.

Dots per inch (DPI) The unit of measurement for image resolution, which specifies how close the dots in the bitmap should appear on the output.

DPI *See* dots per inch.

Element A specific component of a Web page, such as a paragraph or a heading.

Email harvesters Programs that continually explore Web pages looking for email addresses that in turn receive spam emails.

Embedded style sheet A section of CSS code entered in the head element of an HTML document.

Extensible Hypertext Markup Language (XHTML) A successor to HTML 4.01 intended to make HTML interoperable with XML.

Extensible Markup Language (XML) A more generic markup language than HTML that enables users to describe any kind of document, instead of only Web pages.

External style sheet A standalone CSS document containing style information that multiple Web pages can link to.

Favicon A custom graphic file 16 pixels in width by 16 pixels in height, saved in the .ico format, and named favicon.ico, associated with a Web page; browsers display a favicon in the address bar and on the bookmark or favorites menu and bar.

File Transfer Protocol (FTP) A means of communication specifically created for moving files between two networked computers and the most common method of transferring documents to a Web server.

Fixed layout A Web page layout that uses a fixed page width.

Fixed positioning A positioning technique similar to absolute positioning that places an element at the top of the stacking order and positions it relative to the browser window rather than to a Web page element.

Fluid layout A Web page layout that gives a Web page the flexibility to adjust its width based on the width of a user's browser window; *also called* liquid layout.

Font family A collection of a single typeface and its variants.

Font stack A list of font families in order of preference, separated by commas, which is a common format for values of the font-family property.

FTP *See* File Transfer Protocol.

FTP client A dedicated program for transferring files via FTP.

Generic font families Groupings of font families according to shared characteristics.

GIF An image format that works best for art containing limited numbers of colors and areas with defined borders between areas; short for graphics interchange format.

Grandchild element The child element of a child element of the current element.

Grandparent element The parent element of the parent element of the current element.

Hand-coding Creating a Web page by entering HTML directly.

Head section The section of an HTML document containing elements that are not part of the main Web page, such as the title element.

Hexadecimal system A system for specifying colors that uses a pound sign (#) followed by six digits, which may include the numbers 0–9 and the letters a–f; the first two digits specify the red value, the middle two digits indicate the green value, and the final pair of digits represents the blue value.

hsl system A system for specifying colors that uses a set of comma-separated values, each ranging from 0–255 or 0–100%, which represent the amounts of hue, saturation, and light in a color.

HTML *See* Hypertext Markup Language.

http *See* Hypertext Transfer Protocol.

https *See* Hypertext Transfer Protocol secure.

Hyperlink *See* link.

Hypertext Links in and between text-only documents.

Hypertext Markup Language (HTML) A standardized format for specifying the structure of a Web page.

Hypertext Transfer Protocol (http) One of the schemes that Web servers use to make documents available.

Hypertext Transfer Protocol Secure (https) One of the schemes that Web servers use to make documents available.

Id selector A CSS selector that applies code in its associated style rule to the element with the specified id attribute value.

IETF *See* Internet Engineering Task Force.

Inline element A fine-grained element that appears within a block-level element, such as a word or phrase within a paragraph.

Inline style A style rule inserted into the opening tag of an element using the style attribute.

Internet Engineering Task Force (IETF) The organization that defined and published the first two versions of HTML.

JPEG An image format optimized for images that contain many colors, such as photographs; *also called* JPG; short for Joint Photographic Experts Group, the organization that created it.

JPG *See* JPEG.

Layer A new level displayed on top of the basic flow of elements on the Web page, into which a positioned element is placed.

Link Text or another Web page element that users can select to open another document containing related content; *also called* hyperlink.

Link shortener A Web-based service that transforms large, unwieldy links into manageable URIs.

Liquid layout *See* fluid layout.

Local root folder The main directory on the computer, USB drive, or shared network drive where you save all of the files for your Web site.

Mailto link A link that creates a new email to a specified recipient.

Multicolumn layout A layout that involves columns of text and graphics running parallel to each other down the page.

Name-value pair CSS code that specifies the name of a property to apply to a selector, along with the value to assign that property.

Native For a bitmap image, the native dimensions are the original width and height at which the image was saved.

Nav bar A set of links for moving between Web pages in a Web site; *also called* navigation bar.

Navigation bar *See* nav bar.

Nesting An arrangement of Web page elements in which one element is located entirely within another.

One-sided tags HTML tags that are used by themselves, rather than in pairs.

Opening tag The tag you place at the start of an element you are marking.

Ordered list A list in which items are numbered or lettered sequentially.

Page flow The default order of a Web page in which elements are displayed based on the sequence in which they appear in the HTML code.

Parent element An element with another element nested within it.

Path The part of a URI composed of the sequence of folders in which the target document is stored on the server.

Pixels The individual dots that make up an image, used to measure the size of a bitmap image.

PNG A graphics format originally designed as an alternative to GIF that also supports an alpha channel; short for Portable Network Graphics.

Presentational Describes a language such as CSS, which is designed to describe the appearance of items.

Preview To open a Web page in one or more user agents and examine the result.

Project plan A summary of the goals, objectives, and target audience of a planned Web site. *Also called* design document.

Pseudo-class A categorization of a Web page element for CSS purposes based on a relationship or condition of the element at a given moment, rather than on a static property.

Reflowing The process in which browsers change the locations of elements on a Web page to fit a change in available space.

Relative link A link that gives only the path and filename information necessary to locate the target document based on the location of the current Web page.

Relative positioning A positioning technique that lets you make adjustments to the default position of an element while preserving the space allotted to the element in the default page flow.

Rendering engine Software that translates Web page elements into visual, auditory, or tactile representations based on Web standards.

Render To display, as when a user agent displays a Web page.

Resolution Specifies how close the dots in a bitmap should appear on the output; measured in dots per inch (DPI).

rgb system A system that uses rgb triplets to specify colors.

rgb triplet A set of comma-separated values, each ranging from 0–255 or 0–100%, which represent the amounts of red, green, and blue in a color.

Rollover effect A change to a Web page element when a user's mouse pointer is over the element but not clicking it.

Row A horizontal set of cells in a table.

Sans-serif font A font that does not incorporate serifs.

Script More complex Web page code written in another programming language.

Scalable Vector Graphics (SVG) A graphics format that's optimal for encoding line art, and which can be displayed at different dimensions with no decrease in quality.

Scheme The way that computers ask for and communicate about a requested document.

Screen readers Devices that many people with visual impairments use to access the Web, which read aloud Web page text and descriptions that a user selects.

Selectors The parts of a style rule that identify the HTML element or elements to which the rule applies.

Semantic Describes languages such as HTML, which are intended to indicate the meanings of elements such as headings and paragraphs, but not to tell Web browsers how the elements should appear.

Serif font A font that uses serifs.

Serifs Small finishing strokes at the ends of the lines making up each character in some fonts.

Server name The part of a URI that identifies the general location of a target document on the Web.

Sibling elements Two elements that are both children of the same parent element.

Skip link A link at the top of the body section of a Web page that increases accessibility by targeting an anchor at the start of the main page content, allowing users to bypass navigation.

Span element A generic element that allows you to isolate a specific section of a larger element.

Stack To overlap Web page elements using positioning.

Storyboard In Web site planning, a sketch that outlines the components of each page and their places in the layout, as well as the links between the pages in the Web site.

Style rules Lines or blocks of CSS code that specify the presentation of Web page elements.

SVG *See* Scalable Vector Graphics.

Tags HTML codes that specify how user agents should treat each item in a Web document.

Target document The Web page or other document that a link opens.

Template A generic Web site layout that includes a color scheme and element positions, but which uses placeholder images and text.

Testing server A non-publicized Web server for testing purposes, which may require a password for access.

Tiling The default behavior of user agents when displaying small background images, meaning that, like tiles on a floor or wall, the images are displayed repeatedly both across and down a page to fill up the browser window.

Type selectors CSS selectors that use the names of HTML elements, such as h1 or p, and apply associated name-value pairs to every instance of the specified element(s).

Uniform resource identifier (URI) A standard format for specifying how and where to access a resource on the Internet; *also known as* Web address.

Unordered list A list in which the order of list items doesn't matter.

URI *See* uniform resource identifier.

Usability A Web site's ease of use.

Usability testing A crucial part of improving a site's usability, in which a developer sits down with potential or actual users of the site, asks them to accomplish a task, notes how they go about it and whether they are successful, and asks for their feedback.

User agents Programs and devices that interpret Web documents.

Validation Putting your code through an automated comparison against Web coding standards.

Vector graphic An electronic file that describes a graphic using geometric shapes.

W3C *See* World Wide Web Consortium.

WCAG *See* Web Content Accessibility Guidelines.

Web *See* World Wide Web.

Web address *See* uniform resource identifier.

Web Content Accessibility Guidelines (WCAG) A widely used reference for implementing Web accessibility maintained by the World Wide Web Consortium.

Web Hypertext Application Technology Working Group (WHATWG) The organization formed by several major technology companies to begin a process of creating the HTML specification that would become HTML5.

Web pages Documents formatted to be accessible on the Web.

Web server A computer optimized to store and share Web documents and that has an extremely high-speed Internet connection.

Web sites Collections of Web pages that are available to anyone with Web access.

WHATWG *See* Web Hypertext Application Technology Working Group.

World Wide Web A vast collection of publically-accessible, linked documents written in Hypertext Markup Language and related languages. *Also called* Web.

World Wide Web Consortium (W3C) The organization founded to take on the responsibility of maintaining HTML standards after the second version.

XHTML *See* Extensible Hypertext Markup Language.

XML *See* Extensible Markup Language.

Index